Pete Luckett's Complete Guide to Fresh Fruit & Vegetables

PETE LUCKETT'S

complete guide to
Fresh Fruit
&
Vegetables

Kathleen Robinson
with Pete Luckett

Goose Lane Editions

For Aunt Peg

When this book was finally complete, I amazed to discover just how many people had actually contributed to it. First of all, I am profoundly grateful to Pete Luckett, who is so generous in sharing his knowledge of fresh produce and who invited me to help him share this knowledge with others. I am indebted to my brother Peter to whom this book owes its existence. I would also like to thank my parents who kept me going through it all and my sister for her timely moments of inspiration. Finally, I owe a word of thanks to my co-workers at Pete's Frootique, especially one wee Scotsman who shepherded me through the hardest part and introduced me to okra.

Published with the assistance of the Canada Council and the New Brunswick Department of Tourism, Recreation and Heritage.

Cover photos by Brian Atkinson
Interior photos by Brian Atkinson and Sue Tufts
Illustrations by David Langille
Book design by Julie Scriver
Printed in Canada by Gagné Printing

Canadian Cataloguing in Publication Data

Robinson, Kathleen, 1959-

Pete Luckett's complete guide to fresh fruit & vegetables

ISBN 0-86492-118-7

1. Cookery (Vegetables)   2. Cookery (Fruit)
I. Luckett, Pete, 1953-   II. Title.
III. Title: Complete guide to fresh fruit & vegetables

TX801.R62 1990   641.6'5   C90-097582-2

Goose Lane Editions Ltd.
248 Brunswick Street
Fredericton, New Brunswick
Canada E3B 1G9

Contents

The
GREENGROCER'S GUIDE

I love it. I really do. I love workin' wif fresh stuff. There is nuffin' like the feel of a ripe persimmon, or a Passe Crassane pear. The color of mandarins next to Ribier grapes sen's shivers up and down me spine. I never lose me enthusiasm for the look of a box of fresh lychees or a new crate of asparagus or rapini. I love the smell tha' 'its you when you open a box of basil or a crate of coriander. All the colors an' tex'ure, the movemen', the activi'y which surroun's fruit an' veg . . . "Move it while it's at its peak, darlin'." It's a very busy job selling fruit and veg. But you know mos' of all, I enjoy the fruit and veg 'emselves, doin' what they do best, gettin' eaten.

I'd hazard a guess that most cookbooks were written by chefs—chefs, standing, pen and paper in hand in the midst of enormous well-equipped kitchens. This one was written by a greengrocer and his scribe, standing with pen in hand in the midst of a glorious array of fruit and vegetables. And as a chef can tell you about whisks and wooden spoons, so Pete and I can tell you about cardoon and boniato. A cookbook with a twist!

Pete is an excellent, inventive cook and he knows more about fruit and vegetables than anyone I know. You can be sure if you follow the guidelines in this book, not only will you create some wonderful meals but you'll be doing it with the best ingredients available.

The purpose of this book is to pass on some of the enthusiasm and appreciation that Pete and I feel for fruit and vegetables and perhaps a few interesting tidbits that fuel our devotion. Over the three or four years I have worked with Pete, I have been amazed at how my knowledge of produce has grown. Pete has been in the business for twenty years and will tell you, without hesitation, that there is no other business he would rather be in.

Even before I worked for Pete I had begun to be a little adventurous; I would buy the occasional Seckel pear or perhaps a mango if I was feeling really daring, but I did not know how to choose a good ripe granadilla, or how to cook okra. As I learned these things a whole new world opened up. Working with Pete, and being an inquisitive person by nature, I have "overheard" Pete explain 101 ways to cook 101 vegetables, and I have sampled 101 types of fruit at just about every stage of under, over and perfect ripeness. This book can save you years of trial and error and years of working for Pete, a lengthy endeavor for which few of us have time.

Given the access the average consumer has to fresh fruit and vegetables from all over the world, this guide to buying and preparing fresh produce will broaden your culinary repertoire. On any given day, you can find at your local market, apples and kiwi from New Zealand, lychees from Taiwan and Madagascar, Asian pears from Japan and China, papaya from Hawaii, pineapple from the Dominican Republic, Honduras and Costa Rica, figs, cactus pears and persimmons from Brazil, mangoes from Peru, squash from Mexico, pears from France, bananas from Ecuador, grapes from Chile and, of course, everything from broccoli to zucchini from California and Florida.

The leaps and bounds made in the technology of transport and shipping over the last fifteen years means that produce is shipped halfway round the world; it either arrives in the same perfect shape as when it left the tree or, having been picked at the right moment, arrives ripe and ready for eating. As a result, produce is no longer seasonal. The ground may be frozen and covered with three feet of snow in New Brunswick, but we still have everything from grapes to snow peas waiting in the market.

The temperature of shipping containers is controlled to within a couple of degrees. We can unpack grapes for the stall at Pete's and know that the fruit looks and tastes every bit as good at that moment as it did when it was packed, 4,000 miles ago. The bananas you bought yesterday were probably picked green in Ecuador, and during their two-week sea voyage ripened to the lovely yellow that caught your eye when you went shopping. The strawberries, which look so marvellous in January, were probably sitting in a field in California twenty-four hours earlier.

Thanks to modern transport, to air freight, container technology, refrigeration and storage facilities, there is an overwhelming variety of fresh produce arriving daily at supermarkets and fruit stalls. And we take all this freshness and variety for granted, even though the lettuce has probably traveled further than we did in the preceding week.

But the miracle of modern transport is not the only thing that gives us ultra-fresh fruit and vegetables. Pre-cooling has become a major factor in the last thirty years. Have you ever wondered why the broccoli from California you bought at the supermarket on the weekend looks better on Thursday than the broccoli you picked up at the farmers' market on Monday? It's because of pre-cooling—an amazing process by which the field heat is drawn out of fruit and vegetables and ice-cold air is circulated around them so

Can you imagine that your great-grandfather ever had the chance to eat fresh grapes in January, or savor the crunch of a just-picked-apple six months before he would get any from his trees, let alone sink his teeth into the creamy-custard of a cherimoya, or the luscious sweetness of a persimmon?

that within thirty minutes of being picked, produce is at 33° F inside and out. This means that not only can fresh fruit and vegetables stand up to long-distance travel, but once it reaches its destination, its shelf life has increased by ten to twenty times. This is why zucchini from Florida in January tastes every bit as delicious as field-fresh zucchini in July. It may even taste better.

The wonders of modern technology have also brought fresh herbs into the market year-round. At Pete's, basil, dill, mint and coriander are the most common. I worked at a café in a little seaside town one summer not long ago. One week a co-worker's aunt brought in a shopping bag full of bunches of herbs in their own little plastic sacks, the stalks wrapped in damp paper towel. For the next two weeks, everything we served was garnished with fresh herbs: the grilled salmon was accompanied by dill; the scallops with Pernod and cream were garnished with tarragon; the tomato salad was dusted with freshly chopped basil. Every single dish got rave reviews.

I always recommend using fresh herbs; dried herbs are a poor substitute. The difference between fresh and dried is night and day. If you are worried that you might not use a whole bunch of a fresh herb at once, Pete recommends that you chop up any excess herb and place it by the teaspoonful into the compartments of an ice-cube tray; then add water and freeze. Every time you need a teaspoonful of the herb, simply thaw out a cube and the herb will be almost as flavorful as it was fresh.

One day when a customer asked how to preserve herbs I told her Pete's little ice-cube trick. Now every few weeks she comes in and orders a couple of bunches of something rare, takes them home and freezes them. She says that she will never go back to dried herbs again.

Cooking is an art and a good cook an artist (not necessarily vice-versa), and as a good artist knows how to blend colors and how to use light and shade, so a good cook knows how to blend flavors and how to use herbs. Herbs will make or break a meal. A handful of fresh herbs in a lettuce and tomato salad will turn it into a gourmet delight. Knowing how to use fresh herbs is a key to the art of fine cuisine.

There is, in all of this, one thing that Pete and I

would like you to bear in mind. When we talk about how long you can expect to store produce once you get it home, we are talking about A-1 fruit and vegetables. If your celery is wilted when you buy it, make allowances for this. Don't go home and store it for a week. If the only alfalfa sprouts you could get were turning a little brown, eat them on the way home or use them up on your first salad. Don't plan your meal for the day after tomorrow around them, because when you go to use them, they will only be fit for the garbage.

This is a guide book with some unusual recipes, a number of surprising combinations, some of which will win you over right away. Some may take a little more of this or a little less of that to suit your palate.

So explore, be adventurous, be daring... try Midnight Parsnip Snack, taste Fried Ñame, savor Dill with Steamed Carrots. Go on, have a little fun!

Pete
KING of GREENGROCERS

Once upon a time, not so very long ago or so very far away, somewhere around the middle of England, a boy was born who was destined to become a king: King of the Greengrocers. His name was Pete Luckett. He was the third of four children born to an "unwealthy" family who lived in a terraced house in the city of Nottingham. There was nothing special about this family, except that they were his family. When Pete was a little boy, his mum and dad did not have a crib for him, so he slept in a drawer. There was no indoor plumbing; the toilet was in the yard. A family pastime was to take an old pram and gather coke or coal off the railway tracks, where it had fallen from trains. This is a standard beginning for every king. It is believed to build character. It certainly worked for Pete!

Right from his wee nipperhood, the prince loved his future kingdom—the outdoor markets. He was intrigued by the hustle and bustle, the vibrancy of selling fruits and vegetables. He used to go to the markets just to watch the barrowmen ply their trade. Pete would stand for hours and listen to them getting excited, screaming, yelling, hollering, fascinated by the patter, the lingo which is unique to English markets. He admired the beautiful stalls and the pride that the vendors took in their displays. The whole area was a wealth of color and excitement. "It was a really alive place to be."

While still a lad, about ten or eleven, his mum used to give him about one pound fifty—thirty bob—to go and buy the week's fruit and veg for the family. This was his royal duty every Saturday morning. With a shopping bag carefully clutched in his hand, the little prince would climb onto the bus and ride it into the middle of the town, to Nottingham Central Market. Pete would check out all they best buys and wheel and deal and bargain with the barrowmen. He would return home laden with produce and a huge grin on his face, usually munching some fruit he'd nicked off a barrow. His mum would give him a big smile and a pat on the head and say, "Well done, our Pete!"

At sixteen, Pete started working in the produce department of a high-class grocery store and for the next five years, despite occasional forays into the hotel trade, concentrated on learning all that there was to know about the fruit and vegetable business. After two years, he shifted from grocery stores to his first love, the open-air markets. He learned all the chat, the lines, the flattery, the gestures. It wasn't long before he could hold his own with any of the lads.

When he was twenty-one, a stall came up for sale in Nottingham's Victoria Market and Pete opened Pete's Frootique. Competition was fierce. Pete's Frootique was one of twenty fruit stalls all in a line. "All doin' the same as me, all chattin' up the customers, all shoutin' and yellin' their wares, all with fabulous displays." Nevertheless, Pete ran his stall successfully, with a little help from friends and family. After four years, Pete decided that it was time to move, so move he did. He sold everything, lock, stock and barrel, went to Heathrow and boarded the first plane going to North America, with nothing but a handful of money and a suitcase.

The next few years were adventurous ones for Pete. He traveled across the United States, through Guatemala, Belize and Mexico, and even spent some time in French Guyana, working in Texas, Florida and Belize when he needed more money. Eventually, his wanderlust wearing thin, Pete decided to settle down and applied for immigration to Canada. Three months later he moved to Alberta but after a brief year in western Canada, Pete, going against the general trend, moved east and bought a farm in southeast New Brunswick.

Although Pete loved farm life, it quickly became obvious that he was not going to make a living at it. A year or two earlier, a germ of an idea had been sown in Pete's head when he had read about the Saint John City Market in *Harrowsmith* magazine. It sounded like a typical English market, one that could use a greengrocer. When money was dangerously low, Pete decided to go to Saint John to take a look at this market and the possibilities of getting back to what he does best.

The general report about Saint John was not particularly favorable. Pete was warned about "the scruffiest, dirtiest, horriblest city in Canada, smelly, disgusting and not friendly." Undaunted, he got on the bus and headed toward this dragon of a city. The

With $230 worth of produce and ten years of experience, Pete revived Pete's Frootique and a king was crowned!

emerging monarch will never forget his first reaction to the home of his future kingdom. He was wonderfully impressed. "The old 'ouses, the colou', the streets, the way it was all buil', the characters tha' I saw aroun' town . . . I thought it was a real neat place. I though' it was real sharp."

The first thing Pete did was to head for the city market, where he managed to wrangle a deal with the clerk who gave him a twelve-foot bench stall in the middle of the market. Within two months he had shifted to a more appropriate spot with lots of available counter space and the requisite refrigerator.

There are few uptowners who do not remember the arrival of this barrowman to the Saint John City Market and few who frequent the market today who do not know him. Every day, six days a week, one hour before the market opens, Pete's employees arrive to begin the daily task of setting up the stall, getting fruit and vegetables out of the cooler or the warm room, and loading up the Brussels sprouts, green beans, broccoli, cauliflower, bananas, strawberries, anything which would not survive the night without the benefits of either heat or refrigeration. (For Pete's first ten years in the market, there was no heat in winter and no air conditioning in summer.)

It is impossible not to notice the influence of a decade of experience as a barrowman. Pete's Frootique is a blaze of carefully coordinated colours and shapes. The quality of his produce is second to none and his prices are excellent. Every employee keeps a keen eye on color: they never put the broccoli beside the green beans or the beets beside the potatoes, let alone the mandarins beside the navel oranges, or the Macs beside the Red Delicious. Dull colors are used to set off the bright green of broccoli or the vibrant orange of carrots. Quality is also carefully controlled. Pete's advice to his team is, "If you wouldn't buy it you'self, don' put it out."

When I shop at Pete's, I simply put produce in my basket. I don't bother with the 360-degree check. I know that if something is on the stall at Pete's, it is good. If by some unlucky occurrence customers get something that is not the best, they have no doubt but that it will be unquestioningly replaced or their money refunded on the spot, with a smile. Customers are Pete's livelihood and each one of them knows it.

As the day progresses, Pete's part of the market is a hub of activity, humming with conversations, usually in full voice, the phone ringing off the hook, orders being filled, customers being waited on or loading their baskets, Pete's employees keeping the displays "sparklin', " and full to overflowing.

As Pete's Frootique has grown in the City Market, so Pete's Frootique has grown outside the market. There are two more Pete's Frootiques and two Pete's Frootique warehouses. Pete's trucks and vans, which zip along the streets of Saint John and the highways of New Brunswick, cannot be missed with their brightly colored Pete's Frootique logo on the side. In the summer, the busiest season for Pete and his Frootique, there are between thirty and forty employees. Not bad for a man who started with $230 worth of produce and a twelve-foot stall!

Pete's employees are few when compared to his viewers! When Pete first arrived at the City Market he was certainly the loudest vendor there, ready with a comment about anything and everything and a joke or an antic for every occasion. Because he had a friend who worked for CBC radio, his comments were often aired. And because he was lively, informative and funny, he was interviewed frequently. A fan at CBC radio was talking with some friends at CBC television and Pete's name came up. Not long after, Pete's phone rang. It was a CBC producer. The station was starting a new show and would Pete like to have a brief spot as greengrocer?

Two or three times a week, Pete says as much as he possibly can in two minutes about any fruit or vegetable he chooses. These are aired on CBC's Midday and once a week on the CBC News for New Brunswick. Thanks to CBC, Pete and his Frootique have become a main tourist attraction. During the summer at Pete's, there seems to be a long string of people, loyal fans, who "watch Pete every time he's on, without fail," some apparently traveling halfway across the country just to come to the market for an autograph or a photograph, or to buy a T-shirt with Pete's distinctive logo on the front and his trademark, "Toodaledoo" across the back. And Pete greets everyone of them with the charm and enthusiasm which has got him where he is today. He has no lack of fans to cheer him on, no matter what he tries to do!

No matter where Pete is, he is noticeable. If he is not extolling the virtues of his favorite exotic fruit to an amused customer, he is encouraging a cashier to "Take good care of this lady, darlin'. She's a special friend of mine," or ensuring a hesitant shopper that the Spanish onions "really are so sweet, they'll rot your teeth," or giving a delighted child a handful of grapes or strawberries for a treat or, in the manner of a busy politician, carrying on three or four conversations at once.

Vegetables

Artichokes

Artichokes are not something you eat in a hurry. Eating one of these vegetables is a lengthy but delicious task. And, amazingly, after you've finished, there seems to be more on your plate than when you started—all those nibbled leaves and leftover fuzz.

Artichokes could correctly be called flowers; they are the flowers of a variety of thistle. Although there are various types of artichokes available to Europeans, almost all North American, or globe, artichokes are grown in Castroville, California, where they grow more artichokes than anywhere else in the world. If you shop at a specialty market, you may also find artichokes imported from outside North America.

Artichokes are available off and on all year. Their peak season is from March through May, and they may be a little scarce in July and August. Look for tight, compact heads with thick, blemish-free leaves. A good head will be heavy for its size and feel fresh and crisp. Someone once told me that a good artichoke will squeak if you squeeze it. This may be an old wives' tale, but give your intended a squeeze; if it does squeak, you'll only enjoy it more! Avoid artichokes with loose, spreading leaves and discoloration. The exception to this rule are the "winter-kissed" artichokes which appear on the market at the beginning of November. The bronze markings on the leaves are a result of being touched by the first frost, thus slowing the maturing process and enhancing the flavor. Size has nothing to do with taste. Big artichokes are simply easier to stuff and have larger hearts.

Artichokes may be refrigerated in a closed plastic bag, or a plastic container with a tightly fitting lid, for up to a week.

They are a good source of folate and vitamin C, and provide considerable potassium and iron. Four ounces/120 grams of cooked artichoke contain 53 calories.

To prepare the artichokes, simply wash them and, if you can't break off the stems, cut them off flush with the base.

(Until I was lucky enough to buy some inexpensive artichoke steamers, I used to leave the stems on. Then I could stand them up on their stems in a pot and, since they would be out of the water, they would steam rather nicely.) Pull off and throw away the little leaves at the base and any tough discolored leaves. Immediately dip the artichokes into acidulated water, then lay them on their sides and cut off the top one-third. Or cut the spiky tops off each leaf with a pair of stainless-steel scissors. They are now ready to steam.

The usual way of eating a cooked artichoke is to tear off the outer leaves, one at a time, dip them in a sauce and then scrape the flesh off with your teeth. This continues until you reach the central part of the artichoke, the "choke" of inedible, light fuzz. Then scrape or cut off the fuzz, exposing the heart, the most delectable part of the artichoke, which may be eaten with a knife and fork.

Artichokes discolor after they have been cut. To prevent this from happening, have ready a bowl of acidulated water in which to plunge the artichokes. Acidulated water is simply 1 quart/1 L of water mixed with 3 tablespoons/40 mL of vinegar or lemon juice. Contact with carbon, iron, steel or aluminum will also darken artichokes and give them a harsh flavor. So, use a stainless steel knife for cutting and a stainless steel or enamel saucepan for cooking.

Boiled or Steamed Artichokes

This is the simplest way to cook artichokes and particularly delicious. Because there is nothing but you and the artichokes and your chosen sauce, you can experience not only the richness of the vegetable, but also the fun of eating it.

1 tsp	salt	5 mL
4 Tbsp	olive oil	60 mL
4	large artichokes, washed and trimmed	4

Using a saucepan big enough to hold your artichokes, add the salt and olive oil to 3 inches/7 cm of boiling water. Steam the artichokes until the stem end is soft when pierced with a fork. This could take anywhere from 20 minutes to 1 hour depending on the size of the artichokes. Keep an eye on the liquid, adding more boiling water, if necessary, to prevent scorching. Turn the vegetables upside down and let them drain for a couple of minutes.

Serve them with a bowl of melted butter, mayonnaise or Hollandaise sauce. *Serves 4*

Stuffed Artichokes

This stuffing is my favorite. If you are planning to stuff artichokes, it is worth remembering that bread crumbs are especially compatible with this vegetable.

4	large artichokes, washed and trimmed	4
4 Tbsp	melted butter	60 mL
1	clove garlic, minced	1
¼ cup	mushrooms, chopped	50 mL
2 cups	fresh bread crumbs	500 mL
4	anchovy fillets, minced	4
1 Tbsp	capers, minced	15 mL
	Salt and pepper	
1 Tbsp	fresh thyme, finely chopped	15 mL
¼ cup	parsley, chopped	50 mL
¼ cup	Parmesan cheese, grated	50 mL
	Melted butter	
1 cup	chicken broth	250 mL

Steam the artichokes until they are tender enough so that the leaves can be spread apart easily.

While the artichokes are cooking, melt the butter in a skillet and sauté the garlic and mushrooms until the mushrooms are tender; then mix in the bread crumbs, anchovies, capers, salt, pepper, thyme and parsley. Remove from the heat.

Drain the artichokes and let them cool until they can be easily handled; then hold the vegetable upside down on the counter and push down with the palm of your hand to spread the leaves apart. Remove the tiny central leaves and carefully spoon out the "choke." Fill the cavity with stuffing and push a little between the outer leaves. Sprinkle each artichoke with some grated Parmesan cheese.

Tie each vegetable around the middle so that it will keep its shape. Stand the artichokes upright in a casserole and brush with melted butter. Pour the broth around the bottoms of the artichokes and put the whole thing in the oven at 375° F/190° C for 30 minutes. Baste frequently with the liquid in the pan.
Serves 4

Asparagus

The only way to really enjoy asparagus is to eat it when it is as fresh as possible. Despite all the innovations of modern technology, we still cannot preserve asparagus in any truly acceptable form. Some years when we have a good crop, we can get almost enough at a reasonable price; but in those years when the harvest is not particularly plentiful, we all suffer.

Asparagus is available all year but is usually sold at very high prices, since it is imported, except during the North American harvest from April to June. When buying asparagus look for stalks with nice tight, compact heads; some heads may have a purple hue which is natural to the variety. The thickness of the stalks is a matter of taste; some people prefer thick stalks, some like them thinner. It makes little difference in the flavor of the vegetable itself. Avoid asparagus with ruffled tips or wrinkles in the stalks, which indicate that the vegetable is old and probably tough.

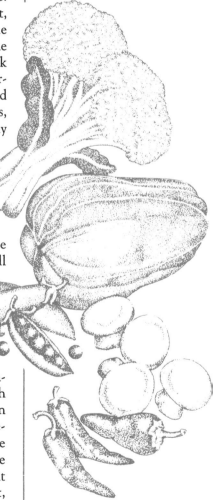

Asparagus, like mushrooms, should not be bought until the last possible moment. They are better off with your supplier than in your refrigerator. But once you get them home, either wrap the stem ends in wet paper towel and put the asparagus in a plastic bag or stand them up with the stem ends in a little water. If necessary, asparagus will keep like this for 4 days in the refrigerator.

Asparagus is an excellent source of vitamin C and folate and a good source of potassium. Four ounces/120 grams of the raw vegetable have only 30 calories.

There are some tips to bear in mind when dealing with this vegetable. The very first thing to remember is never, absolutely never, soak asparagus. To wash this vegetable, simply hold the stalks upside down under cold running water and shake them a bit to release any sand that might be trapped in the tips. The second important thing to remember is that since most asparagus is now a hybrid variety, ninety percent of the stalk is edible. It is not necessary to peel it, even less to cut the stalks right off. When trimming asparagus, you need only cut the smallest inch or so off the stalk, except of course if you buy a particularly old bunch of the vegetable. Then you might need to cut off a little more. The the third and final tip is *do not overcook asparagus*. There is almost nothing worse than overcooked asparagus. Bear these rules in mind and you will be sure to get the most from your asparagus.

The easiest thing to do with asparagus is simply to use it raw, tossed into a salad or with a mayonnaise-based sauce. Asparagus is one of those vegetables which needs little embellishment. As far as Pete and I are concerned, there are only two ways to eat asparagus: lightly steamed with butter and lemon juice or in a cold asparagus sandwich. A good cold asparagus sandwich is a moment of bliss and a good excuse to eat white bread. The cooked, cooled vegetable with a little lemony mayonnaise and some soft white bread is well worth a try!

Steamed Asparagus and Variations

1½ to 2 pounds	asparagus, washed with the bottoms trimmed	750 g to 1 kg
¼ cup	melted butter	50 mL
2 Tbsp	lemon juice	25 mL
1	lemon, thinly sliced	1
	Salt and pepper	

Because the stalks of asparagus tend to be thicker than the tips, they need a little more cooking, so the very best way to cook asparagus is to tie the stalks together in a bunch and stand them up, either in an asparagus pan, if you are lucky enough to have one, or an old coffee pot, such as Pete uses. What I do, because I have neither, is to put the vegetable in the deepest available pot and make a little hood out of aluminum foil to make sure the vegetable is well covered.

Pour a couple of inches of water into the bottom of the pot, put on a lid and bring the water to a rapid boil. Add the asparagus. It should only take about 10 minutes for the vegetable to be cooked perfectly. The asparagus is ready when the stems feel tender when pierced. But don't sacrifice the spears for the stems; if the spears are tender, remove the asparagus from the pot immediately.

Put the cooked asparagus on *warm* plates. Pour the

melted butter and the lemon juice over the vegetable. Garnish with a slice of lemon, and sprinkle with salt and freshly ground black pepper. *Serves 4*

With toasted almonds: instead of lemon juice, throw on a handful of toasted sliced almonds.

With pine nuts: instead of lemon juice, add some toasted pine nuts.

With cream: warm a little cream, either cereal or whipping cream. Cook over low heat until it thickens somewhat and pour it over the cooked asparagus, in place of lemon juice. Grate on a little nutmeg and serve with white pepper and salt.

For a delicious brunch treat, lay the asparagus on a warm plate and slide a poached egg on top. Pour some warm Hollandaise sauce over the egg and, if you want to be truly decadent, sprinkle with a little freshly grated Parmesan. Serve with thin slices of toasted white bread.

Asparagus belongs to the lily family, along with onions, leeks and garlic, not to mention tulips and gladioli . . . rather odd cousins! But we all know perfectly well what a luxury asparagus is.

Danish Asparagus

This is how we used to eat asparagus at my grandmother's. She had an asparagus patch, which explains the rather generous amount of this delicacy for each person. This is a main course, but it can be served in smaller quantities if you don't have an asparagus patch or are unwilling to take out a mortgage to prepare this dish.

4	hard-cooked eggs	4
1 cup	melted butter	250 mL
	Rind of 1 lemon, finely grated	
3 Tbsp	fresh lemon juice	50 mL
¼ cup	parsley, minced	50 mL
4 pounds	asparagus, washed and trimmed	2 kg
1 Tbsp	sesame seeds	15 mL
	Nutmeg (optional)	

Mash the eggs and combine them with the butter and salt in a small saucepan. Cook over low heat long enough to blend completely. Remove from the heat; stir in the lemon rind, juice and parsley. Keep warm.

Cook the asparagus until just tender. Lay the cooked vegetable on a warmed platter; pour the sauce over the vegetable and sprinkle with sesame seeds.

You might like to have some whole nutmeg and a grater handy. My uncles claim that nutmeg makes this dish just that much better. *Serves 4 or 8 as a main course; serves 16 as a small treat.*

Avocado Pears

These extraordinary pear-shaped packages are one of the pure undiluted luxuries of the produce world. Technically they are a fruit, and over the last decade or so, they have become as readily available as tomatoes in most markets, although not in the same quantity. Despite their availability, avocados have not become ordinary.

One either loves or loathes the avocado. Its wonderful velvety, buttery texture and rich, nutty taste either win you over at once or turn you off. Get two avocado lovers together and watch them.

One day while I was working at Pete's, a man who had bought about 10 avocados the week before appeared at my cash. I commented on the fact that he was not buying avocados this week, even though they were less expensive than they had been the week before. He looked at me in astonishment, turned his nose up and said, "Those are a completely different type of avocado and their taste does not compare with the ones I bought last week." It was then that I became aware of the amazing and obvious differences in the varieties.

Avocados are available all year round but their peak season is from December to May. They are ready to eat when they yield to gentle pressure. Often the best bet is to buy avocados before they are ripe and let them ripen at home by putting them in a loosely closed paper bag at room temperature. Keep checking them because there is a fine line between perfect ripeness and over-ripeness. Once the fruit is ripe, you may store it in the warmest part of your refrigerator for up to 3 days. Pete claims that avocados taste better if you take them out of the refrigerator for a while before you serve them. When buying avocados, keep an eye out for dark patches on the skin and soft or sunken spots; an avocado should be uniformly soft or hard.

Avocados are an excellent source of folate and a

good source of potassium and magnesium. The real killer is their caloric content due to the oil in the fruit (thirty percent in some varieties). Four ounces/120 grams, about half a medium-sized avocado, have almost 160 calories! (But they are worth every single one!)

Avocados can be cooked, but few would argue that cooking improves them. Pete says that he has never cooked an avocado and never would, so neither will we. Cut in half, the pit cavity provides a natural spot to pop in a little chicken or shrimp salad, which is especially good with avocado. You can also put a few slices on a green salad or serve them decoratively arranged on a plate and drizzled with a little of your favorite vinaigrette. I make a salad with sliced avocados, minced shallots and cherry tomato halves with snow peas broken over the top. I let the whole thing sit in a vinaigrette for about half an hour and then pour off the excess dressing: it's excellent.

In North America, all avocados come from California and Florida. The Florida avocados have smooth, shiny, green skins and tend to be larger and more watery than those grown in California. Pete's own particular favorite is the Hass avocado, grown in California. It is oval and has a dark green knobbly skin which turns purple or black when ripe; its flesh could not possibly be richer. "A perfectly ripe Hass avocado is almos' a miracle darlin'," exclaims Pete. It is like eating butter out of a shell. Amazing!

Avocados with Shrimp Salad

3	large avocados, halved lengthwise	3
1	lemon, cut up so that you can rub it on the avocados	1
1 pound	cooked shelled shrimp, halved	500 g
½	English cucumber, chopped	½
1	Serrano or Jalapeño pepper, seeded and minced	1
2	hard-cooked eggs, chopped	2
12	pitted black olives, chopped	12
	Mayonnaise	
	Sour Cream	
	Salt	
	Alfalfa sprouts	
	Sprigs of fresh coriander or parsley	

Scoop out the flesh of the avocados without damaging the shells. Discard the pit. Put the flesh into a bowl. Rub the inside of each shell lightly with the lemon to prevent discoloring. Mash the avocado flesh with a fork. Add the shrimp, cucumber, hot pepper, eggs and olives. Mix well. Add enough mayonnaise and sour cream (in a ratio which appeals to you) to hold everything together. Season with salt. Line the avocado shells with a layer of alfalfa sprouts and stuff them with the salad mixture. Top each shell with a sprig of parsley or coriander. *Serves 6*

Avocado Coriander Soup

This recipe comes from a woman who shops at Pete's and regularly buys avocados and bunches of coriander. She says this soup is one of her staples.

2	ripe avocados, peeled and cut up	2
½	English cucumber, seeded and chopped	½
3 to 4	large green onions, chopped	3 to 4
2	cloves garlic, minced	2
1½ cups	yogurt	375 mL
	Juice of ½ lime	
1 cup	chicken broth	250 mL
½ tsp	cayenne	2 mL
¼ cup	fresh coriander, chopped	50 mL
	Salt and pepper	
	Coriander leaves	
	Paprika	

Put everything except the salt, pepper, coriander and paprika into a food processor or blender. Process until smooth. Chill. If the mixture is too thick, thin with a little milk. Season with salt and pepper. Garnish with fresh coriander leaves and a sprinkle of paprika. *Serves 4*

Guacamole

Guacamole is best made just before you are going to serve it, because it darkens considerably if it has to wait.

2	large, very ripe avocados	2
1	medium tomato, peeled, seeded and chopped	1
½	small onion minced	½
3	cloves garlic, minced	3
2	Serrano or Jalapeño peppers, finely chopped	2
	Juice of 1 lime	
	Chili powder to taste	
	Sprigs of fresh coriander or	

parsley
Salt and pepper

Scoop the flesh out of the avocado shells and mash well. Blend the remaining ingredients with the avocado flesh. *Makes about 4 cups/1 L*

Guacamole may be served with corn or tortilla chips (it's especially nice if you heat the chips), fresh vegetables, cooked shrimp, cooked chicken or scooped into a tomato shell. Guacamole is a very personalised creation: feel free to add a little homemade mayonnaise or sour cream. If you like a little crunch, add some chopped sweet peppers, olives or a small diced cucumber.

Beans

Snap and wax beans, as green and yellow beans are commonly called, are available all year, their peak season being from May to August. Look for smooth, crisp beans which are free from blemishes or spots. They should snap easily if they are fresh. Pete buys his yellow beans when they are a little green at either end, like an unripe banana. He says that is the best way to make sure they are fresh and tender. Avoid beans which are flabby or wilted, or those with thick fibrous pods, an indication that they are too mature.

Yellow and green beans are stored the same way. Put them, unwashed, into plastic bags and refrigerate. They will keep for 3 to 4 days.

Beans are a good source of vitamin C, folate and potassium; they also provide some iron. Four ounces/120 grams of cooked beans have 40 calories.

When beans are ready to use, wash them well in cold water. Snip off the stems and tops. Beans can be left whole, or cut or broken straight across in 2-inch/5-cm pieces. The Chinese prefer long oblique slices; the French, long, thin slivers. If the beans are small enough, they are particularly delicious left whole.

A key factor when dealing with beans is cooking time. Beans should be cooked as little as possible—just long enough to take away the raw taste but not so long that they loose their snap. It is important to keep testing them so that they do not overcook.

These little green morsels are one of summer's delights. If you are lucky enough to have a garden, or an above average greengrocer (like Pete), you will know the delicious taste of truly fresh green beans. Green and yellow beans are interchangeable. For a little extra color, mix them together.

Boiled Beans and Variations

2 pounds	beans, washed, trimmed and left whole or cut up	1 kg
4 Tbsp	butter, chopped	60 mL
	Salt and pepper	

In a large saucepan, boil just enough water to cover the beans. Drop in the beans, a few at a time, so that the water never stops boiling. If it does, stop, put a lid on the saucepan and bring it back to a boil. You must remember, however, to cook the beans without a lid on or they will lose their bright color. Boil for 3 to 10 minutes, depending on the age and size of the beans. Taste them as they cook. The instant they are done to your liking, drain them. Put the pot back on the stove and toss the beans with the butter until the butter has melted. Season with salt and pepper.

With toasted almonds: toss the beans with the butter and ½ cup/125 mL toasted sliced almonds.

With garlic and pine nuts: substitute ¼ cup/50 mL olive oil for the butter. In a skillet, heat the oil and sauté 3 finely chopped cloves of garlic until tender. Add ½ cup/125 mL toasted pine nuts. Toss with the beans.

With fresh herbs: toss the beans with olive oil or butter and 1½ tsp/7 mL fresh tarragon, dill, marjoram or garlic and basil.

With cream: toss the beans with butter and add ½ cup/125 mL cream—a mix of whipping and coffee cream is nice, or you can use one or the other.

With tomato: toss the beans with the butter and add some heated tomato sauce. Sprinkle with fresh, chopped parsley before serving. *Serves 4*

Chilled Beans and Variations

Cook the beans as above but toss them with 4 tablespoons/60 mL of olive oil instead of the butter, *after* you have chilled them.

With mustard-flavored mayonnaise: add 2 or 3 Tbsp/25 or 50 mL Dijon mustard to a rich homemade mayonnaise. Toss in a handful of crumbled, crisply cooked bacon.

Dilled vinaigrette: toss the beans in a vinaigrette

made with dill vinegar or add 3 or 4 Tbsp/50 or 60 mL of freshly chopped dill to your favorite dressing. *Serves 4*

Beans etc.

1½ pounds	beans, washed, trimmed and cut up	750 g
1 Tbsp	olive oil	15 mL
1 Tbsp	butter	15 mL
½ cup	mushrooms, sliced	125 mL
1	medium onion, very thinly sliced	1
2	cloves garlic, mashed	2
3	large tomatoes, peeled, seeded and chopped	3
¼ cup	minced fresh basil	50 mL
⅓ cup	parsley, minced	75 mL
	Salt and pepper	

Boil the beans in 1 cup/250 mL salted water for 5 minutes. Drain and chill.

In a skillet, heat the oil and butter. Sauté the mushrooms, onion and garlic until the onion is soft and transparent. Add the tomatoes, basil, salt, pepper and parsley. Cook for 5 minutes, stirring frequently.

Add the beans and mix well. Cook for 3 to 5 minutes or until the beans are just tender. *Serves 4*

Beans à la South of France

1½ pounds	beans, trimmed, washed and cut up	750 g
1	large onion, minced	1
1	clove garlic, minced	1
1	small red pepper, cut in strips	1
3 Tbsp	butter	50 mL
¼ cup	thyme, chopped	50 mL
	Salt and pepper	
¼ cup	parsley, minced	50 mL

Cook the beans in boiling, salted water until tender-crisp. While the beans are cooking, sauté the onion, garlic and red pepper in the butter, stirring constantly, for 5 minutes or until the onion is transparent. Drain the beans and add them to the onion mixture. Season. Cook over medium heat for 4 minutes, stirring to coat the beans with the onion. Sprinkle with parsley and serve hot. *Serves 4*

Yard-Long Beans

I would be doing an injustice to you and to the long bean if I did not mention this Asian wonder—the yard-long bean. Usually only about half a yard long, the yard-long bean is similar to our common green bean, not botanically but in taste. Cut into 2-inch/5-cm sections, yard-long beans are superb in a meaty stir-fry, or added to a stew during the last 15 minutes of cooking. They are also delicious braised. But do not bother cooking them any other way, because the yard-long bean does not do well when compared with our own green bean.

There are essentially two types of dau gok, an alias for this bean: the pale-green type tends to be slightly sweet and fleshy; the dark green variety is a little drier and not quite so delicate in taste. This creature does not keep. Buy it and use it. If you must, you can store it in a plastic bag in the refrigerator for 2 days, but no longer. One cup/250 mL of the Chinese long bean has about 45 calories, lots of vitamin A, some vitamin C and a little potassium.

Beets

Beets are available almost all year round, their peak season being from June to October. They are especially good in the early summer, when we get the delicious beet greens, the leaves still attached to the root. Look for beets having a good round shape, smooth, firm flesh and a rich, deep-red color. The smaller vegetables are tender, the larger ones tougher. If the green tops are attached, they should be fresh in appearance, although it will not affect the quality of the root if the leaves are slightly wilted. Avoid spotted, pitted beets, or those with scales. If you are buying the greens without the beet attached, look for thin-ribbed leaves which are fresh and clean.

If the beet greens are fresh, store them in the refrigerator and use them as soon as possible. The beets themselves will keep for up to three weeks in a plastic bag in the vegetable drawer of the refrigerator.

Beets are a good source of potassium and an excellent source of folate. The greens provide some calcium; they are also a good source of iron and an excellent source of potassium and vitamins A and C. Four ounces/120 grams of cooked beets have about 40 calories. Four ounces/120 grams of cooked beet greens have about 30 calories.

Pete's favorite way to cook beet greens is as quickly as possible, which preserves much of their texture and nutritional value. It is preferable to boil or steam the greens in, or over, a small amount of water for about 10 minutes. Then serve them with black pepper and butter. You might like to add some crisply cooked bacon or some Parmesan cheese for a little extra flavor.

Aunt Gill's Beets

My Aunt Gill is a beet lover and her beets are always a cause for celebration, because they are so delicious. Cooking them is easy enough, but the preparation is a little more work.

Simply put the beets in a large pot and boil them for about one hour, or until the skins slip off. Then peel and grate them. You have to work quickly so that the beets don't get cold. Aunt Gill recommends using a paper towel so that you don't burn you fingers.

If you have a microwave, you can grate the beets after they have cooled off and then heat them up again. When they are all grated, add butter, salt and lots of freshly ground black pepper.

This is pure beet in all its delicious glory. For something a little more exciting, you can blend the beets with anything recommended below, but do try them plain first!

There are four different varieties of beets which are commonly cultivated: the garden beet, which we all know and love; the leaf beet, more commonly known as Swiss chard; the sugar beet, from which we get most of our sugar and the mangold, which is a major source of livestock feed in Europe. Perhaps we should have more respect for the apparently dull beet!

Baked Beets and Variations

Combine cooked beets with any of the following for a delicious treat. Use 1 pound/500 g of beets for 2 to 3 servings.

With onion and herbs: slice the beets and serve with melted butter, chopped onion, vinegar and 2 Tbsp/25 mL of tarragon, marjoram, thyme or dill.

With yogurt: slice and serve with yogurt and black pepper.

With onion and orange: slice and serve hot with chopped onion and orange sections.

Scandinavian Pickled Beets

½ cup	cider or white vinegar	125 mL
½ cup	water	125 mL
½ cup	sugar	125 mL
	Salt and pepper	
6	large beets, cooked, peeled and thinly sliced	6
2 Tbsp	caraway seeds	25 mL
	A sprig of fresh dill, chopped	

Combine the vinegar, water, sugar, salt and pepper. Boil for 5 minutes. Cool. Pour the liquid over the beets and sprinkle with caraway seeds. Cover and refrigerate overnight. Before serving, drain and sprinkle with chopped dill. *Serves 4*

Beets Parmesan

16	tiny beets, cooked and peeled	16
⅔ cup	coffee cream	150 mL
	Salt and pepper	
⅓ cup	Parmesan cheese, grated	75 mL
	A sprig of dill, chopped	

Mix the beets and the cream. Season with salt and pepper. Simmer over low heat, stirring constantly, until the beets and cream are heated through. Add the Parmesan cheese and cook until the cheese is melted. Serve hot. Sprinkle with chopped dill before serving. *Serves 4 to 6*

Chilled Buttermilk-Beet Soup

4	large beets, peeled and grated	4
2 Tbsp	butter	25 mL
4 cups	chicken stock	1 L
½ cup	green onions, finely chopped	125 mL
1 tsp	sugar	5 mL
2 cups	buttermilk	500 mL
1 Tbsp	fresh dill, chopped	15 mL
	Salt and pepper	

Sauté the beets in butter for 5 minutes. Add the chicken stock and simmer until tender. Add the green onions and cook for 5 minutes. Blend in a food processor or blender until smooth. Chill. Stir in the sugar, buttermilk and fresh dill. Season with salt and pepper to taste. *Serves 6*

Belgian Endive

This delicacy has intrigued me ever since I first stuck the price into the basket of Belgian endive at Pete's. French endive, or Witloof chicory as it is also called, is expensive. It comes packed as though it was crystal—in little wooden boxes, beautifully wrapped in waxy purple paper. I quickly understood that this was not just an ordinary vegetable. It is a lovely looking creature. Imagine the end of a baseball bat, shrink it down and make it a little more pointed—that is the shape of Belgian endive. The heads are slender and smooth and almost completely white, except for a little yellow or green around the edge of the leaves. It has a mildly bitter flavor.

Belgian endive is available all year, with its peak season during the summer months. Look for firm, crisp heads with pure-white leaves, light yellow around their edges and tips. Heads should be between 4 and 6 inches/10 and 15 cm long. The vegetable is very clean and only needs to be wiped off with a damp cloth to be ready for eating. It stores well if you are careful. Wrap it in damp paper towel and refrigerate it for up to 5 days, making sure the heads are well covered; the endive needs to be protected from light.

It is important to remember that if you are using Belgian endive simply as a salad green, a little goes a long way. You can slice the heads and add a handful to a salad, or you can serve the individual leaves stuffed with almost anything. The taste of Belgian endive mixes beautifully with mild cheese, apples or beets, almost anything which is a little sweet.

Belgian endive is a good source of vitamin A and potassium and an excellent source of folate. Four ounces/120 grams of the vegetable have 20 calories.

Belgian Semi-Waldorf

My sister named this salad and it does vaguely resemble a Waldorf salad. It is delicious and easy. I find that the taste improves if you let it sit in the refrigerator for a day before you serve it; the flavors mellow.

½ pound	Belgian endive, cleaned and thinly sliced	250 g
2	apples, diced	2
1	carrot, sliced	1
¼ cup	freshly-shelled walnuts	50 mL
¼ cup	raisins soaked for 1 hour in hot water	50 mL
½ cup	mild cheese such as Mozzarella, cubed	125 mL
1 tsp	lemon juice	5 mL
1 tsp	sugar	5 mL
½ cup	vinaigrette	125 mL
¼ cup	fresh parsley, coarsely chopped	50 mL

Mix the fruit and vegetables, nuts and cheese. Add the lemon juice and sugar to the vinaigrette (see recipe below) and blend well. Pour the vinaigrette over the endive mixture and toss well. Sprinkle with parsley and serve. *Serves 4 to 6*

	Vinaigrette	
¼ cup	lemon juice	50 mL
¼ cup	vegetable oil	50 mL
1 Tbsp	wine vinegar	15 mL
1 Tbsp	anchovy paste (optional)	15 mL
1 tsp	dill	5 mL
1 tsp	salt	5 mL
¼ tsp	oregano	1 mL
¼ tsp	pepper	1 mL

In a small bowl, whisk together the lemon juice, oil,

vinegar, anchovy paste, dill, salt, oregano and pepper. *Makes ¾ cup/150 mL*

Belgian Endive with Ham and Cheese

This makes a delicious, different and simple lunch dish. Pete's friend, who gave me this recipe, also says that to spruce it up, you need only pour Hollandaise sauce over the top. Definitely up-market!

4	heads Belgian endive	4
8	slices ham	8
8	slices Swiss cheese	8

Boil the endive in ½ cup/125 mL of salted water, just long enough to soften the heads a bit. Slice each head in half. Wrap each half with a slice of ham. Lay them on a greased cookie sheet or in a buttered casserole, side by side, lay the cheese across the top and broil until the cheese is melted and a bubbly golden. *Serves 4*

Braised Belgian Endive

Most Belgian endive fans prefer the vegetable cooked this way.

3	small carrots, sliced	3
2	small onions, sliced	2
2 Tbsp	butter	25 mL
1 pound	Belgian endive, cut in ½-inch/ 1.25-cm slices	500 g
2 cups	chicken stock	500 mL
1 Tbsp	lemon juice	15 mL
1	bay leaf	1
	Salt, pepper and thyme	
1 Tbsp	cornstarch dissolved in	15 mL
1 Tbsp	water	15 mL

Sauté the carrots and onions in the butter for 5 minutes. Lay the sliced endive on top. Pour the chicken stock over the endive and add the lemon juice and the bay leaf. Season with salt, pepper and thyme. Over medium heat, bring the mixture to a boil and cook gently for 10 to 15 minutes. Add the cornstarch and mix it into the sauce. Adjust the seasoning. Serve hot. *Serves 4 to 6*

Bok Choy

If you ask for Chinese cabbage in some grocery stores, you might be mistakenly led to bok choy. Although its taste is cabbage-like, bok choy bears no resemblance to Chinese cabbage. It is an uncommonly pretty vegetable in its mature stage, with pure, silvery-white central stalks and dark, bluish-green leaves. Baby bok choy is comparatively rare and not as attractive, being all one shade of green, the leaves only slightly darker than the stalks. Like Chinese cabbage, bok choy is two vegetables in one— the leaves and the stalks—which should be cooked separately. The leaves take much less cooking time, having a slightly hot taste; the stalks are succulent and crunchy.

Bok choy is available all year. Look for vegetables with big leaves if you want to use them for soup, and longer narrower stems if you are planning on a stir-fry (bok choy's forté). Buy clean-looking bok choy with clear, white stalks and crisp, bright-green leaves. Brown slippery spots on the leaves indicate overchilling which reduces the vegetable's flavor.

It is better to use bok choy as soon as possible rather than store it. You can, however, refrigerate it, unwashed in a plastic bag, for 2 days. Don't forget that it does not hold up to storage well. To wash it, simply hold it under cold running water just before using it and drain it well.

Like many other Chinese vegetables, bok choy is low in calories, with only 15 in ½ cup/125 mL. Bok choy is also rich in vitamins A and C and a good source of potassium.

Pete likes to add a handful of chopped bok choy stalks and leaves to a salad for a little extra crunch. The next time you are having a simple soup, throw in a few thin strips of bok choy leaves; they only need to simmer for 5 minutes. You can also toss in the stalks, chopped up. Since they need to cook a little longer, put the stalks in before the leaves. Your next stir-fry is simply waiting for bok choy. Slice up the stalk and add it first; then shred and add the leaves. The stalks take about the same time to stir-fry as celery; the leaves, literally seconds. An interesting variation with the bok choy leaves is to cut them into long very thin strips and fry them for an instant in a generous amount of oil. They need only a little salt and pepper for seasoning and can serve as a bed for something special, or as a dish on their own.

Simple Bok Choy Stir-fry

This is essentially a "how-to" recipe. It is fast and couldn't be much easier.

2 Tbsp	peanut oil	25 mL
1½ pounds	bok choy, cleaned, the stems cut into 1-inch/2.5-cm slices, the leaves thinly sliced	750 g
1 tsp	brown sugar	5 mL
¼ tsp	garlic, minced	1 mL
	Salt to taste	
1 tsp	fresh ginger, minced	5 mL
4	slices of bacon, crisply cooked and crumbled	4

In a frying pan or wok, heat the oil until it smokes. Drop in the chopped stems of the bok choy and fry over high heat for about 4 minutes, or less, until the stems are soft on the outside but still crunchy.

Add the bok choy leaves, sugar, garlic, salt and the minced ginger. Cook, stirring constantly, for another 2 minutes or until the mixture is tender but still crispy. Sprinkle with crumbled bacon. *Serves 4*

Broccoli

Broccoli must be as close to perfection as anything in the vegetable world. It is easy to use in a wide variety of ways; it is beautiful to look at, tastes wonderful, has lots of vitamins and minerals and has very few calories. Broccoli is one of North America's favorite vegetables, and rightly so! You can eat it raw, steamed, in a quiche, in a salad, in a soufflé, on its own in a vinaigrette, with a sauce, without a sauce—the possibilities are almost endless.

Broccoli is available throughout the year, the peak season being from October to April. Look for tightly closed, compact bud clusters and firm, tender stems. The head should be a deep green, sometimes with a hint of purple. Avoid broccoli that is wilted, bruised or flabby, or with woody stalks.

To store broccoli, simply put the unwashed head in a plastic bag and place it in the refrigerator for no more than three days. Broccoli is very perishable, so it is a good idea to use it promptly.

There is never a good excuse for boiling broccoli: it is one of the worst things you can do to this fine vegetable. Boiling all but destroys both its flavor and its texture. The best way to cook this vegetable is to steam it, and not for long. Broccoli should be crisply tender when cooked.

Broccoli is also splendid in a stir-fry. Don't forget to eat the stems; just peel and slice them thinly, or cut them into spears. As a rule, it is unwise to cook the stems with the florets as they are tougher and take longer to cook; you risk overcooking the one in order to make the other edible.

Simply add the stems before the florets, and give them an extra 5 to 7 minutes cooking time. When the stem pieces are slightly soft, add the florets.

Italian Broccoli

3 Tbsp	olive oil	50 mL
1	clove garlic, minced	1
1	bunch broccoli, cut into florets	1
3	anchovies, mashed	3
1½ cups	dry wine, red or white	375 mL
	Salt and pepper	

In a deep frying pan, heat the oil. Sauté the garlic until it turns gold; add the broccoli. (If you are using the stems, they should be peeled, cut into 2-inch/5-cm slices and cooked for about 7 minutes. Test them before you add the florets.) Cook, stirring constantly, for 2 or 3 minutes.

Add the anchovies, wine, salt and pepper to taste. Cook over low heat for about 5 minutes, or until the broccoli is tender but not mushy. Stir occasionally. Serve hot. *Serves 3*

Broccoli and Cheese Quiche

This is actually a little more heavy-duty than a quiche.

1	bunch broccoli, cut into florets	1
1 cup	onion, sliced	250 mL
1 cup	mushrooms, sliced	250 mL
3 Tbsp	butter	50 mL
4	eggs, lightly beaten	4
1 cup	cereal or coffee cream	250 mL
½ cup	milk	125 mL
¼ tsp	Dijon mustard	1 mL
	Salt, pepper and nutmeg	
1 cup	old Cheddar cheese, grated	250 mL
1	unbaked 9-inch/23-cm pie shell (Add a little lemon peel to the pastry for this quiche to make it extra special!)	1

Fry the broccoli, onions and mushrooms in the butter until slightly tender. In a medium saucepan, beat the eggs into the cream and milk, add the mustard and season to taste with salt, pepper and nutmeg. Heat very gently until close to boiling but do not boil. Sprinkle the cheese into the pie shell, top with the vegetables and pour the egg mixture over top. Bake at 400° F/200° C for 15 minutes; then reduce the heat to 375° F/190° C and bake for another 30 minutes or until set. Let stand for 5 minutes before serving. *Serves 4*

Broccoli Mushroom Casserole

Broccoli is rich in vitamins A and C, folate and potassium. As a member of the cabbage family, it may be helpful in the prevention of some types of cancer. Broccoli is also low in calories, with only 33 calories in 4 ounces/120 grams of the raw vegetable, or 3/4 cup/175 mL of the cooked.

This casserole is extremely rich and filling.

1	bunch broccoli, florets and stems peeled and sliced	1
1 pound	fresh mushrooms, sliced	500 g
1 cup	chopped onion	250 mL
3 Tbsp	butter	50 mL
1/4 cup	chicken bouillon	50 mL
4	eggs	4
1 1/2 cups	cottage cheese	375 mL
1 cup	sour cream or yogurt	250 mL
3 cups	egg noodles	750 mL
2 Tbsp	butter	25 mL
1/4 cup	fine bread crumbs	50 mL
1 1/2 cups	old Cheddar cheese, grated	375 mL

Sauté the broccoli, mushrooms and onion in butter. Season with salt and pepper and remove from the heat. Toss the vegetables with the bouillon.

Beat the eggs in a bowl; whisk in the cottage cheese and the sour cream or yogurt.

Cook the egg noodles in salted water until slightly underdone. Drain and butter.

Mix the broccoli and cheese mixtures together with the noodles and place in a 9 x 13-inch/23 x 33-cm baking pan. Top with the bread crumbs and grated cheese. Bake, covered, at 350° F/180° C for 30 minutes and, uncovered, for an additional 15 minutes.
Serves 4

Broccoli Soup

1	large onion, chopped	1
1	medium carrot, grated	1
1	clove garlic, minced	1
2 Tbsp	oil	25 mL
6 cups	chicken or vegetable stock	1.5 L
1	bunch broccoli, cut into florets, stems peeled and cut into chunks	1
1 tsp	rosemary	5 mL
	Salt, pepper and nutmeg	
1 cup	sour cream or yogurt	250 mL
	Parmesan cheese	

Sauté the onion, carrot and garlic in a frying pan with the oil. When the onion is soft, add the chicken stock and the broccoli. Bring to a boil and simmer until the broccoli is tender.

Set aside a few florets for a garnish and purée the rest.

Heat the soup and add the rosemary, salt, pepper and nutmeg. Stir in the yogurt or sour cream. Blend thoroughly. Do not allow the soup to boil. Sprinkle with Parmesan cheese and garnish with the reserved florets. *Serves 4*

Brussels Sprouts

I can still remember the first time that I was served these tiny Belgian natives. I sat in open-mouthed astonishment gazing at the tiny boiled cabbages sitting on my plate. Another surprise was tasting them, because they certainly didn't taste like boiled cabbage. That was about twenty years ago. Since then I have almost become fond of Brussels sprouts.

Brussels sprouts are readily available almost all year, the peak season being from September until mid-February. If you have the chance, buy small, firm, bright-green heads which feel heavy for their size. The small heads have the sweetest taste. Avoid soft, wilted, puffy heads with loose or yellow leaves.

To store Brussels sprouts, simply remove any yellowish or loose leaves and put the unwashed sprouts in a plastic bag. They may then be put in the refrigerator and stored for four or five days. But use Brussels sprouts as quickly as possible, since their flavor can get quite strong as they sit around.

Brussels sprouts are rich in vitamin C and folate. They are also a good source of potassium and iron. Like the other members of the cabbage family, Brussels sprouts may be influential in the prevention of certain types of cancer. Four ounces/120 grams of Brussels sprouts contain about 45 calories.

There is a secret to cooking Brussels sprouts which is vital to producing delicious sprouts. Rinse them and make a shallow "X" in the stem ends after trimming: this little "X" will ensure even cooking.

Brussels sprouts are a favorite of many devout vegetable lovers and are considered by some to be the national vegetable of Great Britain. Their taste is certainly unique and can easily be enhanced. But there are two key points to bear in mind when dealing with Brussels sprouts: do not buy them when they're too big and do not cook them too long.

Boiled or Steamed Brussels Sprouts and Variations

It takes less water to boil Brussels sprouts than to steam them. For boiling, use about 1 inch/2.5 cm of water and allow approximately 7 minutes cooking time. For steaming, allow 15 to 20 minutes and use about 2 to 3 inches/5 to 7 cm of water. The cooking time of course depends on the size and freshness of the sprouts. They are cooked when the stem ends feel tender when pierced.

With butter: simply toss the cooked sprouts with melted butter and sprinkle with some freshly ground black pepper.

With mushrooms: mix some sautéed mushrooms with the butter and toss both together with the sprouts.

With sour cream: heat some sour cream and pour it over the sprouts. Crumble some crisply cooked bacon on top.

A real gourmet treat: toss 1 pound/500 g of cooked Brussels sprouts in 4 Tbsp/60 mL of butter, 4 Tbsp/60 mL of finely minced shallots, ½ tsp/2 mL of caraway seeds, a pinch of marjoram and 2 Tbsp/25 mL of vinegar. Serve hot. *Serves 4*

Brussels Sprouts Roma

1 pound	Brussels sprouts, washed and trimmed	500 g
2	cloves garlic, finely chopped	2
2 Tbsp	olive oil	25 mL
	Salt and pepper	
2 Tbsp	freshly squeezed lemon juice	25 mL
	Rind of 1 lemon, grated	
¼ cup	Parmesan cheese	50 mL
1 Tbsp	fresh dill, coarsely chopped	15 mL

Boil or steam the Brussels sprouts until almost tender. Meanwhile, fry the garlic in the oil; when golden, add the sprouts. Season with salt and pepper.

Sauté the mixture, stirring carefully, for 3 minutes. Add the lemon juice and cook for another minute. Sprinkle with lemon rind and Parmesan cheese. Garnish with dill before serving. *Serves 4*

Brussels Sprouts, Sour Cream and Chestnuts

1½ pounds	Brussels sprouts, trimmed and washed	750 g
¼ cup	sliced almonds	50 mL
4 Tbsp	butter	60 mL
1 pound	cooked or canned chestnuts, water chestnuts or jicama, thinly sliced	500 g
	Salt and pepper	
¼ tsp	nutmeg	1 mL
¼ cup	sour cream	50 mL
¼ cup	minced parsley	50 mL

Steam or boil the sprouts until they are almost tender. Drain.

Toast the almonds in the butter; then add the Brussels sprouts and chestnuts. (If you use canned chestnuts or water chestnuts, let them drain and gently pat them dry.) Season with salt, pepper and nutmeg. Cook over low heat, shaking the pan frequently, until the sprouts are tender.

Add the sour cream, stirring carefully. Heat until warm. Sprinkle with the parsley before serving. *Serves 4 to 6*

Cabbage

Red, green and Savoy—all three cabbages are interchangeable, one difference, besides color, being the mild taste of the crinkly leafed Savoy. Some people also find that the red cabbage has a little spicy warmth.

Pete is particularly fond of Savoy cabbage and so, behold some further details on and information concerning Savoy cabbage. In his fondness for Savoy cabbage Pete gives away his roots, for Europeans love this vegetable from its purplish-green outside to its solid, deep green heart. Savoy is probably the most versatile of all the cabbages. Its big, "easy-peel-away" leaves make excellent cabbage rolls. Its crinkly, outer leaves, which resemble napa, can be used instead of the Chinese cabbage in Oriental cooking. As Pete points out, the flavor of cooked Savoy cabbage is so delicious that it needs nothing but butter and freshly

The cabbage family, which includes broccoli, Brussels sprouts, kale, kohlrabi, collards and cauliflower, has the seal of approval of the Canadian Cancer Society; it is believed to be helpful in the prevention of certain types of cancer.

ground black pepper—no sauce, nothing to mask that sweet, distinctive flavor.

Cabbage is available all year and new cabbage is available from May to September. The difference between old and new cabbage is incredible. Pete says that the only time cabbage is good as a cooked vegetable is when new cabbage is available, the taste of the new cabbage being so much more delicious. The rest of the year, stored cabbage is good for salads, soups, slaws, pickling and sauerkraut. When buying cabbage, look for firm heads which are heavy for their size. The outer leaves should be of a soft color, crisp and fresh in appearance and without blemishes. Savoy cabbage is deep green, occasionally with a distinct purplish color, and has a softer head but should still have firm, crisp leaves. Avoid heads which are too white and overmature. If the leaf bases are separated from the stem, the cabbage may be strong in flavor and coarser. The best way to keep cabbage is to refrigerate it, uncut and unwashed, in a plastic bag, where it will keep for up to a week.

Raw cabbage is a wonderful source of vitamin C and an excellent source of fiber. Four ounces/120 grams of raw cabbage have only 30 calories.

Steamed Cabbage

1	medium head of cabbage, cut in wedges	1
½ cup	melted butter	125 mL
	Salt and pepper	

Boil ½ inch/1 cm of salted water in a heavy pot. When steam begins to rise, add the cabbage. Cover tightly and turn the heat down. Test after 5 minutes; it could take up to 10 minutes for the cabbage to become crisply tender. Drain well. Toss with melted butter and season with salt and pepper. A handful of caraway seeds would not go amiss in this recipe.

With vinaigrette: toss the cabbage with a few tablespoons of bacon fat and some crisply cooked, crumbled bacon. At the last moment, add a few drops of vinegar. Pour on a little vinaigrette (see page 33 for recipe). *Serves 4*

Lemon Cabbage

2 to 3 pounds	cabbage, shredded	1 to 1.5 kg
3 Tbsp	butter	50 mL
3 Tbsp	flour	50 mL
	Juice and rind of 2 lemons	
	Salt and pepper	
1	lemon, sliced paper thin	1
	Dill for garnish	

Bring 1½ to 2 cups/375 to 500 mL salted water to a boil, add the cabbage and cook until just tender. Save the cooking liquid.

Melt the butter in a saucepan. Mix in the flour and cook over low heat for a minute. Gradually add the cabbage water. Cook over medium heat until the sauce is smooth. Add the lemon juice, salt and pepper to taste. Put the cabbage in a casserole and pour the sauce over it. Heat at 350° F/180° C for 15 minutes. Garnish with lemon slices and dill. *Serves 4*

Cabbage etc.

1	small onion, sliced	1
1 cup	carrot, sliced	250 mL
½ pound	mushrooms, sliced	250 g
3 Tbsp	butter	50 mL
1	medium-size cabbage, trimmed and shredded	1
1 Tbsp	butter	15 mL
½ cup	chicken stock, heated	125 mL
1 Tbsp	flour	15 mL
3	large tomatoes, peeled, seeded and chopped	3
1 cup	tomato juice	250 mL
¼ cup	parsley, minced	50 mL
3 Tbsp	cream	50 mL
1 Tbsp	fresh basil, chopped	15 mL
	Salt and pepper	

Sauté the onion, carrot and mushrooms in the butter until soft. Add the cabbage and the boiling chicken stock. Cook over high heat for 3 minutes, stirring constantly. Remove from the heat.

Melt the remaining butter; stir in the flour and cook for 1 minute. Add the tomatoes, juice and the parsley, stirring constantly until the mixture begins to thicken. Stir in the cream. Combine the tomato sauce with the cabbage mixture and mix well. Season with the basil, salt and pepper. Cover and simmer for 10 minutes, stirring frequently. Serve very hot. *Serves 6*

Braised Cabbage

¼ cup	butter	50 mL
1	medium head of cabbage, shredded or coarsely cut	1
	Salt and pepper	
1 cup	chicken stock or dry white wine, or a mix of the two	250 mL

Melt the butter in a large, heavy frying pan. Add the cabbage and stir over medium heat until it wilts and turns brown at the edges. Add salt, pepper and the chicken stock or wine. Cover and simmer for about 30 minutes, or until the cabbage is just tender.

You may wish to add some chopped fresh dill or basil and a tablespoon of vinegar. *Serves 4*

Cardoon

Cardoon, occasionally called artichoke weed, looks like a relative of celery but is in fact part of the thistle family. The plant grows wild in the Pampas grass of Argentina and as a weed in Australia. It is almost revered in France and Italy, where it has been considered a delicacy for 300 years. Unfortunately, this rather lovely vegetable is not as popular with North Americans and may be a little difficult to track down. This may be in part due to the fact that some people find that cardoon is an acquired taste, the flavor of the vegetable being a combination of artichoke, celery and parsnip. Its texture, when cooked, is rather soft and fleshy.

Cardoon is available from November to March. The vegetable should look and feel a little soft; don't expect it to be crisp like celery. Cardoon, which is small and slender, will be more tender. The stalks, however, should be firm. Don't worry if the tops of the cut stalks are a little brown or limp; the leaves are often removed just prior to shipping and the cardoon browns quickly once cut. You can keep the vegetable wrapped in plastic in the refrigerator for up to 2 weeks.

Cardoon is a good source of potassium. Four ounces/120 grams of this vegetable have only 26 calories!

Pete says the key to cardoon is that is has to be carefully trimmed and must be precooked before it can be cooked. Chop off the top leafy portion of the vegetable and save it to use as flavoring for soups and casseroles. Remove the outer ribs and use them for flavoring as well. If the sides of any of the inner ribs are tough, remove them. The ribs of cardoon have tough strings, looking like those found in celery but more pronounced and tougher, so pull these off before cooking.

If you can get cardoon from France or Italy, it is nice raw, sliced into a salad. The California cardoon, which is the most common on the North American market, is better cooked as it has a tendency to be bitter.

To cook the vegetable simply cut it into 2-inch/5-cm chunks and boil it in lightly salted water until tender, about 15 to 20 minutes. Although this may sound like a bit of a bother, don't skip the precooking. Otherwise, you'll find yourself serving a nasty, bitter vegetable. You can then add the cooked vegetable to stews or soups, or you can stir-fry it and serve it with a cheese sauce or a delicious Mornay sauce. Cardoon dipped in a light egg batter and deep fried until crisp is a great Italian treat.

If you have a favorite way of cooking celery, substitute cardoon, the two are readily interchangeable. But be careful; use light sauces or dressings with cardoon. This is a delicate vegetable which is easily overwhelmed.

Cardoon looks like a rather long, large, flat celery stalk. Like celery, cardoon grows in bunches but with thicker, fleshier, silvery-gray stalks and larger, longer leaves. It can grow to lengths of more than two feet.

Some people recommend that cardoon be treated treated with acidulated water, since the vegetable discolors quickly once cut; but since it has to be cooked and turns rather brown anyway, Pete says he sees little point in the acidulated water treatment. It has no effect on the taste.

French Cardoon

5	cloves garlic	5
1	large onion, cut into chunks	1
¼ cup	parsley	50 mL
1	bay leaf	1
1½ tsp	fresh thyme	7 mL
1	red pepper, seeded and cut in strips	1
2 pounds	cardoon, cut into ½-inch/1-cm slices	1 kg
4	anchovy fillets	4
¼ cup	fresh parsley, chopped	50 mL
1 Tbsp	olive oil	15 mL
1 Tbsp	flour	15 mL
	Salt and pepper	

Combine 2 cloves of the garlic with the onion, parsley, bay leaf, thyme and red pepper in a pot with 2½ quarts/2.5 L of water. Simmer. Add the cardoon and cook for 30 minutes or until tender. Drain and reserve the cooking liquid.

Crush the remaining garlic in a bowl, and add the anchovies and parsley. If you have a mortar and pestle, crush the three together; if you don't, make a paste out of them, using a bowl and fork.

Combine the olive oil and flour in a saucepan big enough to hold the cardoon. Add the anchovy mixture and stir gently. Add up to 1 cup/250 mL of the cooking liquid, enough to make a thick sauce.

Add the cardoon to the sauce and reheat until the cardoon is good and hot. Season with salt and pepper to taste. *Serves 4 to 6*

Cardoon au gratin

6 Tbsp	butter	90 mL
4 Tbsp	flour	60 mL
1½ cups	milk	375 mL
1 cup	Cheddar or Swiss cheese, grated	250 mL
½ cup	breadcrumbs	125 mL
1 tsp	Dijon mustard	5 mL
1½ to 2 pounds	cardoon, cut up, cooked and drained	750 g to 1 kg
¼ cup	bread crumbs	50 mL

Melt 4 Tbsp/50 mL of the butter in a saucepan. Stir in the flour and cook for about 1 minute. Heat the milk and stir it into the mixture. The sauce should be quite thin because it will thicken as it cooks. Feel free to add more warmed milk as you go along to keep the consistency as you like it. Cook for 2 minutes. Add ¾ cup/175 mL of the cheese and the mustard.

In the meantime, melt the remaining 2 Tbsp/25 mL butter in a large frying pan. Add the cardoon and heat, stirring gently and constantly. When the cardoon and the cheese sauce are both hot, blend the two and pour the mixture into a well-buttered casserole. Sprinkle with bread crumbs and the remaining ¼ cup/50 mL cheese. Bake at 350° F/180° C for 15 minutes or until bubbly and golden.

You can add ½ cup/125 mL of sliced, sautéed onions to this mixture. Or you can omit the cheese and Dijon, add 1 cup/250 mL of sliced, sautéed onions and season with a little nutmeg instead. *Serves 4*

Cardoon and Cream

Hopelessly simple and beautifully delicious.

1½ to 2 pounds	cardoon, cut up, cooked and drained	750 g to 1 kg
½ cup	whipping cream	125 mL
½ cup	cereal cream	125 mL
	Salt, pepper and nutmeg	

Mix everything together well and simmer in a large saucepan until the cream is reduced by half. Serve as hot as possible. *Serves 4*

Carrots

The vegetable world is full of wonderful little treats and the carrot is one of Nature's finest surprises. From carrot soup to carrot muffins, this lowly vegetable doubtlessly has uses we have not even thought of, perhaps some even stranger than the snowman's nose. Carrots are dual purpose: useful simply as a vegetable and, because of their sugar content, as an ingredient in desserts such as carrot cake and carrot pudding. And, wonder of wonders, carrots are one of the vegetables that children truly enjoy eating.

Carrots are available all year round. The stored ones wear rather thin and get a little old at about the same time the new crop Florida and California carrots become available in markets across the country. As well as the traditional large carrots, tiny baby carrots, popular in Europe, are now easily available. Look for carrots with a rich golden-orange color. They should be smooth, clean, firm and well-shaped. Choose even-sized carrots. Usually the smaller the carrot, the more tender and sweet it is. If you are buying bunched carrots, look for fresh-looking, bright-green leaves. Avoid cracked, soft or shriveled carrots. Be especially careful in the spring: if prepackaged carrots have not been stored properly, there will often be soft spots or decay.

To store prepackaged carrots, simply place them in their bag in the refrigerator. For bunched carrots, remove the green tops and store them unwashed in a plastic bag; they store well for two weeks. Pete surprised me by mentioning that fresh carrot greens provide excellent flavoring for soups, stews and casseroles. So next time, don't throw them out!

Ah, yes, we all know, don't we, what a good source of vitamin A carrots are, one of the richest in fact. Vitamin A keeps your eyesight in good condition and is important in bone formation. Carrots are also a good source of vitamin C and potassium. Four ounces/120 grams of raw carrot have only 45 calories.

Take some time and have some fun experimenting with carrots. Try adding puréed or mashed carrots in equal amounts with your favorite mashed vegetables, whether they be potatoes, parsnips or beets.

Steamed Carrots and Variations

2 pounds	carrots, peeled and julienned	1 kg
4 Tbsp	butter	60 mL
	Pepper	

Steam or boil the carrots in salted boiling water until just tender. Drain, toss with the butter and season with pepper. Steamed carrots with butter and pepper are truly delicious without any other additions.

With fresh herbs: toss the buttered carrots in 2 Tbsp/25 mL of chopped fresh dill, tarragon or marjoram.

Steamed, glazed carrots: add 2 Tbsp/25 mL of honey, or for real excitement, maple syrup to the melted butter. Shake over low heat until the butter and honey or syrup combine and glaze the carrots. Sprinkle with chopped parsley and dill.

Nutty, glazed carrots: to make things even more exciting, throw in a handful of toasted, slivered almonds.

Cognac-glazed carrots: for a real treat, add 2 Tbsp/25 mL of cognac to the glazed carrots.

Carrots and Cumin

1 pound	carrots, sliced	500 g
1½ cups	vegetable stock	375 mL
2 Tbsp	butter	25 mL
1 cup	onion, chopped	250 mL
1	clove garlic, minced	1
1 tsp	cumin seed	5 mL
	Salt and pepper	

Simmer the carrots in the vegetable stock for 5 minutes or until almost tender. Save ½ cup/125 mL of the cooking liquid.

Sauté the onion and garlic in the butter until soft and transparent. Add the cumin seed and cook for one minute. Pour in the reserved liquid and add the carrots, salt and pepper. Cook until the carrots are tender, about 5 minutes. *Serves 4*

This is a Moroccan favorite which my brothers enjoy. They brought the recipe home and it has become a family specialty.

Carrot-Alfalfa Winter Salad

Pete has some advice: the next time you go shopping, look for a bag of really fresh carrots or, if you can, get a bunch with their tops on. Take them home, give one carrot a good wash, peel it if you must, and sit down and eat it. Really taste this little wonder. Pete will just about guarantee that you'll be surprised. He claims that we are so spoiled by always having good carrots readily available that we don't appreciate them enough.

This does not have to be a winter salad. A friend of my mother's used to make this salad in the winter about 20 years ago when good vegetables were hard to find. It is so good we never stopped making it, even though good salad vegetables are now available all year round.

2 cups	carrots, grated	500 mL
2 cups	alfalfa sprouts	500 mL
1/4 cup	raisins	50 mL
1/4 cup	peanuts	50 mL
1	clove garlic, minced	1
1 Tbsp	lemon juice	15 mL
1 Tbsp	oil	15 mL
1/4 cup	yogurt	50 mL
2 Tbsp	mayonnaise	25 mL
1 tsp	chopped parsley, chives and/or tarragon	5 mL
	Salt and pepper	

Combine the carrots, sprouts, raisins and peanuts. Toss them together well. Blend the garlic, lemon juice, oil, yogurt, mayonnaise, parsley, herbs, salt and pepper in a bottle; give it a good shake and pour the dressing over the vegetables. Toss and serve at once. *Serves 4*

Carrot Quiche

4 cups	carrots, grated	1 L
1	unbaked 9-inch/23-cm pie shell	1
4	eggs	4
1/4 cup	coffee cream	50 mL
1 cup	Swiss or Cheddar cheese, grated	250 mL
	Salt, pepper and nutmeg	

Spread the grated carrots on the bottom of the pie shell. Beat the eggs and cream together. Stir in the cheese and season as desired. Pour the mixture over the carrots. Bake at 425° F/220° C for 10 minutes. Reduce the heat to 350° F/180° C and continue baking for 30 minutes or until the custard is set. Let stand for 10 minutes before serving. *Serves 4*

Carrot Mincemeat

Now we get to see how versatile carrots really are, just for the real doubters among us.

2 cups	carrots, grated	500 mL
2 cups	raisins, golden and dark, mixed	500 mL
1	lemon, cut into pieces	1
5 cups	chopped apples, preferably Cortlands	1.25 L
1 cup	candied citron peel	250 mL
2 cups	sugar	500 mL
2 tsp	cinnamon	10 mL
1 tsp	nutmeg	5 mL
1 tsp	cloves	5 mL
½ cup	molasses	125 mL
½ cup	cider	125 mL

Toss the carrots, raisins and lemon into the food processor. If you are not the lucky owner of one, put these ingredients in the blender one at a time and crush them. Put the carrot mixture into a medium-sized saucepan and add the apples, citron peel, sugar, cinnamon, nutmeg and cloves. Blend well. Add the cider and molasses, and simmer over low heat until the carrots and apples are soft.

Use your own preferred method for preserving. Carrot mincemeat freezes well. Makes 2½ quarts/2.5 L.

Steamed Carrot Pudding

No one is as fond of steamed puddings as the English, and very few people seem to make them with such proficiency. Pete, being English . . . well, he claims that this is one of the things that makes him look forward to Christmas. This is a real favorite, made at least once a year chez Pete, when it provides a wonderful, light alternative to the traditional plum pudding.

2 Tbsp	sour milk	25 mL
½ tsp	baking soda	2 mL
1 tsp	salt	5 mL
1 tsp	cinnamon	5 mL
½ tsp	allspice	2 mL

¼ tsp	nutmeg	1 mL
½ cup	flour	125 mL
1 cup	grated carrots	250 mL
1 cup	grated potato	250 mL
1 cup	soft bread crumbs	250 mL
1 cup	raisins	250 mL
½ cup	currants	125 mL
½ cup	candied citron peel	125 mL
1 cup	brown sugar	250 mL
¾ cup	suet	175 mL

Combine the sour milk and baking soda, set aside. Add the salt, cinnamon, allspice and nutmeg to the flour and blend well. Add the sour milk and every-thing else to the flour mixture.

After it's been well oiled, fill your best pudding basin with the batter. If you don't have a pudding basin, a ceramic bowl will do. Wrap the basin with a cloth and steam for 3 hours.

If you have a favorite traditional sauce, such as a brandy butter or even a custard sauce, that you serve with plum pudding, it will be as good with this deli-cious pudding.

Cauliflower

An attractive head of cauliflower requires a lot of work and for this reason, cauliflower tends to be expensive. In order to keep the curd (or head) white, the outer leaves are gathered around the bud and hand-tied to protect it from sunlight. There is a new purplish green variety of cauliflower available in some markets which doesn't require as much attention as the white. It keeps its green color when cooked.

Cauliflower is available all year, with peak supplies from September to November. Look for clean, firm, snowy-white heads with nice tight curds. A yellowish hue indicates over-maturity. Often you can find smudgy or speckled heads for sale at a reduced price. If the damage is not too extensive and can be easily removed, just scrape it off or cut it out, unless you are buying the vegetable for its appearance.

The best way to store cauliflower is simply to put it in the refrigerator as soon as you get home. It will keep in a plastic bag for a week, but using it as soon as possible is recommended as old cauliflower acquires a strong taste and smell.

Cauliflower is an excellent source of vitamin C and folate and a good source of potassium. Four ounces/ 120 grams of raw cauliflower have about 30 calories.

Cauliflower is delicious steamed and served with almost any sauce. Try it with a curry, Bernaise or Mornay sauce. The easiest way to steam a cauliflower, if you don't have a steamer, is simply to put it in a saucepan with a tightly fitting lid with a few inches of salted water in the bottom. Put the lid on and boil the water for 10 to 15 minutes. The lower part of the cauliflower will be boiled, but the rest of the vegetable will be steamed.

Cauliflower is equally delicious cooked or raw, with your favorite vinaigrette or mayonnaise. Try adding it to a green salad or include some on a tray of crudités. When searching for a snack, break off a chunk of cold, fresh cauliflower and eat it as though it were an apple. You'll probably find it to be a refreshing change.

The word "cauliflower" comes from blending two Latin words, "caulis" meaning stem or cabbage and "floris" meaning flower. Cauliflower is a cultivated descendant of cabbage and every bit as diverse, adaptable and delicious.

Cauliflower Cheese

This is an English meal, usually served as a main dish with a salad or a green vegetable. It was one of Pete's favorites when he was growing up.

1 Tbsp	butter	15 mL
1 Tbsp	flour	15 mL
1¼ cups	milk	300 mL
1 cup	old Cheddar cheese, grated	250 mL
1 tsp	Dijon mustard	5 mL
	Salt and pepper	
1	medium cauliflower, washed, trimmed and broken into florets	1
¼ cup	old Cheddar cheese, grated	50 mL
¼ cup	fine dry bread crumbs	50 mL
	Paprika	

Melt the butter in a saucepan and stir in the flour. Pour the milk into a saucepan and let it heat a bit before adding it to the butter and flour paste. Cook the mixture over low heat, stirring constantly, until smooth and thickened. Add the cheese and mustard. Season with salt and pepper, if desired. Stir constantly until the cheese is melted. Feel free to add more milk if the sauce gets too thick. Keep warm.

Cook the cauliflower in boiling salted water for 3 or 4 minutes or until almost tender. Drain.

Put the cauliflower into a buttered baking dish. Pour the cheese sauce over top and sprinkle with the cheese and bread crumbs mixed together. Dust with paprika. Bake at 400° F/200° C for about 5 minutes or until the top is nicely browned. *Serves 4*

Cauliflower and Mushroom Bake

1	large cauliflower, washed, trimmed and broken into florets	1
¼ cup	butter	50 mL
3	cloves garlic, minced	3
1 Tbsp	fresh basil, chopped	15 mL
	Salt and pepper	
1 pound	mushrooms, sliced	500 g
1	large onion, chopped	1
1	medium green pepper, cut in strips	1
1	small red pepper, cut in strips	1
3 cups	cooked rice, preferably brown	750 mL
1½ cups	Parmesan, Swiss or Cheddar cheese, grated	375 mL

Sauté the cauliflower in 2 Tbsp/25 mL of the butter with the garlic, basil, salt and pepper. Set aside. Sauté the mushrooms, onions and peppers in the remaining butter. Stir everything together and place in a large well-buttered baking dish. Bake, covered, at 350° F/180° C for 30 minutes. *Serves 6*

Cauliflower-Blue Cheese Salad

½ cup	yogurt	125 mL
1 Tbsp	mayonnaise	15 mL
1 tsp	lemon juice	5mL
3 Tbsp	blue cheese, crumbled	50 mL
1	medium cauliflower, washed, trimmed and broken into florets	1
4 Tbsp	parsley	60 mL

Cream the yogurt, mayonnaise, lemon juice and blue cheese together until blended. Toss the cauliflower and parsley together and add the yogurt mixture. Stir carefully. This salad looks exquisite served with sliced tomatoes and the dressing tastes wonderful with them too. *Serves 4 to 6*

Cauliflower Soup

1	cauliflower, washed, trimmed and broken into florets	1
1	medium onion, chopped	1
¼ cup	butter	50 mL
2 Tbsp	flour	25 mL
3 cups	chicken stock	750 mL
1 cup	cream	250 mL
	Salt and pepper	
3 Tbsp	chervil, chopped	50 mL

Boil the cauliflower in 1 cup/250 mL water. Drain and reserve the water. Set the vegetable aside.

Cook the onion in the butter until soft. Blend in the flour, add the stock and bring to a boil, stirring constantly. Add the cauliflower water along with the cream, salt and pepper. Add cauliflower and heat well.

Let the soup stand for a moment or two, and sprinkle with chervil before serving. *Serves 6*

Celeriac

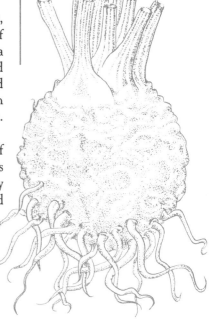

To those unfamiliar with celeriac, or celery root, this particular vegetable varies in size from that of a small apple to that of a large cantaloupe. It has a beige exterior covered with bumps, crevices and grooves; little rootlets protrude from the base and stubby stalks from the top. This ungainly globe, which is often scruffy and dirty, is not an appetizing sight. But it's definitely worth exploring.

Celeriac is available from late fall to early spring. If you have any doubt that what you have located is actually the elusive celeriac, simply check for its very distinct aroma of celery. Choose medium-sized spheres; the larger ones tend to be woody inside. The smoother the exterior, the easier it will be to peel, and although you can leave the skin on if you're going to boil it whole, celeriac needs to be peeled at some point. To store, simply cut off the rootlets at the base and the stalks on the top; put what is left into a plastic bag and refrigerate for no more than a week.

Celeriac is not loaded with vitamins, but is a good source of both potassium and vitamin C. A four-ounce/120-gram portion has 47 calories.

To prevent celeriac from turning brown when peeled, submerge the pieces of the vegetable in a bowl of acidulated water. (Acidulated water consists of 3 tablespoons/40 mL of lemon juice or vinegar to 1 quart/1 L of water.)

This rather unattractive root vegetable has been unjustly ignored by most North American cooks. I have noticed that the majority of people who buy it at Pete's have European origins. When I ask them about how they cook it, their answers vary. When I asked him about it, Pete clarified things a little and made a few suggestions.

Pete's Introductory Celeriac Salad

When I asked Pete how to use celeriac, he gave me this recipe.

½ cup	mayonnaise	125 mL
1 Tbsp	Dijon mustard	15 mL
	Salt and pepper	
½ cup	coffee cream	125 mL
3	medium-sized celeriac (2 pounds/ 1 kg), peeled and cut into pieces a little larger than match sticks.	3
1	Spanish onion, thinly sliced	1
	Lettuce	
½ tsp	caraway seeds	2 mL
¼ cup	minced parsley	50 mL

Fold the mayonnaise, mustard, salt and pepper into the cream. Drain the pieces of celeriac, dry them on paper towel, and fold them into the dressing along with onions. Toss with two forks.

Place the mixture in a salad bowl lined with lettuce and sprinkle with caraway seeds and parsley. *Serves 4 to 6*

Introductory Salad Number Two

Another easy introductory salad involves marinating the celeriac.

3 Tbsp	olive oil	40 mL
2 Tbsp	white wine vinegar	25 mL
1 tsp	sugar	5 mL
1 tsp	caraway seeds	5 mL
1	clove garlic, minced	1
2	medium-sized celeriac (1 pound/500 g), peeled and cut into julienne strips	2
	Salt	
¼ cup	mayonnaise	50 mL
2	green onions, chopped	2

Mix the oil, vinegar, sugar, caraway seeds and garlic; add the celeriac and season with salt. Cover the mixture and leave it at room temperature for 2 hours, stirring occasionally.

Just before serving, drain off the marinade, which can be saved and used as a vinaigrette, and stir in the mayonnaise.

Sprinkle with green onions and serve. *Serves 4 to 6.*

Celeriac and Potato Soup

1	large onion, sliced	1
2 Tbsp	butter	25 mL
3	medium-sized celeriac (2 pounds/ 1 kg trimmed weight), peeled and cut into chunks	3
1 pound	potatoes, peeled and cut into chunks	500 g
1 tsp	fresh tarragon, chopped	5 mL
3 cups	chicken stock	750 mL
2 cups	milk	500 mL
	Salt, pepper and nutmeg	
	Paprika	

Sauté the onions in the butter in a covered pan over low heat until soft. Add the celeriac, potatoes and tarragon. Toss for a minute or two. Then add the chicken stock and the milk. Simmer, covered, for 30

Inside the unattractive exterior of celeriac is a lovely mottled, white flesh with a delicious, unique taste and an intriguing texture. Celeriac is equally at home in soups, salads, fritters and stuffings; it can be baked, boiled, braised, puréed or eaten raw.

minutes or until the vegetables are tender. Purée the soup very quickly in a food processor or blender. (I like to purée about three quarters of the mixture and mash the rest of it with a potato masher, later adding it to the soup.)

The soup does well with a little texture. If you like your soup thinner than it is at this point, add some hot milk until it is the right consistency. Season with salt, nutmeg and pepper (white pepper if you have it). Sprinkle with a little paprika just before serving. *Serves 4*

Celeriac Royale

⅔ cup	homemade mayonnaise	150 mL
⅔ cup	yogurt	150 mL
1 tsp	Dijon mustard	5 mL
1 Tbsp	fresh dill, chopped	15 mL
1 Tbsp	chives, chopped	15 mL
1 Tbsp	parsley, chopped	15 mL
1½ pounds	celeriac, peeled and coarsely grated	750 g
2	hard-cooked eggs, chopped	2

Mix the mayonnaise, yogurt, mustard, dill, chives and parsley together. Pour the sauce over the celeriac and garnish with the eggs. *Serves 6*

Baked Celeriac and Potatoes

Using equal amounts of thinly sliced celeriac and potatoes, arrange them in layers in a well-buttered baking dish. Dot with butter and barely cover with chicken or beef stock. (I prefer chicken.) Bake at 350° F/180° C until tender, about 45 minutes. Sprinkle with some Mozzarella cheese if you like.

Mashed Celeriac and Potatoes

Using twice as much celeriac as potatoes, proceed as if you were going to make mashed potatoes, boiling the celeriac along with the potatoes. When cooked, mash the celeriac and potatoes together, using vegetable stock instead of milk. Add some finely minced garlic, salt, pepper and nutmeg. Purée everything together, adding stock until you reach the desired consistency. Serve very hot. It's a delicious change from ordinary mashed potatoes.

Celery

Celery stuffed with cheese or peanut butter was one of my favorite snacks as a child. I always asked for cheese because I wasn't overly fond of peanut butter, and to this day one of my favorite treats is celery with cheese, or just plain old celery.

At Pete's, the cash registers are squeezed in among the fruit and vegetables: one between the limes, garlic, ginger and grapefruit, one between the turnip and cabbage and one between the romaine and celery. My favorite is the one next to the celery. Occasionally an outer rib or two will fall off the stalk and, presto, I am suddenly standing beside a snack!

Pete trims all the celery that he sells at the stall and when this happens I find I am standing beside a whole box of snacks! Celery is particularly refreshing at Pete's because, sprinkled with ice, it is moist, cold, green and superbly crunchy. It's hard to beat.

I am always amazed by the shoppers who search through the display for a small stalk of celery (it is not a *bunch* or a *head* but a *stalk*) because, they say, they could never eat a large stalk in a week. I help them find a small one and expound on the virtues of celery, encouraging them to eat one piece in the morning and one at night or a couple of pieces at night when they are watching T.V. My efforts are not always in vain. A couple of customers have started buying bigger stalks. Try it yourself; it is a great snack anytime and all but totally devoid of calories. If I begin eating a stalk at night, I will eat at least half of it before I go to bed!

Celery is available all year with no peak season. There are actually two different and distinct types of celery. Golden Heart which is bleached white, and Pascal which is green. Pascal is the type which can

Pete's favorite way of cooking celery is to sauté it and eat it with lots of butter and freshly-ground black pepper.

most often be found in our markets. No matter which variety you are buying, look for the same characteristics. Leaf stalks should be crisp and firm with a pronounced snap when you break them; but guess about this part, greengrocers don't take too well to customers testing their celery by breaking pieces. A nice tight stalk usually means good celery. Leaflets should look fresh. Avoid stalks which look wilted, shriveled or limp.

Store celery in a plastic bag in the refrigerator for up to 2 weeks. You have one and only one chance to revive your celery if you forget it and it wilts. Soak it in icy, salted water until it perks up again.

Celery is full of fiber and is not bad in the mineral and vitamin departments. A "detergent vegetable," raw celery is excellent for your teeth when eaten raw. Best of all, you can it eat to your heart's content, without the cheese, of course, no matter how strict your diet: an entire pound (3 to 4 large pieces) has only 50 calories and most of them are used up when your body processes the vegetable.

It takes a little thought, but you need not waste anything in a stalk of celery. The leaves are delicious in soup. The outer stalks are great cooked. The inner stalks are wonderful on a tray of crudités or stuffed with cheese. Slice the stalk thinly and add it to a stir fry, or sprinkle a handful into your next vegetable, chicken, tuna or egg salad. They key thing is not to forget you have celery in the refrigerator.

Sautéed Celery

1	stalk celery	1
¼ cup	butter	50 mL
	Salt and pepper	
	Tarragon or thyme	

Wash the stalk well. Slice it into 1-inch/2.5-cm pieces, cut at a 45° angle. Melt the butter in a frying pan and add the celery. Sauté for 5 minutes, stirring frequently. Add more butter if needed. Season with salt and pepper, and sprinkle with some chopped fresh tarragon or thyme. *Serves 4*

Chayote

This newcomer to the Canadian vegetable market is a versatile creature. This little squash comes in various colors, from white to dark green, with or without spines, with ribs or without. Weighing close to 1 pound/500 grams, chayotes are roughly pear-shaped, 5 to 7 inches/12 to 15 cm long and about the same in diameter. The female squash, which is smooth and meaty, is preferable to the spiny male.

Chayotes are available all year and are particularly abundant during the winter months, from November to March. Look for firm, young, unblemished vegetables, the harder the better. Avoid chayotes that are wrinkled or even vaguely soft. Pete has tested all three colors of chayotes, dark green, light green and white, and says that they all taste exactly the same. Store chayotes in a cool, dark, well-ventilated spot for up to a month. You can also refrigerate them, lightly wrapped, for 3 weeks.

Chayotes are a good source of fiber and vitamin C. Four ounces/120 grams of raw chayote have 32 calories.

You can use chayote in any recipe which calls for summer squash, and then some. But it is worth bearing in mind that chayote takes longer to cook than most summer squash because of its solid consistency.

Authorities differ on treatment: some recommend vigorous seasoning; others feel that its delicate flavor is one of the chayote's most attractive features. You can choose for yourself. Pete's own choice is to add lots of different tastes to the chayote, as you will see in his stuffed chayote recipe. These little squash also blend especially well with seafood or ham.

A chayote is the fruit of a particularly useful plant, yielding spring shoots which are eaten like asparagus, tuberous roots which are eaten like potatoes and blossoms which are reputed to produce amazing honey. Next time you see chayotes, pick up a few because when they are in good condition, they will keep for up to a month.

Easy Chayotes

This is the easiest way to cook chayotes, as the name suggests, and a good introduction to the vegetable.

Reckon on about half a chayote per person. Cut the squash in half and cook in boiling water until tender. Scoop the flesh out of the shells and mash it with a little butter, toss in some chopped fresh oregano and a little spicy seasoning salt. That's it!

Cheese-Stuffed Chayotes

3	large chayotes	3
3 Tbsp	butter	50 mL
1 cup	Cheddar cheese, grated	250 mL
1 tsp	Dijon mustard	5 mL
	Tabasco sauce	
	Salt and pepper	
¼ cup	dry bread crumbs	50 mL

Cut the chayotes in half lengthwise and cook them in boiling, salted water until tender. Drain and cool. Spoon out the flesh, taking care not to damage the skin, which is alarmingly easy to do. Throw out the cores. Mash the flesh.

Heat 2 tablespoons/25 mL of the butter and sauté the chayote flesh, stirring constantly, for 2 minutes. Stir in the cheese, Dijon mustard and a dash of Tabasco sauce, and cook until the cheese melts. Remove from the heat and season with salt and pepper.

Stuff the squash shells with the mixture and place them side by side in a shallow baking dish. Sprinkle each shell with a pinch or two of the bread crumbs, and dot with the remaining butter. Pour ½ inch/1 cm of water around the base of the chayotes and bake at 350° F/180° C for 30 minutes or until golden. Add more boiling water, if required. *Serves 6*

Chayotes à la Pete, Excellenté

2	medium-sized chayotes	2
6	slices bacon	6
2	cloves garlic, minced	2

1	large onion, chopped	1
2	Serrano or Jalapeño peppers, finely minced	2
1 cup	bread crumbs	250 mL
2	eggs	2
¾ cup	Gruyère or old Cheddar cheese, grated	175 mL
1 to 1½ cups	milk	250 to 375 mL
	Pepper	

Boil the chayotes whole for about 30 minutes or until they begin to feel soft. Remove them from the water and let them cool until you can handle them. Scoop out the flesh very carefully; the skin becomes very tender once it has been cooked.

Put the chayote flesh in a piece of cheesecloth or a clean tea towel and wring it until the squash flesh is quite dry.

With the bacon and garlic, fry the onion until it is soft and translucent and the bacon crisp. Crumble the bacon, and add the hot peppers. Mix the bread crumbs with the chayote. Add the eggs and blend well. Mix in the grated cheese, saving a small amount for a garnish, and the bacon mixture. Add enough milk to make the mixture moist but not soupy. Stir well. Season with pepper.

Spoon the combination back into the chayote shells, heaping up the shells with the filling. Sprinkle with the extra grated cheese. Bake at 350° F/180° C for 20 minutes, or until golden. *Serves 4*

Chinese Cabbage and Napa

This is a wonderful vegetable, perfect for cabbage haters. Very few people dislike this vegetable, even die-hard disdainers of cabbage.

I asked Joe, the man who used to run the Nipa Hut, a little restaurant in the corner of the Saint John City Market, to explain the difference between napa and Chinese cabbage. Joe always buys napa and insists that it is a completely different creature from Chinese cabbage, not even a substitute. He said that the main difference is that napa is a little coarser and its flavor a little hotter. For the average person, there is no difference between napa and Chinese cabbage. For all but the most discerning tastes, the two are interchangeable, except that I like to put the former in sandwiches because it is more succulent. Pete's personal recommendation is that you try the two in the same recipe and see which one you prefer. If you can tell the difference, I will be surprised.

Their appearance, however, is another matter. I can distinguish between Chinese cabbage and napa at twenty paces. Chinese cabbage looks very businesslike, slender like a stalk vegetable. Sometimes the upper parts of the leaves will flare outwards; sometimes they'll curl inwards. Napa is a little more frivolous, tending to be fat with pale-green, crinkled leaves, like the leaves of a Savoy cabbage, tightly bound around a central head. Both are good cooked quickly or eaten raw. They can be used instead of ordinary cabbage in any recipe, but remember that both napa and Chinese cabbage cook more quickly.

Chinese cabbage is available year round. Buy firm, tight heads with nice clean color and crisp texture. If you plan on cooking it, the limper cabbages, which have a slightly milder flavor, are preferable. Napa is also available all year round. Buy tight, heavy heads with unblemished leaves.

Both Chinese cabbage and napa may be stored, wrapped in plastic, in the bottom of your refrigerator for up to 2 weeks. If you plan on using them raw, keep them for as brief a time as possible, only a couple of days.

These vegetables are excellent sources of vitamin C and folate and provide some vitamin A and potassium. One cup/ 250 mL of either vegetable has only 15 calories.

When you buy Chinese cabbage or napa, you are really getting two vegetables in one. The leaves and the central ribs need to be dealt with in different ways in order to get full enjoyment from the vegetable. Both are a welcome addition to a stir-fry. Cut the leaves from the ribs. Slice the ribs like celery and the leaves in very thin strips. Simply put the ribs in to cook a few minutes before you add the leaves. The ribs are delicious raw in salads because of their juiciness, and they are equally good in strips with a vegetable dip. If lettuce is getting boring, or too expensive, try making a salad with chopped Chinese cabbage leaves. Thin laces of the leaves are also good dropped into a soup at the last minute.

Many people will tell you that bok choy, napa and Chinese cabbage are all the same thing, which causes Pete to throw up his arms in despair. Napa and Chinese cabbage not only look alike to the untrained eye, but many books will lead you to the same erroneous conclusion. Pete says very definitely, "No, they are not the same."

Potter's Cabbage

1 Tbsp	butter	15 mL
3	large shallots, sliced	3
6	slices of bacon, cut up	6
1½ inches	fresh ginger root, peeled and grated	3.5 cm
1	large carrot, grated	1
2 pounds	Chinese cabbage, rinsed and cut in quarters lengthwise	1 kg
½ cup	dry white wine	125 mL
1½ cups	chicken stock	375 mL
	Salt and pepper	
1 Tbsp	butter	15 mL

Melt the butter in a skillet, and sauté the shallots, bacon, ginger and carrot until soft. Put half the mixture in the bottom of a 2-quart/2-L casserole. Cover with the cabbage and the other half of the vegetable combination. Bring the white wine and stock to a boil and pour the liquid over the vegetables. Season with salt and pepper. Cover and bake at 350° F/180° C for 60 minutes.

Remove the casserole from the oven and drain off the liquid. Boil the liquid over high heat until only 2 tablespoons/25 mL are left. Add the remaining butter and pour over the cabbage mixture. *Serves 4*

Sweet and Sour Chinese Cabbage

This is also great with other cabbage; use red cabbage for a colorful side dish.

2 Tbsp	butter	25 mL
2 to 3 pounds	Chinese cabbage, coarsely chopped	1 to 1.5 kg
	Salt and pepper	
1 cup	chicken stock	250 mL
2	tart apples, cored and thinly sliced	2
¼ cup	cider vinegar	50 mL
1 Tbsp	honey	15 mL
1 tsp	caraway seeds	5 mL
1 Tbsp	cornstarch, dissolved in	15 mL
¼ cup	cold water	50 mL

Melt the butter in a large saucepan. Add the cabbage, a generous amount of pepper and a little less salt. Sauté, stirring constantly, for about 2 minutes. Add the boiling chicken stock and apples. Cook for about 3 minutes or until the cabbage is slightly tender but still crisp. Add the vinegar, honey and caraway seeds.

In a small bowl, dissolve the cornstarch in the water. Gradually add the cornstarch liquid to the vegetable mixture. Simmer, stirring constantly, until the sauce thickens. Add more honey or vinegar if the sauce is not sweet or sour enough. Simmer for a minute or two. *Serves 6*

Sautéed Chinese Cabbage

3 Tbsp	butter or peanut oil	50 mL
1 pound	Chinese cabbage, trimmed and shredded	500 g
	Salt and pepper	

Heat the butter or oil in a frying pan. Add the cabbage. Cover and cook for two or three minutes, stirring occasionally to keep the cabbage from scorching. Season with salt and pepper.

Fennel seed or ground cumin is especially tasty with this recipe. *Serves 4*

Collards

Collards are one of the oldest members of the cabbage family. The key to their popularity and longevity is hardiness, since they are able to withstand drought and very high temperatures. As for the cold, a light frost only improves their taste.

Collards are available off and on all year round, their peak season being from December to April. Look for young, firm, crisp leaves, and avoid larger, older plants with yellowed, wilted or insect-damaged leaves. Collards may be washed before being stored. But if you don't have the time or inclination to wash them when you buy them, it is not necessary. To wash collards, simply put them in a sink full of lukewarm water. Swish them around a few times and let the sand and dirt sink to the bottom. Rinse in cold water as many times as necessary, until water comes through clean. Refrigerate them wrapped in damp paper towel in a plastic bag for 3 to 5 days.

Collards are very good for you. They are an excellent source of vitamin A and provide some calcium, potassium and zinc. Four ounces/120 grams of raw collard greens have 23 calories.

There are two schools of thought on the cooking of collards. Some experts suggest cooking them as long as possible, others think that collards should be cooked for no longer than 5 or 10 minutes. This is simply a matter of personal preference. If they are cooked for a long time, collards develop a mellow taste and become quite soft. If cooked briefly, the texture is like that of sautéed cabbage and the flavor pronounced. You can serve collards alone or combined with a starchy vegetable like potatoes, or with rice or beans. They are also tasty with a cream or cheese sauce. You can even slide a poached egg or two in there for a little more protein. Feel free to be aggressive when seasoning collards; they blend well with garlic and onions, ginger or anchovies or they can be complemented by crunchy fried croutons or crumbled bacon. Try them with raisins, some grated ginger root and pine nuts.

The flavour of this leafy vegetable wanders somewhere between cabbage and kale. It has thick, meaty leaves like a cabbage but grows in a loose-leafed shape. It bears a remarkable resemblance to English Spring cabbage. African slaves introduced collards to the Southern United States hundreds of years ago, and it is still the South which grows and consumes most of North America's collards. Indeed, some would argue that the only truly traditional way to cook collards is, as they do in the South, boiled with hog jowls or a piece of salt pork.

Southern Collard Greens

This is a traditional recipe for cooking collards. Serve it with corn bread for the real thing.

1	ham hock	1
	or	
½ pound	salt pork	250 g
4 pounds	collard greens, washed, with the stems cut out and the larger leaves shredded or cut up	2 kg
1	Serrano or Jalapeño pepper, finely chopped	1
¼ cup	peanut oil	50 mL
	Salt and pepper	

Put the ham hock or the salt pork with 1½ quarts/1.5 L of water in a large saucepan with a tightly fitting lid. Bring to a boil and reduce the heat.

Simmer for 30 minutes. Add the collards and hot pepper. Simmer for another 2 hours, stirring occasionally. Add the oil and simmer for yet another 30 minutes. Season with salt and pepper. *Serves 4*

African Collards

A friend of mine came back from Ethiopia with this recipe and never misses an opportunity to make it. It is certainly one of my favorites.

1½ pounds	collards, washed and chopped	750 g
6	slices bacon (this addition is not African!)	6
2	large shallots, minced	2
½-inch	chunk of fresh ginger, grated	1.25 cm
1	Serrano or Jalapeño pepper, minced	1
	Salt, pepper, nutmeg, cinnamon and cardamom to taste	
1 cup	dry rice, cooked	250 mL
3 Tbsp	butter	50 mL
¼ cup	raisins, soaked in boiling water for 15 minutes, then drained	50 mL
⅓ cup	slivered almonds, toasted	75 mL
2	green onions, sliced	2

Drop the collards into a large pot of boiling, salted water. Boil until tender, testing often. Drain well.

Fry the bacon until crisp. Set aside and sauté the shallots in the bacon fat until tender, about 2 to 3 minutes. Add the collards and the crumbed bacon along with the ginger, pepper and spices. Stir long enough to heat the collards through. Remove from the heat.

Mix the rice, butter, raisins and nuts. Fold the rice mixture into the collards. Sprinkle with green onions.

Serve at room temperature. *Serves 2*

Corn

Although modern technology has made many kinds of produce not only more available but deliciously fresh, as if we had just picked them from the garden, fresh, affordable corn on the cob is one of those treats still exclusive to summer.

Corn on the cob is the ultimate kid's food because it must be eaten with the hands and invites a mess. In order to truly enjoy corn, even adults tend to get a bit messy. Its juicy sweetness seems to be enhanced by sticky fingers and the feel of melted butter everywhere. Mmmm, dreaming of it yet?

Corn on the cob is available at Pete's all year round and at a pretty reasonable price, but this is not the norm. In most places, the peak season for fresh corn is from June to September. It is during the latter part of the summer that there is an abundance of this delightful yellow vegetable and the price drops accordingly. Select fresh-looking ears with tight green husks and a fresh, sweet smell. The kernels should be plump, juicy and packed tightly onto the cob. Avoid soft, shrivelled ears with spots, signs of decay or worm damage. Large, tough kernels can indicate over-maturity. Pete recommends small kernel corn because it is usually sweet and tender.

The best way to store fresh corn is to wrap it, un-husked, in damp paper towel in a plastic bag in the refrigerator, but for an absolute maximum of two days. Cooked fresh corn is a good source of folate and has about 80 calories in one small ear.

It is almost a crime to eat fresh corn on the cob any other way than all by its glorious self, but just in case

Corn used to be one of the vegetables which had to be eaten almost before it was picked, but thanks to recent developments in the world of hybrids and technology, most of the corn we buy now will keep its sweetness for a few days rather than just a few hours. Pre-cooling, a process which takes place moments after the corn is picked, removes the field heat much more quickly than ordinary refrigeration, thereby slowing the sugar conversion process and prolonging the life of the cob. The corn stays sweeter and fresher longer.

you happen to run into a windfall of fresh corn, or you are a corn farmer who finds himself with a surplus, here are a few recipes with corn as well as a few different ways to cook it.

Roast Corn (2 methods)

1. Pull back the husk and remove the silk. Replace the husk and if necessary, tie with a string to keep it in place. To increase the moisture and create some steam, soak the corn in salted cold water for 5 minutes. Drain and place the ears in a shallow baking dish. Bake at 350° F/180° C for 30 minutes.
2. Husk the corn and rub with butter. Wrap individually in aluminum foil, shiny side in, and roast at 375° F/190° C for 30 minutes.

Barbecued Corn

This is the easiest of all.

Bury the corn, unhusked, in the coals. The husks will turn black; but don't worry, the corn inside will be fine. It should take from 10 to 15 minutes. You will have to carefully turn back one of the husks to test for doneness.

Boiled Corn

In a large pot, boil enough water to cover the corn. Husk the corn just before putting it in the boiling water. Do not salt the water as it may toughen the corn. Put the ears in the boiling water and when it has returned to a boil, cover the pot and boil for 6 to 9 minutes. Be careful not to overcook. Serve with butter, salt and pepper.

Steamed Corn

Arrange on a steamer and steam over boiling water for 6 to 10 minutes, until tender.

Grilled Corn (2 methods)

1. Pull back the husks and remove the silk. Baste the corn with butter or barbecue sauce, or olive oil and salt or any other personal favourite. Pull the husks back up and tie them in place. Soak in cold water for 20 minutes. Drain well. Grill for 20 minutes turning frequently.

2. Husk the corn and grill under the broiler or over an open fire for about 10 minutes turning frequently.

Corn Frittata

1	shallot, minced	1
½ cup	red or green pepper, finely chopped	125 mL
4	ears of corn, kernels cut from the cob	4
2 Tbsp	butter	25 mL
¼ cup	finely cubed ham	50 mL
5	eggs	5
3 Tbsp	milk	50 mL
¼ cup	Cheddar cheese, grated	50 mL
1 tsp	fresh thyme, chopped	5 mL
	Salt and pepper	

Sauté the shallot, pepper and the corn in the butter for 3 to 5 minutes, until tender. Beat everything else together, and pour the mixture over the corn. Fry the frittata over low heat for 5 minutes, shaking the pan occasionally to prevent sticking. When the bottom is brown and set, either flip the frittata (using a plate), or place it under the broiler until the top is set. *Serves 4*

"Corn Pone"

This is not corn pone—a corn bread made in the Southern United States—but rather a corn pudding. My brother insisted on calling it corn pone when we had it as children. The name stuck.

4	eggs	4
1 cup	milk	250 mL

10	ears of corn, kernels cut from the cob	10
½ cup	cereal cream	125 mL
	A sprig of basil, minced	
	Salt, pepper and nutmeg	
4 to 6	slices bacon	4 to 6

Beat the eggs well and add everything else but the bacon. Mix thoroughly. Pour the mixture into a 1-quart/1-L casserole, lay the bacon on the top and bake at 350° F/180° C for almost an hour, or until set. *Serves 4*

Cucumbers

Cucumbers have been a favorite with desert inhabitants because there is little that is more refreshing to eat on a really hot day than a cucumber.

Cucumbers are a rather unusual vegetable. Technically they are a fruit, but we eat them as vegetables, treat them as vegetables and generally think of them as vegetables. Anyway, cucumbers are ready to be exploited. You can cut them up and put them in salads or sandwiches as I do. They can also be peeled and eaten as a fruit. They have an amazing capacity to retain water and to remain cool: the inside of a cucumber can be up to twenty degrees cooler than the outside—a fact which explains the old expression "cool as a cucumber."

Garden cucumbers are available all year, but are at their peak in the summer. There are essentially 3 types of cucumbers. One of these is the long brilliant green English cucumber, grown in greenhouses (the only kind of cucumber available in England), which is favored over our "ordinary" cucumber by Europeans.

The English cucumber is sweeter and more tender than the garden cucumber, and let's not forget that it is also burpless! There is the garden cucumber which is often waxed (for a longer shelf life) and must, therefore, be peeled, resulting in some loss of flavor. And there is the tiny cucumber which is so good for pickling. Some parts of the world are also blessed with lemon cucumbers, which are about the size of an orange, shaped like a kiwi with pale skin and a delicious flavor. Unfortunately, these delicacies do not travel well and are locally available only where they are grown.

When choosing a cucumber, it is important to look

for ones that are firm, fresh and deep green in color. Light green or yellow ones tend to be older. Avoid soft, rubbery cucumbers or very big ones. Greenhouse, or English, cucumbers should be slender and well-shaped.

Cucumbers tend to give off a very strong odor, so refrigerate your cucumbers, cut or whole, in a plastic bag. Cover cut or cooked cucumbers very tightly with plastic wrap or aluminum foil. Unpeeled, a cucumber will last for a week. English cucumbers, however, don't like the fridge so keep them, wrapped, in a cool place.

Cucumbers are a dieter's best friend. A 6-inch/18-cm cucumber has only 25 calories. Four ounces/120 grams of raw cucumber have only 17 calories. An unpeeled cucumber is a fair source of vitamin A and iron. As a further bonus, when you eat a cucumber you do your teeth a favor because it is an important "detergent vegetable," wonderful for dental health. The cucumber's final benefit is to your skin: cucumbers are still considered a beauty aid. To keep your skin soft and smooth, and (reputedly) to lighten freckles, rub a cucumber slice or two over your face.

Sautéed Cucumbers with Cream or Yogurt

3	cucumbers, peeled, split, seeded, and cut in ¼-inch/6-mm slices	3
2 Tbsp	butter	25 mL
	Salt and pepper	
1 Tbsp	tarragon or dill, finely chopped	15 mL
¼ cup	coffee cream	50 mL
	or	
¼ cup	yogurt	50 mL
1 tsp	cornstarch (to prevent curdling)	5 mL

Blanch the cucumber for 3 minutes. Drain well. Melt the butter in a frying pan, add the cucumbers and toss briefly until heated through but still crisp. Sprinkle with salt, pepper and the herb. Gently stir the cornstarch into the cream. Add the cream mixture to the cucumbers and cook for a minute.

With mushrooms: Add 1 cup/250 mL of thinly sliced, sautéed mushrooms to the cucumbers before adding cream or yogurt. *Serves 4*

Poached or Steamed Cucumbers

The easiest way to cook cucumbers is to poach or steam them. They are delicious, especially with fish.

3	average-sized cucumbers, peeled, split, seeded and cut into ¼-inch/.5-cm slices	3
2 Tbsp	butter	25 mL
	Pepper	

Poach the cucumbers in or steam them over boiling salted water for 2 minutes or until they are pale and clear. Drain and stir in the butter; when the butter has melted, grind pepper over them. Or sprinkle the cooked cucumbers with freshly chopped mint, dill, chives, tarragon or parsley. *Serves 4*

Cool Cucumber-Buttermilk Soup

4	average-sized cucumbers, peeled and cut into chunks	4
1 cup	chicken stock	250 mL
3 cups	buttermilk	750 mL
1	clove garlic	1
1 tsp	fresh mint leaves	5 mL
1 Tbsp	fresh dill	15 mL
	Salt and pepper	
	Fresh chives, chopped	

Purée everything in a blender or food processor. Chill for at least 4 hours and garnish with fresh, chopped chives. *Serves 4*

Danish Cucumber Salad

2	English cucumbers, sliced	2
	Salt	
2 cups	plain yogurt	500 mL
1 Tbsp	fresh dill, chopped	15 mL
1	clove garlic, chopped	1
1 Tbsp	wine vinegar	15 mL

Sprinkle the cukes with a little salt. Combine the yogurt, dill, garlic and vinegar. Fold the cukes into the yogurt mixture and refrigerate for at least 2 hours before serving. *Serves 4 to 6*

Cucumber Chips

3	cucumbers, peeled, split, seeded and sliced 1 inch/2 cm thick	3
⅓ cup	flour	75 mL
	Salt and pepper	
2 Tbsp	butter	25 mL
1 Tbsp	grated onion	15 mL
1	clove garlic	1
¼ cup	parsley, finely chopped	50 mL
2 Tbsp	fresh dill, minced	25 mL

Dry the pieces of cucumber by laying them on paper towel, or on a clean tea towel. Mix the flour, salt and pepper in a paper bag. Add the cucumbers and shake.

Melt the butter in a frying pan and sauté the onion and garlic for one minute. Add the cucumbers. Sauté the mixture over medium heat for 4 or 5 minutes, stirring constantly with a fork. Do not overcook or the cucumbers will get mushy.

Drain the chips on paper towels. Sprinkle with parsley and dill before serving. *Serves 4*

Curly Endive and Escarole

This is a rather confusing vegetable, in name only. It is called not only curly endive but also chicory and on occasion, incorrectly, escarole. It is indeed chicory, but not escarole: escarole is Batavian endive. Curly endive is a very attractive leafy, green vegetable which resembles an excited leaf lettuce, having narrow, ragged-edged leaves which curl at the ends. North Americans tend to use curly endive as a salad vegetable where its pungent flavor adds a little sparkle. In European and Middle Eastern cooking, curly endive is used as a cooked vegetable or in soups. I remember being distinctly *unfond* of it as a child, but Pete has a few ideas which provide a chance for those of us who who have been reticent to try it again, or those of us who have never been daring enough to give it a taste.

Curly endive is available all year, its peak season being from July to October. Look for fresh, clean heads which have crisp ribs and leaves. Avoid flabby, wilted-looking heads of yellowish-green color. Curly

Curly Endive and Escarole are not the same thing but they can substitute for each other. Not only do they look quite similar, they are both strong-flavored leafy vegetables and can be used in salads, sparingly, in soups or alone.

endive is one of the few vegetables which should be washed before storing. Wash it under cold running water and shake as much water off as possible; pat it dry with paper towel; put it in a plastic bag and store it in the refrigerator, where it will be happy in the cold for 3 days.

Curly endive is a good source of vitamin A and it contains some iron too. Four ounces/120 grams of raw curly endive have 23 calories.

The easiest way to use curly endive is to use the inner whitish leaves in salads, along with lettuce. You can use the darker outer leaves too, but they tend to be too bitter for most people's taste. The outer leaves can be torn up and added to soups, stews or casseroles, where they will add a little bite.

Escarole is, in fact, endive but not curly endive. It is a broad-leaved variety. The heads look rather flat with coarse, broad, white-ribbed, somewhat curly leaves which join in a yellowish heart. Escarole has a slightly bitter flavor and a crisp texture. It tends to be used as a salad vegetable where the tender, yellowish inner leaves add a little sparkle. The outer leaves are good in a soup. You can safely use escarole in any recipe for curly endive and vice-versa.

Curly Endive, Sesame and Mushroom Stir-fry

6	slices bacon	6
2 Tbsp	sesame seeds	25 mL
2 Tbsp	pine nuts	25 mL
1	medium head endive, trimmed, washed and coarsely shredded	1
½ cup	scallions or green onions, thinly sliced	125 mL
¾ cup	mushrooms, thinly sliced	175 mL
	Salt and pepper	
¼ cup	raisins, plumped in very hot water for 20 minutes	50 mL

In a wok or large frying pan, fry the bacon until crisp. Remove the bacon and let it drain on paper towel. In the bacon fat, sauté the sesame seeds and pine nuts until they are golden. Add the endive, scallions and mushrooms. Season with salt and pepper. Continue cooking and stirring for several minutes, until the endive is tender.

Crumble the bacon and sprinkle it and the raisins over the endive. Serve immediately. *Serves 4*

Braised Escarole and Anchovies

2	cloves garlic, minced	2
2 Tbsp	olive oil	25 mL
4 to 6	anchovy fillets, minced	4 to 6
1	large head escarole, trimmed, washed and coarsely shredded	1
8	capers, whole	8
	Salt and pepper	

Brown the garlic in the oil. Stir the anchovies into the oil and sauté for 1 minute. Add the escarole and capers; mix well. Cook over high heat for 3 or 4 minutes, stirring constantly. Season with salt and pepper. *Serves 4 to 6.*

Daikon

Daikon—also known as Chinese or Japanese radish—is a super vegetable for dieters because it speeds up the breakdown of fat in the body. If you ate enough, you would become very skinny. It tastes just like radish, although somewhat hotter, and it cooks wonderfully! Shaped like a carrot, daikon is pearly white, smooth and usually fairly large, between 1 and 2 pounds/500 grams and 1 kilogram. It can grow up to 50 pounds/25 kilograms, but I would be astonished if you ever encountered one that big on this continent. The other day a man came to my cash with a sack full of daikon. I guess I must have had a peculiar expression on my face because he laughed and said, "I only come to Pete's once every two weeks and I can't get daikon anywhere else. I eat a lot of it." That was obvious. He had almost fifteen pounds of the vegetable!

Daikon is available all year but is at its mildest and most tasty during the winter and fall; in the spring and summer it tends to be hotter and weaker in flavor. Look for smooth, clean, firm roots which should appear to be slightly shiny. Size has little effect on the

Use daikon as you would radish, but with more variety. It is delicious raw, with a dip, so include daikon sticks in your next tray of crudités. Grated, it can be included in coleslaw or served with fish, poultry or meat.

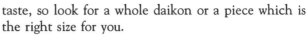

taste, so look for a whole daikon or a piece which is the right size for you.

Contrary to its appearance, daikon does not keep particularly well. It tends to dry out, becoming spongy and losing most of its flavor if kept for too long. If you are going to eat it raw, don't keep it for any more than 2 or 3 days. If you are going to cook it, you can keep it for up to a week, wrapped lightly in plastic and placed in the refrigerator. Daikon is fantastically low in calories, with only 15 in 4 ounces/120 grams. It is also an excellent source of vitamin C and a good source of folate.

Daikon is very versatile. In addition to all its raw possibilities, it is delicious in soups or stews, although it should be added only for the last few minutes of cooking. If you have an artist inside you, try carving daikon into an edible garnish. If daikon had been popular with Michelangelo, we would have eaten his work by now. Imagine finding a mini-David with your next tray of dipping vegetables!

Daikon Soup

4 cups	beef stock	1 L
1	clove garlic, minced	1
1 Tbsp	soy sauce	15 mL
1 tsp	sesame oil (if you can't get sesame oil, sauté some sesame seeds in oil)	5 mL
½ cup	carrot, grated	125 mL
½ cup	daikon, thinly sliced	125 mL
2	green onions, thinly sliced	2
2 Tbsp	dill, finely chopped	25 mL

Mix together the stock, garlic, soy sauce and sesame oil. Bring the mixture to a boil. Add the carrot and continue boiling for 2 minutes. Add the daikon, cover and turn the heat down. Simmer for 10 minutes, or until the daikon is tender. Garnish with green onions and dill. *Serves 4*

Daikon, Zucchini and Red Pepper Salad

2	small zucchini, thinly sliced (about ¾ pound/375 g)	2
½ pound	daikon, scrubbed, halved lengthwise and sliced	250 g
1	small red pepper, cut into strips	1
2 Tbsp	white wine vinegar	25 mL
2 Tbsp	peanut oil	25 mL
2 Tbsp	sesame or walnut oil	25 mL
	Salt and sugar	
¼ cup	freshly shelled walnuts	50 mL

Mix the zucchini with the daikon and red pepper. Blend the vinegar and oils, and add a little salt and sugar to taste. Toss the vinaigrette with the vegetables and chill for about 1 hour.

Sprinkle with walnuts just before serving. *Serves 4*

Daikon and Carrot Crunch

1 Tbsp	sugar	15 mL
1 Tbsp	Dijon mustard	15 mL
½ cup	white wine vinegar	125 mL
	Salt	
½ pound	carrots, peeled and cut in fine julienne strips or coarsely grated	250 g
¼ pound	snow peas, trimmed and broken in half	125 g
1 pound	daikon, peeled, cut in fine julienne strips or coarsely grated	500 g
½ cup	sour cream or yogurt	125 mL
3	green onions, thinly sliced	3
1 cup	radish or alfalfa sprouts	250 mL

Stir the sugar, mustard and vinegar together; sprinkle with a little salt. Pour the mixture over the carrots, snow peas and daikon, and toss. Chill for 1 hour.

Drain the vegetables, squeezing them to get rid of the liquid. Blend in the sour cream or yogurt. Sprinkle with the green onions and sprouts. *Serves 4*

Sautéed Daikon

1 Tbsp	peanut oil	15 mL
¾ pound	daikon, scrubbed and thinly sliced	375 g
	Salt and sugar	
1 Tbsp	parsley, minced	15 mL
2 Tbsp	fresh chives, minced	25 mL
2 Tbsp	toasted sesame seeds	25 mL

Pour the oil into a frying pan or wok. Heat. Add the daikon and toss to cover with oil. Sprinkle with a little salt and sugar to taste. Toss over high heat until the daikon has mellowed a little, about 5 minutes. Remove from the heat; toss with parsley and chives. Sprinkle with sesame seeds and serve hot. *Serves 2*

Eggplant

If you are at all like me, you will be amazed to learn that eggplant is a berry. It belongs to the nightshade family which includes tomatoes, potatoes, tobacco and petunias. No matter what it is, it is undeniably beautiful. Its shiny patent-leather skin is most often purple; but it can also be whitish, reddish, yellowish or striped. It can be anywhere from 2 to 10 inches/5 to 25 cm in length, and anything from round to pear-shaped. More often than not our markets tend to stock the deep purple, largish eggplants, although baby or Italian eggplants are becoming more popular and easier to find. They are used in the same way as the large eggplants, with some allowance made for their size.

Eggplant is available all year. The peak season is from July to the end of September. Whether you are buying the little European eggplant or the larger variety, look for fruit which is firm, heavy and with a smooth, glossy skin of uniform color. Avoid overly large eggplants, those with rough spongy spots or those with dark brown signs of decay.

Eggplant is perishable so don't plan on storing it for too long. If you must, keep it unwashed in a plastic bag in the refrigerator or in a dark, humid place. It can be kept up to 4 days, but the sooner you use it the better.

Eggplant isn't going to make you fabulously

healthy; it isn't a particularly rich source of vitamins or minerals. Four ounces/120 grams of cooked eggplant have only 34 calories.

Eggplant tends to have a bitter taste which will disappear after about 20 minutes of cooking. If you are going to be cooking it for less than that, lightly salt the cut vegetable and let it stand for about 20 minutes. The salt will draw out the bitter juices. Salting the eggplant is also recommended in recipes where the vegetable needs to be drier.

It is not unusual for a recipe to call for eggplant to be fried, but anyone who has fried the vegetable knows just how much fat this involves because eggplant is very absorbent. If you wish to cut down on the fat, you may bake the eggplant in a 325° F/165° C oven for 25 minutes on an oiled cookie sheet, or brush the slices with oil and broil them for 5 minutes on each side, until golden.

Sautéed Eggplant and Variations

1½ pounds	eggplant, trimmed and cut into ½-inch/1.25-cm slices	750 g
	Flour seasoned with salt and pepper	
⅓ cup	olive oil, or less, if you can get away with it	75 mL
4 Tbsp	butter	60 mL

Dip the eggplant slices into the seasoned flour. Heat the olive oil and butter in a large frying pan. Sauté the eggplant until tender and golden on both sides. Drain the slices on a paper towel and keep warm in a low oven.

With Parmesan cheese: simply sprinkle the sautéed slices with Parmesan cheese and broil for 2 or 3 minutes.

With tomato: top the sautéed eggplant with slices of fresh tomato, sprinkle with fresh oregano or basil and broil. For a real treat, sprinkle with grated Mozzarella cheese for the last 2 or 3 minutes of broiling.

With bacon: crumble hot, crisp bacon on top of the cooked sliced eggplant.

With onion: top the cooked eggplant with sautéed onion. *Serves 4*

Eggplant has a wonderfully subtle flavor and a dense texture. It has a terrific ability to absorb the flavor of whatever it is cooked with, while adding a smooth, rich thickness.

Eggplant Casserole

Sauté the eggplant as indicated above, but do not cook the eggplant completely. Arrange the slices in a well-buttered casserole dish, alternating with layers of sliced onion, sliced green and red pepper and sliced tomato. Drizzle a little olive oil on each layer. Season with salt, pepper and some garlic if you like. Cover with bread crumbs mixed with Parmesan cheese and dot with butter. Bake at 350° F/180° C until the vegetables are tender, about 40 minutes. *Serves 4*

Eggplant Parmigiana

3	eggplants, trimmed but not peeled, cut in ¼-inch/6-mm slices, salted and left to drain	3
	Flour	
2	eggs beaten with 2 tsps/10 mL olive oil	2
	Fine dry bread crumbs	
2 Tbsp	olive oil	30 mL
2 or 3	large tomatoes, peeled and sliced	2 or 3
2 Tbsp	fresh basil, minced	25 mL
1 cup	Mozzarella cheese, sliced	250 mL
⅔ cup	Parmesan cheese, grated	150 mL

Wipe the eggplant dry. Dip each slice into the flour and shake off the excess. Dip into beaten eggs, shake again and dip into bread crumbs. Heat the oil in a large frying pan. Brown each slice until golden on both sides, turning only once. Drain on paper towels.

In a 2-quart/2-L casserole, arrange three layers of tomato, eggplant, basil, Mozzarella and Parmesan cheese. Bake at 350° F/180° C for 20 or 30 minutes. For a lighter dish, bake or broil the eggplant as described above and omit the egg and flour coating used when frying. *Serves 6*

Stuffed Eggplant

3	medium eggplants	3
1 cup	onion, chopped	250 mL
2	cloves garlic, crushed	2

1	bay leaf	1
2	medium tomatoes	2
1 Tbsp	basil, minced	15 mL
½ tsp	tarragon, minced	2 mL
½ tsp	oregano, minced	2 mL
2 cups	ricotta or cottage cheese	500 mL
¼ cup	Parmesan cheese, grated	50 mL
1 cup	fine bread crumbs	250 mL
	Salt, pepper and nutmeg to taste	

Slice the eggplants in half lengthwise and bake the halves face down on a oiled tray at 350° F/180° C for 20 to 25 minutes. Scoop out the flesh and mince it.

Sauté the eggplant flesh with the onions, garlic, and bay leaf until the onions are transparent. Combine with the tomatoes, basil, tarragon, oregano, ricotta cheese and half of the Parmesan. Let stand 20 minutes; then drain off the excess liquid.

Stuff the shells with the eggplant mixture. Arrange the stuffed eggplant skins in a baking pan so that they are supported by one another. Top with the remaining Parmesan and bread crumbs, and season with salt, pepper and nutmeg. Bake at 350° F/180° C for 40 minutes. *Serves 6*

Vegetarian Moussaka

3	medium eggplants, unpeeled, sliced into ½-inch/1.5-cm slices	3

Salt the eggplant slices lightly and bake on an oiled baking tray at 350° F/180° C for 15 minutes or until tender.

Mushroom Sauce		
2 cups	mushrooms, sliced	500 mL
3 Tbsp	butter	50 mL
1	large onion, chopped	1
2	cloves garlic, minced	2
¾ cup	tomato paste	175 mL
2 Tbsp	coriander, chopped	25 mL
2 tsp	parsley	10 mL
2 tsp	basil, minced	10 mL
¼ cup	dry red wine	50 mL
	Salt, pepper and cinnamon	

If you wish to cut down on the fat used when frying eggplant, bake the eggplant in a 325° F/165° C oven for 25 minutes on an oiled cookie sheet, or brush the slices with oil and broil them for 5 minutes on each side, until golden.

½ cup	dry bread crumbs	125 mL
½ cup	Parmesan or Cheddar cheese, grated	125 mL
4	eggs, beaten	4

Sauté the mushrooms in butter with the onion and the garlic. Add the tomato paste, coriander, parsley, basil, red wine and spices. Simmer until the liquid is absorbed. Add the bread crumbs, cheese and eggs, and remove from heat.

White Sauce

½ cup	butter	125 mL
½ cup	flour	125 mL
2½ cups	warm milk	625 mL
4	egg yolks	4
1 tsp	cinnamon	5 mL

Melt the butter and blend in the flour. Whisk in the milk and simmer, stirring vigorously until thick. Beat in the egg yolks and cinnamon.

Cover the bottom of a large well-oiled casserole dish with the eggplant slices and half of the mushroom sauce. Layer on the rest of the eggplant and the rest of the mushroom sauce. Top with white sauce. Sprinkle with bread crumbs and a little extra grated cheese. Bake, covered, at 350° F/180° C for 35 minutes. Uncover and bake for another 15 minutes.
Serves 8 hungry people

Baked Eggplant Italiana

4	small eggplants, about 6 inches/ 18 cm long, trimmed, peeled and cut into ¼-inch/6-mm slices	4
2	hard-cooked eggs, sliced	2
3	large, firm, ripe tomatoes, cut into ¼-inch/6 mm slices	3
2 cups	Mozzarella cheese, grated	500 mL
4	anchovies, drained and minced	4
	Salt and pepper	
¼ cup	coriander	50 mL
¼ cup	fresh basil leaves	50 mL
2	cloves garlic	2
¼ cup	olive oil	50 mL

Lay the eggplant slices on a large tray and sprinkle with a little salt. Let stand at room temperature to dry off the excess moisture. Drain and dry between paper towels.

In a pie plate, make overlapping layers of eggplant, egg, tomato and Mozzarella. Top each layer with anchovies. Sprinkle with pepper and a little salt.

Mince the coriander, basil, garlic and olive oil together. Sprinkle over the eggplant mixture. Cover the pie plate with aluminum foil and bake at 350° F/180° C for 20 minutes. Remove the foil and bake for another 10 minutes. This is good hot, lukewarm or cool, but not chilled. *Serves 4*

Earthy Eggplant Soup

2 cups	potato, chopped	500 mL
1½ cups	onion, chopped	375 mL
1 cup	celery, chopped	250 mL
1 tsp	curry powder	5 mL
1 tsp	ginger root, grated	5 mL
3 Tbsp	butter	50 mL
4 cups	chicken stock	1 L
2	eggplants, peeled and chopped	2
2 tsp	thyme, minced	10 mL
3 tsp	basil, minced	15 mL
1 cup	thick tomato sauce	250 mL
2 Tbsp	tomato paste	25 mL
	Salt and pepper	
¼ cup	coriander, chopped or broken into sprigs	50 mL

Sauté the potato, onion, celery, curry and ginger root in the butter for 15 minutes, stirring frequently. Add the stock and bring to a boil. Add the eggplant and herbs, and turn down the heat. Simmer for 30 minutes. Stir in the tomato sauce and paste. Season with salt and pepper. Simmer until good and hot. Garnish with coriander. *Serves 4 to 6*

Fennel

There was no doubt in Pete's mind that fennel and anise were the same thing, until I bet him twenty dollars that they weren't. I won, sort of, but so did he, sort of. Fennel and anise *are* the same thing—fennel and the *vegetable* anise. But there is also the *herb* anise, and fennel and the herb anise are not the same thing. In England, fennel is usually called anise; on this side of the ocean, fennel is usually called fennel. Except at Pete's. This section is about the vegetable, sometimes known as anise.

Fennel is a particularly beautiful vegetable, especially appealing as winter draws to a close because its dark feathery leaves are so reminiscent of spring. A fennel plant looks like celery which has had an accident. It's a bulbous vegetable with thick, broad leaf stalks which overlap one another at the bottom of their stems to form a firm, white, crisp bulb, 3 to 5 inches/7 to 12 cm in diameter. The stalks end in feathery, bright-green leaves which can grow up to two feet tall. It looks rather like dill growing from a celery stalk. Although fennel tastes vaguely like licorice, like the herb anise, they are related only by taste.

Fennel, called finocchio by the Italians, is a winter vegetable, available from October to the end of April. Look for firm, crisp, white bulbs with feathery bright-green leaves. The stalks should be at least 10 inches/25 cm long, a length which will guarantee juiciness. Avoid soft, coarse, discolored or cracked bulbs with brownish-edged bases or wilted stalks and tops. Wrap the bulbs and stalks in a plastic bag, and fennel will keep in your refrigerator for up to 4 days.

Fennel is a good source of potassium and iron and an excellent source of vitamins A and C. For a vegetable, it is also relatively high in calcium. Four ounces/120 grams of raw fennel have 33 calories.

To trim fennel, simply cut off the feathery leaves close to the bulb and remove any tough or discolored outer leaves. Slice off the tough base. Do not trim the vegetable until just before you use it to ensure that it stays fresh and crisp. To keep fennel tender, cut it *with* the grain, in quarters if it is large; in half if the bulbs are small. The leaves can be used as a garnish or to flavor soups, salads or stews.

The easiest way to use fennel is raw, as a salad ingredient. I remember the first time I tasted fennel was at Pete's when he was trimming it for the stall. He handed me a piece of the vegetable and it was a wonderfully crunchy, refreshing little thing. It makes a delicious little salad all by itself. Just slice it up and drizzle your favourite vinaigrette over it, or add slices of fennel to your next salad. It is especially good with romaine lettuce and a lemony dressing. It is also a tasty addition to a tray of crudités. Don't be afraid to explore with raw fennel. It tastes super in the most unlikely places!

Fennel and Celery Parmesan

4	large heads of fennel, trimmed and cut lengthwise in quarters	4
2 cups	chicken stock	500 mL
4	ribs celery, sliced diagonally	4
1/4 tsp	dried, crumbled oregano	1 mL
2/3 cup	melted butter	150 mL
	Salt and pepper	
3/4 cup	Parmesan cheese, grated	175 mL
	Paprika	

Simmer the fennel in boiling chicken stock with the celery for about 5 minutes, or until just tender. Drain thoroughly.

Stir the oregano into the butter. Put half the fennel and half the celery in a shallow, well-greased baking dish. Sprinkle with salt and pepper, brush with half the butter mixture and sprinkle with half the cheese. Top with the remaining fennel, celery, butter and cheese. Sprinkle with paprika. Bake at 400° F/200° C for about 10 minutes or until it is golden brown. *Serves 4*

Braised Fennel

Fennel is one of those vegetables which was made to be braised. It's simple and delicious.

2	heads of fennel, trimmed and cut lengthwise in quarters	2
4 Tbsp	butter	60 mL
1 cup	chicken stock	250 mL
	Salt and pepper	
2 Tbsp	fresh basil or dill, chopped	25 mL

Lightly brown the fennel in the butter in a large frying pan. Add the stock and bring it to a boil. Turn down the heat and cover the pan. Simmer the fennel for about 30 minutes, or until tender. Season with salt and pepper.

Remove the fennel and keep it warm. Boil the liquid until it is reduced by half, and pour it over the fennel as a sauce. Sprinkle with the chopped herb. *Serves 4*

Hellenic Fennel

1½ cups	dry white wine	375 mL
1½ cups	chicken stock	375 mL
2 Tbsp	olive oil	25 mL
2	medium-sized tomatoes, peeled and chopped	2
	Rind of 1 lemon, grated	
1	bay leaf	1
2 Tbsp	fresh dill, chopped	25 mL
	Salt and pepper	
4	large heads of fennel, trimmed and cut lengthwise in quarters	4

Mix the wine, chicken stock, olive oil, tomatoes, lemon rind, bay leaf, dill, salt and pepper together in a large saucepan and bring it to the boil. Turn the heat down and add the fennel. Simmer for 15 minutes or until the fennel is just tender.

Transfer the fennel to a deep serving dish. Cook the pan liquid over high heat, until it is reduced by one third to intensify the flavor. Pour the liquid over the fennel. Serve chilled. *Serves 4*

Fiddleheads

If you frequent gourmet restaurants in any of North America's larger cities, you may have seen this exotic little item on the menu accompanied by a pretty hefty price tag. It seems that many an educated palate is more than willing to pay dearly for this delicate green which has the flavor of an earthy asparagus. To many easterners, fiddleheads are the first sign of spring. Indeed, it was not until I moved to New Brunswick that I was introduced to this spring wonder.

Fiddleheads are small green fern shoots, about 1 to 3 inches/2.5 to 7.5 cm high, which before they have uncurled look remarkably like the heads of violins, hence the name. If Canada had provincial vegetables, fiddleheads would be New Brunswick's. Telling a Maritimer how to cook fiddleheads is like telling an Irishman how to cook potatoes. However, this vegetable is not unique to New Brunswick. It grows throughout Canada, profusely in the east and in British Columbia, and sparsely in the Prairies. In the United States, fiddleheads grow in New England and in the central States and as far south as Virginia. The season for fiddleheads is short—just before the ostrich ferns unfurl. If we are lucky enough to get a warm spring, the season is only a couple of weeks. But fiddleheads *are* spring, the first fresh Canadian green in the markets! No wonder their arrival is greeted with such excitement and awaited with such impatience.

Fiddleheads are available from mid-May to mid-June in most parts of eastern Canada. Lots of distributors will import them if they are located in one of the places where the fiddlehead season begins a little later. You can find them frozen, since they freeze quite well, or you can freeze them yourself by blanching them for one minute in boiling water. They should then be drained, plunged into ice-cold water, and drained again. They can then be put on a baking sheet, placed in a freezer and bagged once they are frozen.

There is nothing quite like truly fresh fiddleheads. Look for deep green fronds which are tight and springy, and which have short tails, no more than 1½ inches/4 cm in diameter. Fiddleheads don't keep

Fiddleheads are especially favored by New Brunswickers. During late spring, Pete's resounds with the question, "When will you be getting fiddleheads?" It is different every year because their arrival depends on the winter, on how high the river has flooded and on how early the snow melted. There are a lot of variables, but New Brunswickers wait for the first fiddleheads with great anticipation and can never seem to eat enough of them before the season is over.

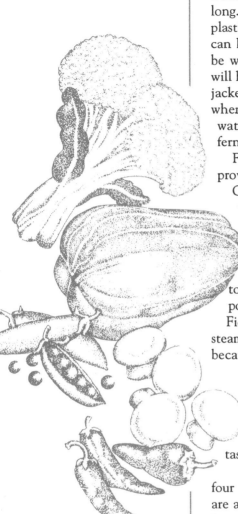

particularly well. They don't actually go bad, but they are so delicate that they lose their wonderful fresh, woodsy flavor and get a little tough if kept for too long. However, if you must store them, put them in a plastic bag with water; change the water daily and you can keep them for up to a week. Fiddleheads should be well washed before you eat them. Some of them will have a papery brown covering over the frond; this jacket does not affect the taste and comes off easily when rubbed between your hands under running water. Trim the tails very close to the curl of the fern.

Fiddleheads are a good source of vitamin C and provide some fiber.

Contrary to some authorities, the delicate taste of fiddleheads is not conducive to heavy or strongly flavored sauces. If you like, you can make a Hollandaise sauce to go with them, or a white sauce flavored with nutmeg. But anyone who knows fiddleheads will tell you that the best way to enjoy them is to prepare them as simply as possible.

Fiddleheads only take about 5 to 10 minutes to steam or boil, and it is important to keep testing them because undercooked or overcooked fiddleheads are not at their best. Fiddleheads may be steamed, chilled and then sautéed in butter. You may also steam and chill them, pouring your favorite vinaigrette over them. Try adding some hot mustard to the dressing: it complements the taste of the fiddleheads well.

One pound/500 grams of fiddleheads will serve four if you have never tasted them before; two, if you are a devoted lover of the green fronds; and one, if it is your first feed of the season and you thought it would never come.

Jerusalem Artichokes

Jerusalem artichokes are delicious raw or cooked, hot or cold. Although they are not easy to find, they are rapidly becoming more popular and are no longer the specialty item they once were. If you have not yet introduced your body to Jerusalem artichokes, don't gorge yourself on them because they contain a starch which your body needs time to get accustomed to.

Jerusalem artichokes, sometimes called sunchokes, are available from November to February. Look for firm roots with no signs of mold. Steer clear of roots which are sprouting or blotched with green. You can keep them unwashed, in a plastic bag in the refrigerator, for up to a week. Artichokes are a good source of iron; they also contain some vitamin B and a small amount of vitamin C. Four ounces/120 grams of the raw vegetable have about 60 calories.

Jerusalem artichokes should be peeled or given a hefty scrub before, using. In order to prevent their white flesh from turning brown, it is a good idea to have a bowl of acidulated water on hand in which to plunge the cut vegetable. (Acidulated water consists of 3 tablespoons/50 mL of vinegar or lemon juice in one quart/1 L of water.)

Sliced, raw artichokes are a great addition to a tray of crudités. Throw a handful into your next salad; or grate them, adding a mayonnaise dressing, a generous dose of black pepper, some chopped parsley and you'll have a delicious and unusual salad.

You can broil Jerusalem artichokes, steam them, boil them or toss them in a stir-fry; pile them around your next roast and savor them roasted. Boil them in about one inch of water for 15 minutes and eat them with butter, sprinkled with fresh, chopped tarragon. They are also tasty drizzled with a Hollandaise sauce.

These rather dull looking vegetables are often called sunchokes, and although that is really a brand name, it is perhaps more appropriate than Jerusalem artichokes. This North American native has absolutely nothing to do with artichokes, except in taste, and even less to do with Jerusalem. They are thin-skinned, knobby roots of a type of sunflower. Their resemblance to ginger root is unmistakable, but their taste is fresh and sweet, and their texture, crisp and slightly fleshy, like that of water chestnuts or jicama.

Jerusalem Artichoke Soup

The delicate flavor of this vegetable makes the most wonderfully delicious soup. Rather a special occasion creation.

1	large onion, sliced	1
1	small clove garlic, minced	1
2 pounds	Jerusalem artichokes, peeled or scrubbed and chopped	1 kg
4 Tbsp	butter	60 mL
3 cups	chicken stock	750 mL
	Salt and pepper	
2½ cups	milk	625 mL
½ cup	whipping cream	125 mL

1 tsp	fennel seeds, crushed	5 mL
¼ cup	parsley, chopped	50 mL

Sauté the onions, garlic and Jerusalem artichokes in the butter for 10 minutes, stirring frequently. Add the chicken stock, salt and pepper to taste. Cook for another 10 minutes. Purée in a blender or food processor. Heat the milk and cream. Blend the cream mixture with the Jerusalem artichoke purée. Add the fennel seed. Heat the soup thoroughly. Sprinkle with parsley before serving. *Serves 4*

Creamy Jerusalem Artichokes

½ cup	whipping cream	125 mL
½ cup	cereal cream	125 mL
2 pounds	Jerusalem artichokes, peeled or scrubbed, cooked and cut into ½-inch/1.25-cm slices	1 kg
2 Tbsp	butter	25 mL
	Salt and pepper	
¼ cup	parsley, chopped	50 mL

Mix the creams and heat slowly. Sauté the artichokes in the butter. Blend the cream and vegetable carefully. Season with salt and pepper and warm over the lowest heat. Sprinkle with parsley and serve when heated through. *Serves 4*

Jicama

This versatile little vegetable is becoming more readily available due to the growing popularity of Oriental and Latin cooking. (Actually, it need not be little; it can range from 1 to 6 pounds/.5 to 3 kg.) Jicama are equally delicious cooked or raw and are very easy to use; all you need to do is peel off the dark beige skin and fibrous underlayer and slice the flesh.

Jicama are rather like water chestnuts in taste and texture but considerably less expensive. Water chestnuts are an excellent addition to a stir-fry if you can afford them; but if you can't, you have no excuse for not using jicama!

This tuberous vegetable is available off and on all year, its peak season being from December to June. Look for firm, smooth, nicely shaped jicama. The skin should be thin, the flesh very juicy. Although size has little to do with the flavor, the larger jicama tend to be fibrous and a little dry. Avoid blemished or scarred jicama, or those with breaks in the skin. You may store jicama in the refrigerator for up to three weeks if it is uncut. Once you have cut it, wrap it tightly in plastic and use it within a week.

Jicama is an excellent source of vitamin C and folate and contains some potassium. One cup/250 mL of shredded, raw jicama has about 50 calories.

Jicama can be used in almost anything. The more you experiment with it, the more useful you will find it. Toss a handful of cubed jicama into your next seafood, poultry or fruit salad, or add it to your next stir-fry. Add it in thin slices or julienne strips to a tray of crudités; it is particularly good with a chili dip. Try it as an appetizer with a little lime juice and your favorite seasoned salt. There are only two things to remember about jicama: it must be peeled, because the skin is inedible, and it must be kept in acidulated water once it is cut or peeled, because it discolors quickly when exposed to air. (Acidulated water consists of 3 tablespoons/50 mL of vinegar or lemon juice per quart/1 L of water.)

Jicama originated in Mexico, and from there spread to Asia and through the Pacific. It has a rather bland, slightly sweetish taste, which makes it a delicious addition to almost anything from a fruit salad to stir-fry.

Jicama for Supper

¼ cup	soy sauce	50 mL
¼ cup	tahini	50 mL
1 inch	ginger root, peeled and grated	2.5 cm
1 Tbsp	brown sugar	15 mL
5 to 8 ounces	tofu, drained and cut into cubes	150 to 225 g
6 Tbsp	butter or oil	90 mL
1 pound	jicama, peeled and sliced	500 g
1	large onion, thinly sliced and separated	1
1 pound	russet potatoes, sliced into ¼-inch/6-mm slices	500 g
	Salt and pepper	

6	green onions, thinly sliced	6
1/8 cup	coriander, chopped	25 mL
1/4 cup	sesame seeds	50 mL

In a medium-sized bowl, blend the soy sauce, tahini, ginger and brown sugar. Add the tofu and leave it to marinate, stirring occasionally. Melt the butter or heat the oil in a large frying pan over moderate heat. Sauté the jicama, onions and potatoes until the potatoes are golden brown, about half an hour. Season with salt and pepper. Add the tofu and any of the marinade it has not soaked up. Cook until the tofu is warmed through and the vegetables and tofu are well mixed. Stir in the green onions and sprinkle with coriander and sesame seeds. Stir to blend. Serve hot. Add more soy sauce, if desired. *Serves 4*

Indy Salad

Jicama can be used in almost anything. This is a salad with Indonesian origins. It is unusual and delicious in its difference.

1 cup	small jicama, peeled and cut into cubes	250 mL
1 cup	fresh pineapple, cut into cubes	250 mL
1	English cucumber, peeled and thinly sliced	1
1 cup	alfalfa sprouts	250 mL
	Watercress	

Lightly toss together the jicama, pineapple and cucumber. Chill and garnish with the sprouts and watercress. (I like to add a peeled mandarin orange and some of its grated rind just before serving.)

Peanut Dressing		
2 Tbsp	lime juice	25 mL
2 Tbsp	honey	25 mL
1/4 cup	peanut butter	50 mL
1/4 cup	water	50 mL
1	Serrano or Jalapeño pepper, minced	1
	A pinch of salt	

Place the ingredients in a small saucepan and heat, stirring constantly until well blended. Chill and pour the dressing over the salad. *Serves 6*

Kale

Kale, along with collards, most closely resemble wild cabbage. Like collards, kale does not come in a head; rather it is a bunch of leaves connected to a central stem. It has a sprightly taste. Its curly leaves look like sprigs of parsley, and this amazing "curly" texture remains even when the vegetable is cooked. Kale comes in the most wonderful colors: everything from dark green and lavender to an earthy, apple green.

The flavor is not unlike cabbage, rather a surprise considering the texture, although somewhat stronger. Like collards, kale improves with a frost; it can also withstand very high temperatures.

Kale is good cut into strips and added to a stir-fry. It is also delicious sautéed in almost any fat. Try adding onions, garlic or caraway seeds for a little extra enhancement. You can also braise kale in stock and add it to a soup.

Kale is available all year, but is most abundant— and most flavorful—from December to April. Look for small bunches of kale with a deep color in the leaves. It should be slightly moist and crisp. Avoid dry-looking kale with wilted, bruised, crushed or yellowed leaves, or with coarse stems. If you are buying it in the summer, make sure that the kale itself is not too warm as it deteriorates quickly if it is not kept cold. Kale does not like to be stored too long. Keep it in a plastic bag in the coldest part of the refrigerator, but for no more than 2 days.

Kale is an excellent source of vitamins A and C. One cup/250 mL of the raw vegetable has about 20 calories.

If this particular vegetable is too strong for your taste, blanching it will moderate the flavor. Because the stems tend to be tough and very strongly flavored, it is generally recommended that you cut them out, although this is unnecessary when you are using tiny kale.

Once you have the leaves free from the stems, wash them in a sink full of lukewarm water and rinse them under cold water several times.

Kalepota

In colder countries this vegetable has come into its own. The Scottish eat it puréed with potatoes, added to barley soup or cooked with oatmeal and cream to make a thick porridge.

Great as a main dish with a tomato salad.

2 Tbsp	olive oil	30 mL
2	large cloves garlic, minced	2
2	carrots, grated	2
1 cup	dry lentils	250 mL
1½ pounds	kale, stemmed, washed and cut in ½-inch/1.25-cm strips	750 g
1 cup	beef broth	250 mL
1 or 2	Serrano or Jalapeño peppers, chopped	1 or 2
28 oz can	tomatoes and juice	875 mL can
6	anchovy fillets, drained and cut into ½-inch/1.25-cm pieces	6
	Lemon juice	
1 Tbsp	olive oil	15 mL
	Pepper	

Heat the oil in a large saucepan and sauté the garlic until lightly browned. Add the carrots and lentils, and stir to coat with oil and garlic. Add the kale, broth and peppers. Cover and simmer over low heat until lentils are just tender, about 30 minutes, stirring occasionally. Add the tomatoes and juice, and cook for another 10 minutes. (Keep an eye on the liquid as it cooks and add more beef broth if it looks like things might scorch.) Add the anchovies and lemon juice to taste. Toss with olive oil. Sprinkle with black pepper and serve. *Serves 2 to 4*

Creamed Kale and Mushrooms

2 pounds	kale, stemmed, washed and cut into bite-size pieces	1 kg
4 Tbsp	butter	60 mL
4 Tbsp	flour	60 mL
1 cup	milk	250 mL
1 cup	coffee cream	250 mL
½ pound	mushrooms, sliced	250 g
	Salt, pepper and nutmeg	

Put the kale in a saucepan, adding just enough salted

water to cover. Bring to a boil and cook, covered, for 20 minutes or until tender. Drain well and chop.

Melt the butter, stir in the flour and cook for 2 minutes, stirring constantly. Stir in the milk and cream; it is a good idea to have them heated and ready to add. Cook over low heat, stirring constantly, for 10 minutes. Add the mushrooms for the last 5 minutes of cooking time. Season with salt, pepper and nutmeg. Add the kale and heat through. *Serves 4*

Kohlrabi

The name of this little oddity means "cabbage turnip" in German. Unfortunately, kohlrabi has been underrated. It is perhaps a peculiar vegetable, but that is not to say that it is not delicious. It is one of those things that people either love or hate, and those who love it are beginning to outnumber those who don't. Steamed and buttered, it is wonderful with most meats; it is also delicious raw, as a dipper, and as an ingredient in salads. But be warned: as a rule, children are not fond of it.

If you have not tried kohlrabi in a while and are of two minds about it, or if you think you are a kohlrabi hater but would like to consider a change in camps, *or* if you are a kohlrabi devotee from way back, read on. If your mind is made up that you hate kohlrabi, or if you have no worries that you may be missing out on something special, shame on you!

Kohlrabi is available from late May to November, its peak months being June and July. Look for kohlrabi with small, smooth bulbs and a thin, crisp rind. If the tops have not been cut off, the leaves should be firm, fresh and green. Larger kohlrabi are not as sweet and tend to be woodier than the smaller ones.

If you get the leaves with the bulbs, cut them off and use them within a day or two as a soup seasoning. You may wrap the bulbs and keep them in the refrigerator for up to a week.

Kohlrabi is a wonderful source of vitamin C and a good source of potassium. It is low in calories, with only 40 calories in ½ cup/250 mL of the raw vegetable.

If none of the recipes below appeal to you, don't give up on kohlrabi: peel them, parboil them or stuff them with your favorite meatloaf (a little spicier than usual), simmer them in beef stock in a large frying pan and add a white sauce made with some of the liquid left over from the simmering. If this doesn't tickle your tastebuds, give up; you have Pete's permission, you'll have done your best. Seriously, this is a delicious little vegetable and deserves a couple of chances to prove itself to the unbeliever.

Marinated Kohlrabi

The Spanish serve this dish with additional anchovies and a bowl of black olives.

I first had something like this in Spain. This recipe is only a close imitation of the original.

3 Tbsp	olive oil	50 mL
1	large clove garlic, minced	1
1	small onion, finely diced	1
1	Serrano or Jalapeño pepper, seeded and minced	1
1 tsp	fresh thyme	5 mL
3 Tbsp	red wine vinegar	40 mL
12	large black olives	12
6	whole capers	6
6	anchovies, or more for anchovy lovers	6
12	small kohlrabi, peeled, boiled for 3 minutes and chilled in ice water	12
1 Tbsp	parsley, chopped	15 mL
¼ cup	green onion, chopped	50 mL

Heat the olive oil in a skillet and sauté the garlic, onion, peppers and thyme. Add the vinegar. Simmer to reduce the liquid, and allow the mixture to cool. Mix in the olives, capers and anchovies. Pour the pepper mixture over the kohlrabi in a fairly narrow bowl. Marinate for about 1 hour, stirring frequently. Before serving, sprinkle with parsley and green onions. *Serves 6*

Pete's Kohlrabi

1 pound	small kohlrabi, peeled and grated	500 g
2 Tbsp	butter or oil	25 mL
	kohlrabi leaves, shredded and boiled	
	Salt and pepper	

Sauté the kohlrabi for a few minutes in olive oil or butter, until tender. Add the kohlrabi leaves and sauté for an additional minute. Sprinkle with salt and freshly ground black pepper. For an interesting variation, sauté ½ pound/250 grams of mushrooms with the kohlrabi.

Greek Kohlrabi

2 cups	chicken stock	500 mL
1 tsp	ground fennel	5 mL
1 tsp	thyme, minced	5 mL
8	small kohlrabi, trimmed, peeled and quartered	8
1½ tsp	cornstarch	7 mL
2	egg yolks	2
	Juice of ½ a lemon	
	Salt and pepper	
2 Tbsp	chives, chopped	25 mL

In a medium saucepan, combine the stock, fennel and thyme. Heat to the boiling point, add the kohlrabi, lower the heat and simmer partially covered, until tender, about 15 minutes. Drain, saving the liquid. Arrange the kohlrabi on a serving dish and place in a warm oven.

Mix the cornstarch with 1 tablespoon/15 mL of the cooking liquid. Beat in the egg yolks. Add the lemon juice and another 1¼ cups/300 mL of the broth. Cook over low heat, stirring constantly, but do not allow the mixture to boil. Season with salt and pepper. Add more broth if the sauce is too thick for your taste.

Pour the sauce over the warm kohlrabi. Sprinkle with chives and serve. *Serves 4*

The next time you are making up a tray of crudités, include some peeled and sliced kohlrabi. Or you might blanch, chill and marinate it in your favorite dressing and add it to your next salad. There is some dispute as to whether kohlrabi is better in the midst of an elaborate creation, or whether it is best simply steamed and seasoned. There are some pretty complex recipes for kohlrabi, but these ones are fairly simple because for Pete, kohlrabi belongs in the legion of vegetables under the column headed, "Best steamed with lots of butter and pepper."

Leeks

Leeks are available in winter, from late autumn until the middle of spring. Buy leeks that are clean and white, are well blanched 2 to 3 inches/5 to 7.5 cm from the base, and have crisp, fresh green tops. Avoid leeks with soft spots, fibrous bases, or yellowish, wilted or bruised tops with unduly loose leaves. Small leeks are the most tender. If you are serving leeks as a vegetable dish, cut off the limp green ends of the leaves. If you are making soup, don't cut anything off: use the entire vegetable.

To store leeks, cut off the rootlets and throw away the coarse outer leaves; trim off the tops of the leaves and place the remaining vegetable in a plastic bag in the refrigerator. Do not leave unwrapped leeks near any other foods because they will absorb some of the leek's flavor.

Leeks are an excellent source of folate and vitamin C and a good source of iron. Four ounces/120 grams of raw leek have about 75 calories.

Because sand and dirt always gets caught between the layers of leaves, leeks are a bother to clean. To make sure you get all of the dirt out, Pete recommends a good wash with a sharp knife. Cut the leeks lengthwise, halfway through, so that as you wash them you separate the layers of the leek, letting the water pour through them. Pete says this gives him nice clean leeks every time—something he considers of utmost importance. "There is nothin' more 'orrible" says he, "than bitin' into a beautiful, soft, luscious lookin' leek and gettin' grit in your mouth . . . So my darlin's, give those gorgeous leeks a good wash." If you're going to be using the leeks sliced, the easiest thing to do is to slice them, put them in a colander and wash them under running water.

Braised Leeks

A luxurious and delicious treat.

3 Tbsp	oil	50 mL
12	average-sized leeks, trimmed and cleaned	12
	Salt and pepper	

2 tsp	fresh thyme, finely chopped	10 mL
½ cup	chicken stock	125 mL
	Lemon juice	
	Parsley, chopped	

Put a little oil in a shallow baking dish, lay the leeks in the dish and bake in a 350° F/180° C oven for 5 to 10 minutes, turning the leeks every few minutes.

Transfer the leeks to a large saucepan cutting the leek in half if necessary. Season with salt, pepper and thyme. Add the stock, bring to a boil, reduce the heat, cover and simmer for 15 minutes.

Sprinkle with some lemon juice and the chopped parsley. *Serves 6*

Leeks au Gratin

1¼ cups	chicken stock	300 mL
12	medium to large leeks, well washed with all but the first 2 inches/5 cm of the green cut off	12
1 cup	mushrooms, sliced	250 mL
4 Tbsp	butter	60 mL
4 Tbsp	flour	60 mL
1 cup	mild Cheddar cheese, grated	250 mL
	Salt and pepper	
½ tsp	Dijon mustard	2 mL
	Nutmeg	
2 Tbsp	dry sherry	25 mL
¼ cup	parsley, coarsely chopped	50 mL

Put the stock in a medium saucepan and bring to a boil. Lower the temperature, and add the leeks and mushrooms. Simmer over low heat for 5 to 7 minutes, until the leeks are barely tender. Drain, reserving cooking liquid. Place the leeks and mushrooms in a buttered baking dish.

Melt the butter in a skillet and stir in the flour. Stir constantly for one or two minutes, taking care not to brown the mixture. Stir in 2 cups of the cooking liquid, adding more chicken broth if required. Simmer the mixture, stirring constantly. Add ¾ cup/175 mL of the cheese. Taste and season with salt, pepper, Dijon mustard and nutmeg. Cook until the cheese is melted. Add the sherry.

Looking like an overgrown green onion, leeks are a common and relatively inexpensive vegetable in Great Britain and continental Europe. As a member of the onion family, they are versatile and delicious in combination or on their own.

Pour the sauce over the leeks and mushrooms. Sprinkle with the remaining cheese. Broil for a few minutes or bake at 425°F/220° C until the top is golden brown.

Sprinkle with parsley just before serving. *Serves 4 to 6*

Vichyssoise

No cookbook can possibly mention leeks and not give a recipe for Vichyssoise, the soup invented by the French chef Louis Diat which some claim introduced the leek into North American kitchens.

2 Tbsp	oil	25 mL
4	medium potatoes, thinly sliced	4
4	medium white onions, thinly sliced	4
4	leeks, white parts only, thinly sliced	4
1	clove garlic, mashed	1
4 cups	chicken stock	1 L
1½ cups	milk	375 mL
½ cup	yogurt	125 mL
	Salt and pepper, preferably white pepper	
2 tsp	fennel	10 mL
½ tsp	mace	2 mL
2 Tbsp	minced chives or parsley	25 mL

Heat the oil in a saucepan. Add the potatoes, onions, leeks and garlic and 1 cup/250 mL of the chicken stock. Simmer, covered, over very low heat until the vegetables are very soft, stirring frequently.

Add the rest of the chicken stock to the leek mixture. Simmer, covered, for 10 minutes. Add the milk, and bring to the boiling point, but do not boil. Cool the mixture, and stir in the yogurt. Season to taste with salt, pepper, fennel and mace.

Purée the soup in a blender. If it is too thick, thin with a little cold milk. Chill thoroughly. Sprinkle with chives or parsley before serving. *Serves 6*

Lettuce

Unfortunately, it seems that a lot of the wonderful world of lettuce slides right past most of us. We tend to stick to iceberg lettuce, or occasionally we will use romaine, but there are many other varieties of lettuce which are not used to full advantage.

I was surprised when I started asking the cooks and chefs who shop at Pete's what their favorite type of lettuce was. None of them said iceberg. This is not to put down this trusted North American standard but to encourage those who are not by nature adventurous to step out on a limb and try something different.

One day I noticed a woman examining the red and green peppers with a confused expression. I asked her if I could help her with anything. She said that she was having a salad party and wanted to know what else she could put in her salads. She put down her basket and displayed her choices. She had a wealth of wonderful additions, but all she had for lettuce were a few heads of iceberg and a couple of romaine. I grinned and said that I thought that all she needed was a little variety in her lettuce. When she looked a little surprised, I showed her the Bibb, Boston and green leaf lettuces. "That's it!" she exclaimed. She added two of each and went home to her salad party, which she later told me was a great success. I can't help noticing that although she now buys lettuce every time she shops, it is rarely iceberg.

From the wonderfully delectable Bibb lettuce to the robust romaine, there is something in your market just waiting for you to taste. I am ashamed to admit that I had worked for Pete for 2 years before I bought anything but iceberg or romaine lettuce, and then it was only because someone else was making the salad for supper. I am jealous of all of you who discovered the diversity of the world of lettuce before I did.

Crisphead Lettuce is more popularly known as iceberg lettuce, which technically is incorrect. This is the most common lettuce largely because it is perfectly suited to the rigours of long-distance travel and the stresses of harvesting and marketing. Crisphead lettuces have firm heads, usually about 6 inches/15 cm in diameter with pale green leaves and a crisp, juicy texture. The taste is very mild.

Butterhead Lettuce has small loose-leaved heads with soft, delicate leaves and a subtle, wonderfully buttery taste. The chief commercial varieties are Boston and Bibb lettuce. Boston is medium-sized, with a firm, clearly defined head which tends to be a little pointed and has thick, broad, smooth, meaty leaves. Bibb lettuce is regarded by many as the ultimate lettuce, the lettuce to end all lettuces. It is small, with dark green leaves which are perfectly tender and have a delicate buttery flavor. Bibb lettuce has five times the nutrients of iceberg lettuce.

Romaine Lettuce has long, almost rectangular, heads with broad, stiff upright leaves which are crisp, coarse and rather sweet. It is, of course, essential to Caesar salad and is particularly good in combination with other lettuce. It is beautifully suited to cooking.

Looseleaf Lettuce is so called because rather than growing in a head, it grows from a stem. The leaves are curly, smooth, tender and a little more meaty than crisphead lettuce. Their color varies from a fresh to a rusty green. The flavor is clean and delicate.

Lettuce is available all year round. Bibb can be harder to find but the others are readily available. Look for fresh, crisp heads, bright green in color and free from blemishes. Lettuce should be refrigerated immediately after buying. It needs some moisture during storage but must not be kept wet. Rinse it with cold water, give it a little shake to get rid of the excess water, wrap it in paper towels and put it in a plastic bag in the refrigerator where it will keep for 3 to 5 days.

Darker leaf lettuces are good sources of vitamin A, and some varieties are excellent sources of folate. Most are good sources of fiber and low in calories. Four ounces/120 grams of raw lettuce have only 17 to 22 calories.

One of the most important things when making a salad is the preparation of the lettuce. It should be washed in a sink of ice-cold water and then dried. It is imperative that the lettuce be as dry as possible so that the dressing may be evenly distributed. A salad spinner gives good results, except for Bibb and Boston lettuce, which are so delicate that they should be drained on a clean tea towel or paper towel.

Caesar Salad

1 to 2	cloves garlic, one minced	1 to 2
1	large head romaine, washed and dried	1
6 to 8 Tbsp	olive oil	90 to 125 mL
12	anchovy fillets, chopped	12
2 Tbsp	lemon juice	25 mL
	Salt and pepper	
1	egg, slightly warmed in boiling water, about 1 minute	1
½ cup	grated Parmesan cheese	125 mL
½ to 1 cup	croutons	125 to 250 mL
6	slices bacon, cooked and crumbled	6

Mash the whole clove of garlic against the inside of a glass, pottery or wooden salad bowl. Tear the romaine into bite-sized pieces, and toss into the bowl. Pour the oil over the lettuce and toss well. Add the anchovies, lemon juice, salt and pepper. (Don't forget how salty the anchovies are, so be sparing with the salt.) Toss again. Break the egg over the salad, add the cheese and toss once more. Sprinkle with the croutons and bacon, and serve immediately. *Serves 4 to 6*

The key to a good Caesar is to serve it before it is made! The dressing should be tossed in, olive oil first, then served immediately. Never let your Caesar wait. It is a salad, not a marinade. Don't be afraid to add more or less lemon juice, oil, Parmesan, anchovies or croutons, but be careful not to overdo any one thing. And please don't leave out the anchovies; if you only add a few, fine, but a Caesar really isn't a Caesar without the anchovies. Right, Pete?

Bibb Lettuce in Cream

This recipe calls for fresh, young, tender lettuce.

3	small heads Bibb lettuce, trimmed and washed	3
¼ cup	sugar	50 mL
¼ cup	white vinegar	50 mL
¾ cup	cereal cream	175 mL
	Salt and white pepper	

Wrap the lettuce in a tea towel and chill for 1 hour. Tear apart the lettuce and put into a salad bowl. Stir the sugar into the vinegar until it is dissolved. Stir in the cream. Pour the sauce over the lettuce and toss. Chill for 10 minutes. Before serving, pour off any excess dressing. Season with salt and pepper. *Serves 4*

Bibb Lettuce, Pepper and Mushroom Salad

4	heads Bibb lettuce, washed, dried and broken up	4
½ pound	fresh white button mushrooms, washed and thinly sliced	250 g
1	small red pepper, sliced	1
2 Tbsp	chopped parsley	25 mL
2 tsp	fresh basil, chopped	10 mL
¼ cup	vinaigrette	50 mL

Place the lettuce, mushrooms and pepper in a salad bowl. Sprinkle with the herbs. Pour the vinaigrette over the lettuce just before serving and toss. (See page 33 for vinaigrette recipe.)

You may wish to toss in a handful of small shrimp or some thinly sliced hard-cooked eggs for a little more protein. *Serves 4 to 6*

Stuffed Iceberg Lettuce

1	medium-sized iceberg lettuce	1
½ pound	cottage cheese, at room temperature	250 g
⅓ cup	blue cheese, crumbled, at room temperature	75 mL
¼ cup	mayonnaise	50 mL
1	rib celery, finely chopped	1
3 Tbsp	red pepper, minced	50 mL
1	green onion, chopped	1
	Chives	
¼ cup	walnuts, finely chopped	50 mL
1 tsp	Worcestershire sauce	5 mL
	Tabasco sauce	
	Sliced tomatoes	
	Sprigs of parsley	

Core the lettuce and hollow out the centre, leaving a shell about 1 inch/2.5 cm thick. Wash and drain the lettuce carefully, drying it on a paper towel.

Mix the cottage cheese, blue cheese and mayonnaise. Blend in the celery, red pepper, onion, chives, walnuts, Worcestershire sauce and a dash of Tabasco. Mix thoroughly.

Fill the lettuce with the cheese mixture, wrap it in

wet paper towels and foil and tie it with a string to keep its shape.

Chill for at least 2 hours. To serve, cut in wedges and garnish with sliced tomatoes and sprigs of parsley. *Serves 4 to 6*

Lettuce and Bacon

2	heads romaine, washed shaken dry, and cut into quarters	2
½ pound	bacon, diced	250 g
1	large onion, sliced	1
1	large tomato, peeled and seeded	1
½ pound	mushrooms, sliced	250 g
	Basil, thyme or marjoram	
	Salt and pepper	
	Chicken stock	

Cook the lettuce in boiling water for two minutes, ensuring that it does not become soggy. Drain the lettuce and lay it in a strainer to allow any excess moisture to drip off. Dry between paper towels.

Cook the bacon until crisp in a large frying pan. Pour off most of the fat. Sauté the onion, tomato and mushrooms in the bacon fat, stirring constantly until the onion is tender. Add the lettuce. Season with a pinch of the herbs, salt and pepper. Sauté over low heat for ten minutes. If there is any danger of scorching, add some chicken stock. Serve very hot. *Serves 4 to 6*

Cape Cod Salad

A great salad, especially for lovers of red wine. My aunt and uncle picked this up in Cape Cod and it quickly became a family favorite.

4	heads Bibb lettuce, washed and dried	4
1	small head romaine, washed and dried	1
1	bunch watercress, washed and dried	1
½ cup	walnut halves	125 mL

½ cup	Mozzarella cheese, grated	125 mL
½ cup	olive oil	125 mL
2 Tbsp	red wine	25 mL
1 Tbsp	red wine vinegar	15 mL
	Salt and pepper	

Tear the lettuces into a salad bowl; add the watercress, walnut halves and cheese. In a separate bowl, blend the oil, wine, vinegar, salt and pepper. Pour the vinaigrette over the salad just before serving and toss. *Serves 6*

Mushrooms

Pete's advice on storing mushrooms is clear: "Don't." When I asked him to expand a little he said: "Don't keep 'em, eat 'em!"

This odd little creation is a peculiarity in the vegetable world. It is really the fruiting body of a variety of fungus. Having no leaves, flowers, seeds or roots, this plant depends on non-living organic matter, rather than photosynthesis, for food. The mushroom has been thought of as exotic and slightly mysterious for thousands of years. The Pharaohs ate mushrooms, and today it is only the fabulously wealthy or the fabulously lucky who eat truffles, perhaps the most exotic, most rare, most expensive and most delicious fungus available.

Although button mushrooms are easy enough to find, they are not cheap; growing them is a precise and time-consuming process. Because of their perishable nature, mushrooms are picked, packed, and shipped to market in less than 24 hours. Many types of mushrooms grow only in the wild and this makes them not only expensive, but also hard to find. Unless you make daily visits to your market, it is unlikely that you will be lucky enough to catch the rarer mushrooms as they arrive. But to keep things simple button mushrooms are widely cultivated and always in good supply. And all that you need to enjoy these little delights is a frying pan, some butter and black pepper. Right, Pete?

Button mushrooms are available all year round, having no peak season, and in most markets and produce departments of large grocery stores, it is possible to bag your own mushrooms. Look for plump, smooth, white mushrooms with tightly closed caps. Avoid shriveled, wide-open or slimy mushrooms or any with blemishes or dark spots.

Mushrooms are not suited to storing. However, if you have no choice and must store these delicate little fungi, ensure that they are wrapped in paper towel or put in a paper bag before refrigerating. And do not forget that mushrooms are fragile and need to be handled carefully. Give them enough space; don't squash them up against anything. If you plan to use them raw, with a dip, or if you want to keep them perfect for a day or two, cover them with a paper towel which has been dipped in water and wrung half-dry, put them on a shallow tray and store them in a refrigerator.

Mushrooms are mostly water so they can absorb a lot of fat or cream in cooking. But raw, four ounces/120 grams of of the delicate fungi have only 35 calories. Mushrooms are a fair source of minerals, especially potassium and a good source of a number of the B vitamins including riboflavin and niacin.

When cooking mushrooms for a large number of people, bear in mind that they release a considerable amount of water and can turn a dish watery. Mushrooms also shrink when cooked so what looks like a good-sized serving of raw mushrooms may be too little when cooked. One pound/500 grams will generously serve three mushroom devotees, or it will keep four ordinary mortals quite happy.

Another consideration is the best way to wash mushrooms: soaking them all but destroys their flavor; wiping them with a damp cloth is a time consuming but effective way to clean mushrooms. A faster and easier option is to put them in a metal sieve and hold them under cold running water, swishing them constantly until they are clean. Then pat them dry with paper towel. However, when asked about washing mushrooms, Pete said that the only time he bothers to wash them is if he is using them in a dip. In stew, soup or even for pan-frying, Pete pointedly refuses to wash mushrooms. He likes to keep his mushrooms as dry as possible because, as he explains, his preference is for golden-brown fried mushrooms which is all but impossible if there is too much moisture in the vegetable.

Mushroom Sauce for Pasta

1 cup	onions, thinly sliced	250 mL
3	cloves garlic, finely minced	3
4 Tbsp	butter	650 mL
2 pounds	mushrooms, thinly sliced	1 kg
1 cup	yogurt	250 mL
½ tsp	nutmeg	2 mL
2 Tbsp	basil, finely chopped	25 mL
	Salt and pepper	
¼ cup	parsley, chopped	50 mL
	Parmesan cheese, grated	

Sauté the onions and garlic in half the butter over medium heat for about 4 minutes, stirring constantly until the onions begin to turn transparent.

In the meantime, sauté the mushrooms in the rest of the butter for about 4 minutes, until tender but still firm. Lower the temperature. Add the onion mixture. Sauté for about 15 minutes.

Add the yogurt, nutmeg, basil, salt and pepper. Heat through, stirring constantly and ensuring that the mixture does not boil. Pour the sauce over the pasta and toss gently. Sprinkle with chopped parsley, and serve with a generous amount of grated Parmesan cheese. *This makes enough sauce for 1 pound/500 g of cooked pasta.*

Stuffed Mushrooms

1 pound	fresh spinach	500 g
1 pound	large fresh mushrooms, cleaned and stemmed, putting the stems aside	500 g
	Melted butter	
¼ cup	fine bread crumbs	50 mL
¼ cup	grated Parmesan cheese	50 mL
⅓ cup	Cheddar cheese, grated	75 mL
⅓ cup	Blue cheese, crumbled	75 mL
6	green onions, minced	6
½ cup	parsley, chopped	125 mL
1 Tbsp	fresh basil, chopped	15 mL

Sprinkle the spinach with water and steam in a large saucepan with a tightly fitting lid. Drain in a sieve, pressing out the excess water. Chop the spinach and set aside.

Mince the mushroom stems and sauté in a little butter. Combine the spinach, mushroom stems and remaining ingredients. Mix well.

Brush the outsides of the mushroom caps with butter and generously fill each cap with the spinach mixture. Bake on a cookie sheet at 375° F/190° C for 20 minutes or until mushrooms are soft. Serve immediately.

Mushrooms and Cream

This combination is especially good on buttered rice.

3 Tbsp	butter	50 mL
½ cup	onion, chopped	125 mL
1 pound	mushrooms, trimmed and sliced	500 g
⅔ cup	coffee cream	150 mL
¼ tsp	nutmeg	1 mL
	Salt and pepper	
3 Tbsp	parsley, finely chopped	50 mL

Melt the butter in a deep frying pan. Sauté the onion for about 2 minutes; then add the mushrooms and sauté for another 2 minutes. In the meantime, heat the cream, add it to the mushrooms and season with nutmeg, salt and pepper. Simmer, stirring constantly, for another 3 minutes or until the cream has thickened. Sprinkle with parsley before serving. *Serves 4*

Mushroom and Leek Soup

6	leeks, well washed and thinly sliced	6
½ cup	butter	125 mL
½ pound	mushrooms, sliced	250 g
¼ cup	flour	50 mL
	Salt and pepper	
1 cup	chicken stock	250 mL
3 cups	milk	750 mL
1 Tbsp	sherry	15 mL

	Fresh chives, chopped	
1 tsp	fresh tarragon	5 mL

Sauté the leeks until soft in ¼ cup/50 mL of the butter. Put aside.

Sauté the mushrooms in the remaining butter until soft. Blend in the flour, salt and pepper. Add the stock and milk and simmer, stirring until mixture is thick and creamy. Add the leeks and simmer for 10 minutes. Stir in the sherry and sprinkle with chives and tarragon. Serve immediately. *Serves 6*

Okra

Okra is not on Pete's list of favorite vegetables. He is, nonetheless, full of information on how to select good okra and how to store it; he even has a few recipes. He claims that the best way to use it is as thickener for soups, gumbos or Creole stews, where its gummy, gluey quality serves it well.

Okra, in good condition, is quite an attractive vegetable. Eight-sided, about 2 to 3 inches/5 to 7.5 cm long, deep green in color with a cute little cap at one end and a nice neat point at the other, okra looks a bit like a Chinese knick-knack.

It is available all year round, with its peak season being from July to September. When buying okra, look for small to medium-sized young pods; mature okra pods tend to be fibrous. Okra should be deep green, crisp and free from blemishes. Avoid dry, shriveled or discolored pods, or those which are stiff and woody. The pods should snap easily, but unless you are out to annoy a lot of greengrocers, checking okra by snapping the pods should be done stealthily. If the pods are pliable, they are too old. You can keep okra for up to 4 days in an open plastic bag in the refrigerator.

Okra is a good source of potassium and an excellent source of vitamin C and folate. Four ounces/120 grams of cooked okra have 35 calories.

Never cook okra in a tin or iron pan because the pods will turn black. They will still be edible but they will look unappetizing. And, unless you want to take full advantage of its gummy quality, do not cut the pods until after the vegetable is cooked; then you can

Okra is a favorite vegetable with people of the southern United States who specialize in Creole cooking. But despite its popularity with West Indian, Arabian and tropical-American cooks, it is not well known in North America and is virtually unheard of in Europe.

safely remove the little caps and cut them any way you like. A drop of lemon juice or vinegar in the cooking water helps reduce their mucilaginous quality.

Steamed Okra and Variations

This is the simplest way of preparing okra and if you are unfamiliar with the vegetable, it gives you a chance to see whether or not you like it.

Wash and trim 1 pound/500 g of okra, pods as small and as young as you can find. Cook in a small amount of boiling water for 10 minutes, or until just tender. Drain well.

With butter and lemon: pour ¼ cup/50 mL melted butter and the juice of a quarter-lemon over the okra. Toss well.

With garlic and oil: pour a little olive oil over the okra and sprinkle with some very finely minced garlic. Toss well.

With garlic-anchovy butter: blend some butter with mashed anchovies and minced garlic. Pour the butter over the okra and and toss.

In vinaigrette: chill the okra completely and pour your favorite vinaigrette over the pods. Toss well. *Serves 4*

Okra, Tomato and Rice

1 cup	onion, chopped	250 mL
½ pound	okra, washed, trimmed and sliced	250 g
2 Tbsp	olive oil	25 mL
1 cup	uncooked rice	250 mL
1 pound	canned Italian plum tomatoes, or use fresh ones if they are readily available	500 g
	Salt and pepper	
¼ tsp	cloves	1 mL
1 or 2	Serrano or Jalapeño peppers, minced	1 or 2
	Chopped parsley	

Sauté the onion and okra in the olive oil until the onion is soft. Add the rice, tomatoes, salt, pepper, cloves, peppers and ½ cup/125 mL water. Bring the mixture to a boil and pour into a greased 2-quart/2-L casserole. Bake at 350° F/180° C for 1 hour or until the rice is tender. Sprinkle with chopped parsley before serving. *Serves 6*

Okra Plus

If this looks like it is becoming too dry, keep a little warm beef stock on hand and add it as necessary.

¼ pound	sliced bacon	120 g
2	medium onions, minced	2
2	potatoes, almost cooked in boiling water, sliced	2
2	ribs celery, chopped	2
1	red pepper, cut into strips	1
1 pound	young okra, trimmed and cut into ½-inch/1.25-cm slices	500 g
1 cup	corn kernels	250 mL
	Salt and pepper	
6	plum tomatoes, peeled and chopped	6
4 Tbsp	fresh basil, minced	60 mL
2 or 3	Serrano or Jalapeño peppers, chopped	2 or 3
2 tsp	celery seed	10 mL
½ cup	coriander, minced	125 mL

In a large frying pan, cook the bacon until crisp. Crumble and put to one side. Save 5 tablespoons of the bacon fat, and in it, sauté the onions, potatoes, celery and red pepper. Stir constantly until the pepper is almost soft; then add the okra. Sauté the mixture, stirring constantly until the okra is golden. Add the corn, tomatoes, basil, peppers and celery seed. Simmer, covered, for 10 to 15 minutes or until okra is tender, taking care not to overcook the mixture. Sprinkle with bacon and coriander and serve hot. *Serves 4*

Fried Okra

1 pound	okra, trimmed and washed and cut into ½-inch/1.25-cm slices (I prefer cooking it whole and cutting it once it's cooked.)	500 g
2	eggs, beaten with	2
½ tsp	salt	2 mL
1 cup	cornmeal	250 mL
	Peanut oil	
	Dried mustard	

Put the okra in a bowl. Pour the beaten eggs over the okra and toss until the pods are completely coated. With a slotted spoon, transfer the okra to a bowl filled with the cornmeal, and toss again until well coated.

Heat ½ inch/1.25 cm of peanut oil in a large frying pan. Add the okra and stir. Cover the frying pan and cook over medium heat, stirring frequently, until the okra is golden brown and crisp. Sprinkle with a pinch of dried mustard. Drain on a paper towel and serve immediately. *Serves 4*

Vegetable Gumbo Soup

Okra is traditionally used as a thickener in soups and stews in southern cuisine. Here is a typical recipe. If you have some left-over chicken on hand, it makes a wonderful addition.

4 Tbsp	butter	60 mL
1	onion, finely chopped	1
4 cups	chicken stock	1 L
1	green pepper, finely chopped	1
1 cup	okra, chopped	250 mL
	Pinch cayenne	
2 cups	canned tomatoes, chopped	500 mL
	Salt and pepper	

Melt the butter in a large pot. Add the onion and sauté, stirring frequently, until transparent. Add the chicken stock, green pepper, okra, cayenne and tomatoes. Simmer, partially covered, for 1 hour. Season with salt and pepper to taste before serving. *Serves 6-8*

One day at Pete's a man came up to my cash with a sack of okra. "Now," he said "I can go home and have my favorite for supper." When I asked him how he planned to prepare it, he gave me this recipe. "Eat it with lots of salt. You will love it. I know." I don't quite love it but it does taste good.

Onions

Onions were so highly thought of in Ancient Egypt that there was actually an onion cult. Although we do not esteem onions quite so highly these days, it would be hard to imagine a lot of our favorite dishes without the onion. Few of us would be willing to eat cooking onions whole and raw, but Spanish onions (of which there are many, many varieties) can really make a salad special or a sandwich extra delicious. From chives to the huge, sweet, eating onions is a world of taste and flavorings just waiting to excite our palates and enhance our meals.

The realm of the onion is enormous and confusing, so to make things a little clearer we'll explore them type by type.

Chives are usually regarded as an herb. These long, slender green shoots are available as fresh as fresh can be early in the summer. The green shoots are delicious finely chopped and sprinkled on sandwiches or salads or used as a garnish on vegetables. The plant should be clipped at least three times during the course of the summer; otherwise, the shoots develop beautiful, although inedible, purple flowers.

Green Onions or Scallions. Although these two terms are used interchangeably, they shouldn't be. Scallions are the shoots of white onions, which are pulled before the bulb has formed. Green onions are harvested while they are still green, and the bulb is obvious. Nevertheless, the two can be substituted in recipes. Both scallions and green onions have a mild flavor and are delicious chopped and added to a salad, sprinkled on scrambled eggs or as a last-minute addition to a stir-fry.

Shallots are a key ingredient in many delicious and wonderful sauces and butters. Their delicate intriguing flavor is enhanced by cooking, blending superbly with fish and poultry. Shallots are superb in a vinaigrette or simply minced and added to a salad. They are usually dried and used like garlic.

Eating Onions are sometimes called "short day" or "early maturing" onions. Their skin is thin and their moisture content high. Pete refers to them as eating onions because their exceptionally mild flavor and crisp juiciness make them delicious for eating when raw. They are also known as sweet onions, and although there are many varieties, the best known is the **Spanish onion**. Depending on the season, year and country of origin, Spanish onions will be of varying strengths. Although they can be cooked, they are best eaten raw. Slice them paper thin and toss a handful onto a green salad, slip a few slices into your next sandwich or try putting out a few chunks of these delicacies with your next tray of crudités.

Cooking Onions, or "long day" onions, are the main crop. They have several thin, dry layers of skin; their flesh has a strong flavor and is not as moist as the flesh of eating onions. Most of us are familiar with these onions; they are the yellow ones which we buy in mesh bags and use all the time.

Onions are available all year. Chives, of course, are really only available if you grow them yourself or purchase small plants at florists or greenhouses. When buying green onions look for young, tender, clean shoots with firm, well-trimmed bulbs and fresh, bright green tops. Avoid withered or damaged green onions with broken or bruised leaves. Store them in your refrigerator, unwashed, for up to 5 days. For shallots and the larger eating and cooking onions, look for hard, firm, dry onions with crackly, unblemished skin and small necks. As a rule, do not buy dry onions which have sprouted, but if they sprout while you are storing them, just cut off the green shoot. If the onion is not mushy, you can still use it.

Dry onions are a good source of vitamin C. Shallots and green onions provide some vitamin A. Although one would never consider eating a cup of chives, the number of calories contained in a cup of green onions is fairly close to that contained in a similar quantity of dry onions. Four ounces/120 grams of raw onion has 40 calories.

Baked Onions

Put unpeeled medium or large onions in a baking dish. Bake at 350° F/180° C for about 30 minutes or until they are soft. Slip off the skins before serving. They will come off easily.

If you are eating the onions hot, serve them with

Whole onions may be stored, unwrapped, in a dry, cool, well-ventilated place for up to two months. Once cut, they should be wrapped in plastic and refrigerated for up to four days.

salt, pepper and butter, like baked potatoes. If you eat them cold, drizzle them with a little olive oil and lemon juice.

Boiled Onions and Variations

Simply boil 1 pound/500 grams of peeled, sliced onions in just enough salted water to cover them. Small onions need not be sliced and will take about 15 minutes to cook; larger onions will require about 20 minutes. Drain the onions well.

Buttered onions: toss the onions with melted butter and black pepper.

With nutmeg: toss the onions with melted butter and nutmeg.

With tomato sauce: pour tomato sauce, seasoned with pepper and freshly chopped garlic over the onions and garnish with chopped parsley.

Creamed onions, creamed onions in a cheese sauce: make a white sauce, or a cheese sauce by adding some grated Gruyère or Cheddar cheese to a white sauce, and pour it over the onions after they have been drained. *Serves 4*

Curried Onions

¼ cup	golden raisins	50 mL
¼ cup	dry sherry	50 mL
1 pound	small white onions, peeled	500 g
	or	
1 pound	sliced onions	500 g
4 Tbsp	butter	60 mL
2 tsp	celery seed	10 mL
	Salt and pepper	
1 Tbsp	curry powder, more or less	15 mL
1 cup	milk	250 mL
1 Tbsp	cornstarch	15 mL
¼ cup	freshly grated coconut	50 mL

Soak the raisins in the sherry for one hour.

Put the onions, 2 tablespoons/25 mL of the butter, celery seed, salt, pepper and 1 cup/250 mL of water into a saucepan. Bring to a boil and lower the temperature. Cover and simmer for 10 minutes, until the onions are tender but still firm. Remove the onions with a slotted spoon and set the liquid to one side.

In the top of a double boiler, melt the other 2 tablespoons/25 mL of butter and blend in the curry powder. Add the onions and simmer over hot water for 10 minutes. Drain the onions into a bowl.

Measure the reserved liquid, add just enough milk to make 1¼ cups/300 mL and put the liquid into the top of a double boiler. Stir the cornstarch into the liquid and simmer, stirring frequently, until the liquid is thick and smooth. Add the onions, raisins and sherry, and cook over hot water until heated through. Sprinkle with fresh coconut. *Serves 4*

Braised Onions and Variations

20	small onions, or 1 pound/500 g sliced onions	20
¼ cup	butter or oil	50 mL
½ cup	chicken or beef stock	125 mL
	Salt and pepper	

A slightly more exciting way to prepare onions is to braise them. The method is a little complicated, but still easy and delicious.

Sauté the onions in the fat until lightly browned. Add the stock, salt and pepper to taste. Cover the pan and cook the onions about 20 minutes, until tender-crisp.

With Parmesan cheese: sprinkle the onions with lots of freshly grated Parmesan cheese just before serving.

With pasta: braised onions make a super pasta sauce. Just pour the onions over cooked pasta and sprinkle with Parmesan cheese.

Fowl braised onions: (Fowl not foul!) add ½ cup/125 mL dry sherry, Madeira or Bourbon to the braised onions, and simmer for about 3 minutes or until the liquid is reduced by half. *Serves 4*

Onion Frittata

2 Tbsp	olive oil	25 mL
2	large onions, sliced as thinly as possible	2
½ pound	mushrooms, sliced	250 g
1 Tbsp	flour	15 mL

2 Tbsp	milk	25 mL
6	eggs, beaten	6
½ tsp	cayenne	2 mL
	Salt, pepper and nutmeg	

In a medium skillet, heat the oil and sauté the onions and mushrooms until the onions are soft and transparent.

In a bowl, mix the flour and milk together, and add the eggs and cayenne. Beat thoroughly. Season with salt, pepper and nutmeg. Pour the egg mixture over the onions and mushrooms, and fry the frittata until the bottom is set. Flip the frittata, using a plate, or broil the top until it is set. *Serves 4*

Parsnips

Pastinaca sativa, the Latin name for parsnips, means "cultivated food." The poor parsnip! This odd-looking vegetable, which looks like an albino carrot, is often relegated to stews. But with a wonderful, sweet, nutty flavor, it is also delicious glazed, battered and deep-fried, puréed, or served in a soup.

Parsnips are available all year; the peak season is from October to May. When buying parsnips, look for ones which are fat and round at the top, not less than 1½ inches/3.5 cm in diameter. Buy small to medium-sized parsnips, which are firm, well shaped and clean; the larger ones have a tendency to be woody.

To store parsnips, simply refrigerate them in a plastic bag. You can happily leave them there for up to two weeks.

Cooked parsnips are a good source of vitamin C and folate. When raw, they are a good source of potassium. Four ounces/120 grams of raw parsnip contain about 85 calories.

Parsnips are easier to peel after they have been cooked. If you do happen to get some large parsnips, simply halve them lengthwise, core them and use them as though they were small.

Sautéed Parsnips and Variations

2½ to 3 pounds	parsnips, unpeeled	1.25 to 1.5 kg
4 to 6 Tbsp	butter	60 to 90 mL
	Salt and pepper	

Steam or boil the parsnips in a small amount of water, until they are easily pierced. This process may take between 20 to 45 minutes, depending on the size of the vegetable. Immerse the parsnips in cold water, and peel them when they are cool enough to handle. Cut off the tough ends, and slice the parsnips very thin. Sauté them in butter for 5 or 6 minutes. Season with salt and pepper.

Glazed: sprinkle white sugar on the parsnips while they are sautéing. Stir well to make sure each piece of the vegetable is coated.

Nutty-glazed: stir ¼ cup/50 mL finely chopped walnuts with the white sugar and glaze as above.

With sour cream: blend 1½ cups/375 mL of sour cream with some mace, ginger or cardamom. Stir the sour cream mixture into the parsnips and heat through. *Serves 4*

Nutty Parsnip Fritters

2 pounds	parsnips, cooked and peeled	1 kg
6 Tbsp	melted butter	90 mL
1 Tbsp	flour	15 mL
2	large eggs	2
¾ cup	milk	175 mL
½ tsp	cardamom or ginger	2 mL
	Salt and pepper	
½ cup	shelled nuts, almonds, hazelnuts or walnuts, coarsely chopped	125 mL

Parsnip fritters make wonderful hors d'oeuvres or are a delicious accompaniment to white fish.

Purée the parsnips in a food processor or blender. Add the butter, flour, eggs and milk, and make a smooth paste. Season with cardamom or ginger, salt and pepper. Stir in the nuts. Ease spoonfuls of the mixture onto a well-oiled cookie sheet. Bake at 350° F/180° C for 15 to 20 minutes, or until golden brown. Drain the fritters on a paper towel. *Serves 6*

Parsnip Soup

The sweetest parsnips are those which have been left in the ground until after the first frost has turned some of the starch to sugar. Parsnips keep very well; in fact, some people claim that parsnips are better after they have been stored for a while.

½ cup	onion, chopped	125 mL
1 cup	carrots, thinly sliced	250 mL
2	large parsnips, peeled, cored and diced	2
1	Serrano or Jalapeño pepper, minced	1
2	cloves garlic, minced	2
3 Tbsp	oil	50 mL
1 tsp	curry powder	5 mL
4 cups	hot beef stock	1 L
½ cup	sour cream	125 mL
	Chopped chives	

Sauté the onion, carrots, parsnips, peppers and garlic in the oil for 10 minutes. If it appears that the vegetables might scorch, add some of the beef stock. Add the curry powder and gradually blend in the beef stock. Simmer until the parsnips are cooked. Purée the mixture in a blender or food processor. Return to the heat and adjust the seasoning. Add the sour cream and sprinkle with chives.

The parsnip taste becomes richer if this soup is allowed to mature for a day or two. *Serves 6*

Braised Parsnips

3 Tbsp	butter	50 mL
2 pounds	parsnips, scrubbed and cut into chunks	1 kg
1 Tbsp	onion, grated	15 mL
¼ tsp	sugar	1 mL
	Salt and pepper	
6	large lettuce leaves	6
3 Tbsp	minced parsley	50 mL

Melt the butter in a large saucepan. Add the parsnips, onion, sugar and some salt and pepper, and simmer the mixture, stirring occasionally. Wash the lettuce leaves and, leaving them wet, cover the parsnips with the lettuce. Put the lid on the saucepan and simmer over low heat for 15 minutes, or until the parsnips are tender. Shake the saucepan often to keep the parsnips from sticking. If the parsnip mixture seems too dry, add a little water, a tablespoon at a time. Sprinkle with parsley before serving. Serve with the lettuce leaves. *Serves 4 to 6*

Parsnip French Fries

8	medium-sized parsnips, cooked, cored and cut into the shape of french fries, or cubed	8
	All-purpose flour	
2	eggs, lightly beaten	2
	Fresh bread crumbs	

Dip the parsnip in the flour and the beaten eggs, and roll the pieces in the bread crumbs. Fry the coated parsnip in oil at 400° F/200° C until tender. Drain the fried parsnip on a paper towel, keeping the pieces warm until they are all cooked. *Serves 4*

Midnight Parsnip Snack

Whenever I run out of popcorn, this is my favorite midnight snack. It's hopelessly easy.

Coarsely grate a parsnip or two. (I like to use the vegetable peeler as a grater, since it produces thick strips of parsnip!) Heat some peanut oil in a wok and drop in the parsnip. Stir-fry them for a moment or two and voîlà! Parsnip curls! Yum!

Peas

Peas have been around for more than 11,000 years, but until about 200 years ago they were usually dried and eaten in soups or porridge. Owing to the fact that they freeze and can so well, over eighty percent of the North American pea crop is preserved in one of these two ways.

Garden peas are available from April to August. Edible-pod peas are available from February through June, except of course for snow peas which are available all year round. Incidentally, for those of you who were wondering, there is little difference between sugar snap and snow peas, except that snap peas are

Like mushrooms, fresh peas are not meant to be kept in your refrigerator for more than a few hours. If you simply have to store your peas, put them in a plastic bag to retain their juiciness, but for no more than 2 days.

smaller than snow peas and have a definite thread. They are, however, interchangeable in recipes.

When buying green or garden peas, look for fairly large, angular, bright green pea pods that are packed with medium-sized peas. There is no way of telling by the outside how sweet and juicy they are inside, so—if you can be sneaky—snap a pod open and pop one of those little round green things into your mouth and test them for yourself. When buying edible-pod peas look for bright green, glossy, crisp pods. In both cases, avoid peas with marks, soft spots or yellowish, swollen pods.

Pete points out that peas are one of the few vegetables which are not available fresh all year, imported from somewhere or another, but adds with great enthusiasm that, thanks to twentieth-century technology, frozen peas are only a hair's breadth away from being every bit as wonderful as fresh peas. So next time you go shopping, if it's not fresh pea season, buy a bag of frozen ones with Pete's blessing.

Don't bother washing garden peas after shelling; they stay nice and clean in their shells. Give edible-pod peas a quick rinse just before trimming them, then just snap off both ends and remove the string if there is one. Try not to keep them for more than 2 days.

Peas are a good source of fiber, potassium and niacin and an excellent source of vitamin C, folate and thiamin. They are a good source of potassium, and contain higher than average amounts of protein and iron. Four ounces/120 grams of fresh garden peas, raw and shelled, have 95 calories. Four ounces/120 grams of edible-pod peas contain 60 calories.

Boiled Peas and Variations

3 to 4 pounds	unshelled peas	1.5 to 2 kg
1 tsp	sugar	5 mL
	Butter	
	Salt and pepper	

Shell the peas seconds before they are to be cooked. Cook them as briefly and gently as possible in boiling water with a little sugar . . . until just tender. Drain well and toss with butter, salt and freshly ground pepper. *Serves 4*

With herbs: after tossing the cooked peas with the butter, sprinkle them with freshly chopped parsley, tarragon, savory or mint.

With mushrooms: combine the peas with an equal quantity of sautéed mushrooms and a sprig of chopped, fresh tarragon.

With shallots: slice 2 or 3 shallots as thinly as possible. Sauté them in a little butter and toss them with the cooked peas.

With green onions: thinly slice green onions or scallions. Heat them in butter and toss with the peas.

With yogurt or sour cream: heat some yogurt or sour cream and a little minced dill. Stir the yogurt in with the buttered peas.

Snow Peas, Red Pepper and Almond Salad

½ pound	snow peas	250 g
2	cloves garlic, finely chopped	2
1 Tbsp	white wine vinegar	15 mL
1 Tbsp	lemon juice	15 mL
1 tsp	sugar	5 mL
	Salt and pepper	
⅓ cup	salad oil	75 mL
½ pound	fresh mushrooms, sliced	250 g
1	large red pepper, in thin strips	1
½	green pepper, in thin strips	½
¼ cup	slivered almonds, toasted	50 mL
4	hard-cooked eggs, sliced or cut in quarters	4

Snow peas and red peppers are a glorious color combination. Not only is this salad gorgeous in appearance, it is a meal in itself.

Top and tail the peas, and remove the strings. Blanch for one minute in boiling water. Drain the peas and plunge them into ice water to chill. Dry on paper towels.

In a small bowl, combine the garlic, vinegar, lemon juice, sugar, salt and pepper. Beat well. Continue beating and slowly drizzle in the oil to make a smooth dressing.

In a large bowl, toss the peas, mushrooms and peppers together. Add the dressing and almonds just before serving and toss once again. Garnish with the eggs. *Serves 6*

Most peas are picked when immature because this is when they are at their sweetest. As they mature, the sugar turns to starch and their protein content increases. The more mature peas are picked to be dried. And we get to eat the most immature peas as sprouts! Versatile little things, peas!

Cold Dilled Pea Soup

3 pounds	peas, freshly shelled	1.5 kg
1	small onion, chopped	1
1	clove garlic, minced	1
1 tsp	tarragon, chopped	5 mL
2 or 3	whole cloves	2 or 3
6 cups	chicken stock	1.5 L
	Salt and pepper	
3 cups	sour cream or yogurt	750 mL
	Fresh dill	

Boil the peas, onions, garlic, tarragon and cloves in the chicken stock, just until the peas are tender. Remove the cloves. Season with salt and pepper. Purée the mixture. Blend in the sour cream or yogurt. Chill for at least 4 hours. Sprinkle with dill before serving. *Serves 8*

Jewish Style Eggs and Peas

3	shallots, very thinly sliced	3
2 Tbsp	melted butter	25 mL
2 pounds	unshelled peas, shelled	1 kg
	Salt, pepper, mace, nutmeg and sugar	
5	eggs	5
6 Tbsp	yogurt	90 mL

Sauté the shallots briefly in a buttered skillet. Add the peas, ¼ cup/50 mL water and a pinch each of salt, pepper, mace, nutmeg and sugar, and continue to cook, covered, for a few minutes. Season the peas with a little more salt and/or sugar. When the peas are half-cooked, make four depressions in the peas with the back of a spoon, and slide an egg into each of the holes. Cover the skillet, and let the eggs and peas simmer for 5 minutes, or until the peas are done and the eggs are set but not hard. Beat the fifth egg into the yogurt and pour the mixture over the peas. Broil for a moment or two. Serve immediately. *Serves 4*

Snow or Sugar Snap Peas

The best way to cook edible-pod peas is to stir-fry them in peanut or olive oil no more than 2 minutes so that they keep their wonderfully crisp nature. Sugar snaps are a delicious addition to any stir-fry or as a dish all on their own. Serve them with melted butter and a little lemon juice. One pound/500 grams of peas will serve three people.

North Americans are especially lucky because we have access to sugar snap peas, garden peas and the lovely little snow peas which we can get all year round.

Peas and Lettuce

2 Tbsp	butter	25 mL
6	green onions, thinly sliced	6
1	head Boston or Bibb lettuce, finely shredded	1
½	small red pepper, sliced or cut into cubes	½
4 pounds	peas, shelled	2 kg
4 Tbsp	chicken stock	60 mL
	Fresh thyme	
	Salt, pepper and nutmeg	
¼ cup	parsley, minced	50 mL

Melt the butter in a skillet. Stir in the green onions, lettuce and red pepper. Add the peas, chicken stock, thyme, salt, pepper and nutmeg. Cover tightly and simmer for no more than 10 minutes, or until the peas are tender. Sprinkle with parsley before serving. *Serves 4*

Peas Italiana

1	small onion, minced	1
2	cloves garlic, minced	2
2 Tbsp	butter	25 mL
4 pounds	peas, shelled	2 kg
½ cup	chicken stock	125 mL
	Salt, pepper and sage	
4	eggs, beaten	4
½ cup	Mozzarella cheese, grated	125 mL

Sauté the onion and garlic in butter until soft and golden. Add the peas, the stock and seasoning. Cover tightly and cook over low heat for 10 minutes or until the peas are just tender, stirring frequently.

Beat the eggs and Mozzarella together, stir the mixture into the peas and remove it from the heat. Let stand, covered, 5 minutes. Sprinkle with additional Mozzarella before serving. *Serves 4*

Peppers

There is something about peppers that is aesthetically pleasing: they look beautiful, feel gorgeous, and taste heavenly. At Pete's, where everything looks superb anyway, one of the most attractive displays are the mountains of red and green peppers.

Bell peppers are available all year in green and red and, during the summer months, in purple and yellow. (Red peppers, incidentally, are simply riper green peppers.) Their peak season is from July to November. Look for bright, glossy, firm peppers, well-shaped and thick-fleshed. Avoid shriveled, bruised peppers and those with soft spots. Refrigerate your peppers, unwashed in a plastic bag, where they will keep well for up to 5 days.

All peppers are excellent sources of vitamin C, and red peppers are particularly high in vitamin A. Four ounces/120 grams of raw green pepper have only 30 calories; four ounces/120 grams of raw red pepper have 35 calories.

When recipes call for peeled peppers, simply broil them in the oven, turning frequently until the skin is black and blistered. Let the peppers cool until you can handle them and slip the skins off.

Peppers Mexicana

1½ cups	onion, thinly sliced	375 mL
3	cloves garlic, crushed	3
	Salt, pepper and paprika	
4 Tbsp	olive oil	60 mL
6	medium bell peppers, red and/or green, cut in thin strips	6
2 Tbsp	flour	25 mL
8 ounces	old Cheddar cheese, grated	250 g
4	large eggs	4

Nothing perks up a salad like a handful of long, thin slices of red or yellow pepper; their sweet flavor sets off the rather nonchalant taste of lettuce. If you are feeling especially extravagant the next time you go shopping, pick up a couple of peppers and eat them like an apple, or cut them into strips to munch on while you're watching T.V. They are a refreshing delicious change from junk food, and they're good for you, too.

1½ cups	sour cream (or part yogurt)	375 mL
½ tsp	dry mustard	2 mL
1 tsp	cumin	5 mL
1 tsp	coriander	5 mL

Sauté the onions and garlic with the salt, pepper and paprika in the olive oil. When the onions are transparent, add the peppers. Sauté over low heat for another 10 minutes. Sprinkle the pepper mixture with the flour. Mix well and continue cooking until there is no extra liquid. Spread a layer of sautéed vegetables in a well-oiled 2-quart/2-L casserole; cover with a layer of cheese and continue the layers until everything is in the casserole.

Beat the eggs and sour cream together and mix in the mustard, cumin and coriander. Pour the egg mixture over the cheese and vegetable layers. Sprinkle with paprika. Bake, covered, at 375° F/190° C for 30 to 35 minutes and, uncovered, for an additional 15 minutes. *Serves 6*

Stuffed Peppers

I asked Terry, a chef who is a regular at Pete's, for a recipe for stuffed peppers. He said "No one eats stuffed peppers!" This delicious concoction is for you, Terry.

4	tomatoes, peeled and chopped	4
1	onion, finely chopped	1
½ cup	pine nuts, lightly toasted	125 mL
3 Tbsp	raisins	50 mL
1 cup	brown rice, cooked	250 mL
1½ cups	old Cheddar cheese, grated	375 mL
¼ cup	Italian parsley, chopped	50 mL
½ tsp	cinnamon	2 mL
	Salt and pepper to taste	
4	green peppers, cored and seeded, with the tops reserved	4
⅓ cup	chicken stock	75 mL

Mix the tomatoes, onion, pine nuts and raisins with the cooked rice. Stir in the cheese, saving a little for the topping. Add the parsley, cinnamon, salt and pepper.

Stand the peppers upright in a baking dish, cutting a little slice off the bottoms, if necessary, to give them a firm base. Fill each pepper with the rice mixture. Sprinkle with the reserved cheese and pop on the lids. Pour the stock into the casserole and cover with foil. Bake at 375° F/190° C for 30 to 45 minutes or until the peppers are tender. Serve hot or cold. *Serve 4*

Pepper Frittata

1	medium onion, sliced very thin	1
1	large clove garlic, minced	1
3 Tbsp	olive oil	50 mL
2	large green or red sweet peppers, cut in strips	2
½ cup	slivered ham	125 mL
2	large tomatoes, chopped	2
	Salt and pepper	
2 Tbsp	water	25 mL
8	large eggs, slightly beaten	8

Sauté the onion and garlic in the olive oil over medium heat for 5 minutes or until the onions are soft. Add the peppers and ham, and cook for another 3 minutes or until the peppers are soft.

Add the tomatoes and simmer gently for 10 minutes. Season with salt and pepper.

Beat the water into the eggs. Pour the egg mixture around the vegetables in the frying pan. Cook over low heat until the bottom of the frittata is set. If you think you can manage to flip the frittata without spilling it, go ahead. If you are not so daring, simply pop the whole thing under the broiler for 2 or 3 minutes, until the top is set. Serve hot or at room temperature.

For a heartier variation, add 2 cups/ 500 mL of cooked, peeled, thinly sliced potatoes to the frittata. Just add the potatoes with the onions, using 1 additional tablespoon of olive oil. *Serves 4*

Hot Peppers

Unless you have grown up eating hot peppers or are a very dedicated culinary explorer, you have probably limited your exposure to hot peppers, adding a pepper here or there as called for in a recipe. Yet, once you've become accustomed to fiery dishes made with chilli peppers, they quickly become an addiction (or so I'm told).

There is an enormous variety of spicy peppers, varying from the rather mild Anaheim to the Scotch Bonnet, which is only eaten by extreme enthusiasts. Surprisingly enough, the heat of a chilli pepper is in the ribs inside the pepper, not in the seeds or the skin. If you want to lessen the bite of a hot pepper, carefully slice out the ribs.

It is wise to wear rubber gloves when dealing with hot peppers; the juice can give you a nasty, painful and lasting burn. Pete learned a handy trick from a wise Jamaican. If you get a pepper burn, simply peel a banana and lay the inside of the peel on the afflicted area. The banana peel will soothe the burn immediately.

To ward off nasty surprises, you should also make sure you give anything which comes in contact with the peppers a good wash, the knife and cutting board especially, because the heat of the peppers will last on almost anything. If you use the same knife to cut an apple that you have just used to cut a pepper, you will probably get a burn from the apple. So cut your peppers and then wash everything, including your cutting board.

If you're not accustomed to cooking with hot peppers, then practise moderation and be wary; too many chilli peppers can spoil a dish. Sample each pepper and the mixture to ensure that you're creating the desired effect. The best way to test a hot pepper is to cut off a slice, remove the rib and enjoy the flavor without suffering the burn, unless you're a masochist or you have an asbestos tongue. In either instance, don't bother with the rib. You can also add chillies at the end of the cooking, a little at a time, until you reach a comfortable amount. Don't forget that many people will not be as tolerant of the heat as you. If you make a dish too hot, provide barley sugar for cooling down. Water won't help.

Hot peppers can be used interchangeably, as long as you use the taste test method to determine the quantity required for the degree of "heat" you want.

Some authorities feel that hot peppers should be peeled before they are added to a dish. Pete argues that he can't see the point. He chops his peppers so small that peeling them is unnecessary.

Hot peppers are available all year. Look for smooth, glossy, firm peppers. Certain types of peppers may look like they have cracks which have healed over; but don't worry about out their appearance, the healed cracks will not affect the taste. Hot peppers can also be blanched and frozen with little loss of piquancy, or refrigerated in a paper bag for a week to 10 days.

Although most of the recipes in this book call for Serrano or Jalapeño peppers, any hot pepper will do. As you become more familiar with the varieties, feel free to experiment a little.

Pete's Pickled Peppers

2 cups	hot peppers, large peppers cut into 2-inch/5-cm pieces (for small peppers, simply cut 2 slits in the skin)	500 mL
¼ cup	granulated sugar	50 mL
½ cup	distilled white vinegar	125 mL
	Salt	
1	clove garlic, minced	1

Cook the peppers for 5 minutes in boiling water, until just tender. Place the peppers in a colander, drain well and transfer to a bowl.

Stir the sugar and vinegar together until the sugar is dissolved. Add a pinch of salt and the minced garlic. Pour the liquid over the peppers, stir well and place the peppers with the liquid in a pint jar.
Makes 1 pint/500 mL

Plantain

This first cousin of the banana is in fact a vegetable and it must be cooked to be edible. I remember being intrigued by huge boxes of what looked like enormous rotten bananas every Saturday morning at Toronto's Kensington Market. I had no idea what they were except that West Indians and South Americans treated them as if they were something special. They bought bags of them. Not until I began working for Pete, did I discover what they were for or how to eat them. They can be baked, boiled or fried. A tasty addition to any diet, they can be eaten alone or mixed with other things.

Plaintain are much larger than bananas, weighing up to 3 pounds/1.5 kg. They are sold separately rather than in bunches and can be dark green, yellow or black in color, often appearing rather mouldy. The flavor varies at each stage of ripening, but they are considered ripe when they are black and vaguely soft. When green, they are quite starchy and they taste rather bland. As the skin darkens, the vegetable takes on the sweetness and the aroma of a banana, yet will keep its shape when cooked. Whether you prefer plantain green or black is a matter of taste. Experience is about the only thing that will serve you there.

Plantain are available all year. If you want to buy the fruit green and ripen it at home, it will go through all the stages—from green to black—and will keep for quite a while. Do not refrigerate plantain unless you wish to stop them from ripening.

Plantain is high in carbohydrates and an excellent source of potassium and vitamin C. For a vegetable, it is relatively high in calories: four ounces/120 grams of raw plantain have about 150 calories.

If you need to peel a green or yellow plantain, cut the tips off. Slit the skin several times from top to bottom, taking care not to cut so deeply that you cut the flesh, and remove the skin with a knife. If the plantain is ripe, ie. black, you may be able to peel it like a banana, but a knife definitely speeds up the process.

Plantain is a kind of tropical potato, as common in the tropics as potatoes are here and serving the same purpose. It is especially versatile because it can also be sweetened and used in desserts.

Baked Plantain

Choose plantains that are between dark brown and black if you want them to be full flavored and soft. Baked plantain is especially good with stews and with roasted or fried meats.

Allow about 1 medium plantain per person. Rinse each vegetable and trim off the tips. Make a lengthwise slit in each plantain and place them in a pan, slit side up. Bake at 375° F/190° C for about 40 minutes or until soft, but not mushy.

Because it keeps its shape so well, you can remove the plaintain from its skin, slice it in diagonal strips and either sprinkle it with lime or lemon juice, or drizzle it with some melted butter. If you are serving it with roast meat, simply split the peel and pour in a little of the pan juices. Once baked, plantain can be reheated in a frying pan and served with your favorite sweet or savory sauce.

Dessert Plantain

2	large plantain, at the black-ripe stage, halved, peeled and slit lengthwise	2
1	cinnamon stick, broken up	1
3	cloves	3
3 Tbsp	lime juice	50 mL
1 Tbsp	cold butter, cut into small cubes	15 mL
2 Tbsp	brown sugar	25 mL
3 Tbsp	rum	50 mL
	Freshly grated coconut	

Arrange the plaintain in a buttered 1-quart/1-liter casserole. Scatter with the spices and lime juice and dot with butter. Bake for 10 minutes at 450° F/230° C. Sprinkle with half the brown sugar. Flip the pieces carefully and sprinkle with the rest of the sugar. Bake another 10 minutes, or until the plantain is tender and warm. Baste with the rum and bake for another 5 minutes. Sprinkle with coconut and serve hot.

This dessert is truly decadent with yogurt, ice cream, sour cream or coffee cream! *Serves 4*

Sautéed Plantain

2 Tbsp	peanut oil	25 mL
2 Tbsp	butter	25 mL
2	half-ripe plaintain, peeled and and cut into ¼-inch/6-mm diagonal slices	2
	Salt and pepper	

Heat the peanut oil and butter in a large frying pan and sauté the plantain slices for 4 minutes on each side, until golden brown. Sprinkle with salt and pepper and serve as you would fried potato. *Serves 3*

Potatoes

Whether boiled, mashed, scalloped or French fried, the potato is one of the most popular vegetables in North America. We eat potatoes all year, every season, in a multitude of different ways. And at Pete's, when the new potatoes arrive from Florida, they sell like proverbial hot cakes at three times the price of winter potatoes. But who can blame us? The taste of the small thin-skinned new potato is one of the first tastes of spring.

Because they store well, potatoes are available all year round, with the new potatoes having a peak season from mid-March to July. For baking, buy firm, well-shaped potatoes that are clean and relatively smooth. Avoid shriveled, bruised or blemished potatoes. Don't purchase potatoes that have frostbite, signs of decay or sprouts. If you're buying new potatoes, look for well-shaped, firm, clean potatoes with thin skins that break easily. Cracked or green-tinged potatoes should generally be avoided.

It is wise to buy your potatoes only two to three weeks ahead of time. If you have no choice but to buy them in bulk, you can store the potatoes in a cool, dry, well-ventilated place for up to 2 months. Don't keep your potatoes in the refrigerator; the low temperature will cause some of the starch to turn into sugar.

Like most fruit and vegetables, potatoes are low in fat and sodium; they are a good source of potassium,

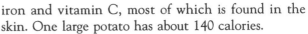

iron and vitamin C, most of which is found in the skin. One large potato has about 140 calories.

Because so much of the potato's nutrition is in or near the skin, it is preferable to cook potatoes with the skins on, wherever possible. Moreover, if peeled potatoes are not used immediately after peeling, they should be kept in cool water to prevent them from turning gray. I remember once making a chowder full of gray potatoes because I did not know enough to keep them in water after peeling and cutting them. They tasted fine; they just looked horrible! Do remember that soaking potatoes in cold water will remove some of the starch, but you also lose some nutrients.

To **bake:** scrub the potato and dry it with paper towel. Pierce the skin to let the steam escape. Inserting a nail or an aluminum or stainless steel skewer into each potato will ensure even baking. If you are only baking potatoes, a 450° F/230° C oven will take 40 minutes. If you are baking the potatoes with a roast, they may take about 1½ hours at 350° F/180° C. Potatoes can be baked at almost any temperature; all that varies is their cooking time.

To **pan roast with meat:** cut up large peeled potatoes, or use new ones that have been scraped. About an hour before the roast is done, roll the potatoes in the drippings and place them cut side down in the pan. Turn the potatoes several times to make sure they are evenly roasted. Baste frequently to keep potatoes soft and moist. If you are short of time, boiling the potatoes until they are almost done will shorten their roasting time considerably and yield almost the same result.

For **mashed potatoes:** cut peeled potatoes into even-sized chunks; wash and drain. Cook the potatoes in boiling salted water until tender. Drain and shake them dry over medium heat to make the potatoes mealy. Mash, adding butter, salt, pepper and hot milk or potato water. Mashing over low heat will ensure that the potatoes stay hot and fluffy. Mashed potatoes should be served at once. Do not leave them standing at room temperature; rather, keep them warm in a 275° F/135° C oven.

To **boil new potatoes:** new potatoes are the only potatoes which should be boiled, and boiling is the only way new potatoes should be cooked. If you don't buy your new potatoes bagged but choose them individually, choose small ones, for these boil the most quickly. Bring a pot of salted water to the boil and add the potatoes and a sprig of fresh mint or dill. Boil just until the potatoes are tender when pierced with a fork. Remove the potatoes from the water and sprinkle them with fresh mint or dill and lots of black pepper and some butter.

Danish New Potatoes

2 pounds	new potatoes	1 kg
2 Tbsp	butter	25 mL
2 Tbsp	sugar	25 mL
1 tsp	salt	5 mL
	Sprig of fresh mint, chopped	

Cook the potatoes in boiling salted water until tender. Drain and peel. (If you want to be a genuine Dane, peel the potatoes; if you want the extra fiber and vitamins, don't.) Heat the butter in a skillet, and stir in the sugar and salt. Cook over low heat, stirring constantly, just until the sugar is golden-brown. Add the potatoes. Sauté over low heat until the potatoes are browned on all sides. Stir gently or shake the pan frequently to avoid sticking. Sprinkle with fresh mint. *Serves 4 to 6*

Potato Soup à la Pete

This is a great soup, and it's quick to make. Perfect for those cold winter days. It's filling and will warm you from the top of your head to the soles of your feet.

2 cups	potatoes, peeled and cut into ¼-inch/6-mm cubes	500 mL
3	medium onions, thinly sliced	3
2 Tbsp	butter	25 mL
6 cups	chicken stock	1.5 L
1 tsp	mace	5 mL
1 tsp	nutmeg	5 mL
4	slices bacon, fried crisp and crumbled	4

Winter potatoes have more starch than new ones, and since it is the starch content which determines the cooking quality of the potato, new potatoes and stored potatoes should be cooked in different ways. Starchy potatoes are well suited for mashing and for making French fries. Potatoes low in starch tend to be dry when baked; they are also excellent pan-fried and good in salads and casseroles.

Fresh parsley, chives or dill,
chopped

Melt the butter in a medium-sized saucepan, and add the potatoes and onions. Cook, covered, over low heat, for about 5 minutes or until the potatoes are almost tender. Stir frequently. If there appears to be some danger of scorching, add a couple of tablespoons of the stock. Add the remaining stock, and season with salt and pepper. Simmer, covered, for 5 or 10 minutes or until the potatoes are very tender. Stir in the mace and nutmeg. You can purée this mixture in a blender or food processor. And if you don't mind the extra calories, you can make the soup richer by adding a cup of cereal cream. Return the mixture to the saucepan and heat gently until the soup is good and hot. Sprinkle with the bacon and parsley, chives or dill. *Serves 4*

Potato Pancakes

I had a discussion with a friend who considers himself to be a potato pancake specialist. He claimed that the best potato pancakes were made in a little restaurant in Winnipeg. But he ate his words when he tried this version!

3	eggs, separated	3
4 cups	grated potatoes, well drained	1 L
6 Tbsp	grated onion	90 mL
3 Tbsp	very fine bread crumbs	50 mL
	Dash of cayenne	
	Salt and pepper	
	Peanut oil	
	Sour cream	

Beat together the egg yolks, potatoes, onion, bread crumbs, cayenne, salt and pepper. In a seperate bowl, beat the egg whites until stiff, and fold them into potato mixture. Place a heaping teaspoon of the batter in a skillet and fry the pancakes in ½ inch/1.25 cm of hot oil. Flip the pancakes when the edges are golden brown.

Keep the pancakes warm in an oven until all of pancakes are cooked. Serve with sour cream. *Serves 6*

Pete's Perfectly Exquisite Creamed Potatoes

4	big potatoes, peeled and cut into ½-inch/1.25-cm chunks	4
2 Tbsp	onion, minced	25 mL
⅛ tsp	mace	.5 mL
¼ tsp	nutmeg	1 mL
1 cup	coffee cream	250 mL
	Salt and pepper	
	Paprika	
2 or 3	green onions, chopped	2 or 3

Soak the potatoes in cold water for half an hour. Drain the potatoes and dry with a paper towel. Place the potatoes, onion, mace, grated nutmeg, coffee cream, salt and pepper in the top of a double boiler. Steam, covered, over boiling water for 45 minutes or until the potatoes are tender and the sauce is thick. If the potatoes are too dry, add a little more cream or hot water, but only 2 or 3 tablespoons/25 or 50 mL at a time. Sprinkle with paprika and green onions just before serving. *Serves 4*

Potato Scallop au Gratin

Even without the cheese, this recipe is every bit as delicious.

2 pounds	potatoes, peeled and cut in ½-inch/1.25-cm slices	1 kg
2 cups	carrots, sliced	500 mL
8 to 12 ounces	Gruyère cheese, grated	225 to 340 g
2	eggs	2
2 cups	milk	500 mL
2 Tbsp	dry sherry	25 mL
½ tsp	grated nutmeg	2 mL
1 tsp	Dijon mustard	5 mL
	Salt and pepper	

In a well-buttered casserole, layer potatoes and carrots alternately with cheese.

Beat the eggs, milk, sherry, nutmeg, mustard, salt and pepper, and pour over the mixture over the potatoes. Bake in a 1-quart/1-Litre casserole at 350° F/

180° C for 1½ hours, or until the liquid is absorbed and potatoes soft. *Serves 6*

Potato Salad

I am not sure where this recipe came from, but I have been eating it for 25 summers. I remember watching my grandmother making it and although there are lots of potato salads around, I think this one is something special.

Dressing		
¼ cup	sugar	50 mL
¼ cup	flour	50 mL
1½ tsp	Dijon mustard	7 mL
	Salt	
4	egg yolks	4
1 cup	milk	250 mL
½ cup	cider vinegar	125 mL
½ cup	yogurt	125 mL

Mix the sugar, flour, mustard and some salt in the top of a double boiler. Stir in the egg yolks and milk; cook until thickened, stirring constantly. Add the vinegar, stir it in and then add the yogurt. Blend well and cool.

Salad		
6	potatoes, cooked and cut into chunks	6
6	hard-cooked eggs, sliced	6
1 cup	chopped parsley, preferably Italian	250 mL
2	ribs celery, chopped	2
½ cup	chives or green onions, chopped	125 mL
½ cup	red and/or green pepper, chopped	125 mL
½ cup	chopped radishes	125 mL
¼ cup	chopped red onion	50 mL
	Paprika	

Put all the ingredients in a large bowl and toss them with the cooled dressing. Sprinkle with the paprika and chill.

You can turn this salad into a meal by adding some chopped meat. *Serves at least 8*

Potato Soufflé

½ cup	hot milk	125 mL
½ cup	Mozzarella cheese, grated	125 mL
2 or 3 Tbsp	butter, at room temperature	25 or 50 mL
1 tsp	nutmeg	5 mL
1 tsp	cayenne	5 mL
3 Tbsp	minced parsley	50 mL
2 cups	fresh hot mashed potatoes	500 mL
4	eggs, separated	4
	Salt and pepper	

Beat the milk, grated cheese, butter, nutmeg, cayenne and parsley into the potatoes while they are still hot.

Beat the egg yolks until thick.

Beat the egg whites until stiff.

Add the egg yolks to the potato mixture. Check the seasoning and add salt and pepper to taste.

Fold in the beaten egg whites, and spoon the mixture into a well-buttered 1-quart/1-L baking dish. Bake at 400° F/205° C for about 15 minutes or until puffed and golden. Serve immediately. *Serves 4*

Radicchio

This gorgeous red and white vegetable has wormed its way into North American kitchens with surprising speed and ease. Ten years ago, it was virtually unheard of, and today, although not yet as popular as it will be, it is not that hard to find. It is no great wonder, for this little beauty is one of the most decorative vegetables on the market. The name, radicchio, is Italian for chicory. Indeed, this leafy creation has been a favorite in European kitchens for a long time.

The Italians have many different varieties of radicchio and use it a hundred different ways. (Pete would argue that the Italians produce the best radicchio.) The type that North Americans usually have access to is the radicchio rosso or radicchio di Verona. It is shaped like a cabbage rose and has reddish leaves with white ribs. It tends to be on the small side, similar to the Bibb lettuce. It also comes in shades of red or green, with solid or variegated leaves. One wonderful thing about radicchio's growing popularity means that

Radicchio is one of the best garnish vegetables available to the cook, and for taste and texture it's wonderful too. It is deliciously crunchy and has a taste rather like an intense lettuce with a hint of radishy warmth. You can use it in any recipe which calls for Belgian endive or escarole.

eventually it will be easier to find and less expensive to purchase.

Radicchio is available all year. If you look carefully, you should be able to find a virtually perfect head. Look for a pure, clean white base, a firm head with bright color and crisp leaves. Radicchio packs a lot more into a head than lettuce, so choose accordingly. And, since you use much less radicchio than you would lettuce, you will probably not need as much as you might expect. Avoid radicchio with brown edges, leaves with holes, or tired-looking heads.

Radicchio stands up to storing much better than you might think. You can keep it in the refrigerator, loosely wrapped, for up to a week. Don't bother washing it until about an hour before using. Then trim the bottom, separate the leaves, hold them under running water and either spin them dry or lay them between layers of paper towel. The leaves may be wrapped in a damp paper towel or tea towel and chilled for about an hour before using them.

Radicchio is an excellent source of vitamins A and C, and is high in fiber. One cup/250 mL of raw radicchio has only 10 calories.

If you are using radicchio di Verona, the leaves make excellent little dishes; they keep their cup shape well and will hold in the juices from moist salads. Radicchio also grills and bakes wonderfully; just brush on a little melted butter or olive oil. Unfortunately, it loses its ruby color once cooked. Of course, when raw, it looks tremendous with whatever you put it next to. If you are including it in a salad or serving it with a dressing, keep the vinaigrette light; enhance the flavor, don't drown it. Try making a brilliant looking salad with avocados, red peppers and radicchio; include a lime juice vinaigrette and you'll have a treat you won't soon forget!

Radicchio, Peppers, Mushrooms and Fennel

5	large shiitake mushrooms (you can use button mushrooms if the Oriental ones are not available)	5
1 pound	fennel	500 g
½ pound	radicchio	250 g
2 Tbsp	butter	25 mL
2 Tbsp	olive oil	25 mL
½	green pepper, cut in strips	½
½	red pepper, cut in strips	½
	Salt and pepper	
¼ cup	toasted pine nuts	50 mL

Radicchio is delicious warmed up by a quick sauté. Try it warm with sliced olives and julienne strips of a mild cheese, such as Mozzarella. Sprinkle on a few toasted pine nuts or walnuts for a little more crunch.

If you are using dried shiitake mushrooms, pour 1 cup/250 mL of very hot water and 1 tablespoon/15 mL of the olive oil over them, letting the mushrooms stand for at least 30 minutes. Remove the mushrooms from the water, dry them and slice the caps into strips.

If you are using fresh mushrooms, simply slice the caps into strips.

Cut the fennel into pieces the size of baby carrots.

Core the radicchio and cut it into thin slivers.

Heat the butter and 1 tablespoon/15 mL of olive oil. Add the fennel and peppers and toss over medium heat until tender for about 5 minutes. Add the radicchio, mushrooms, salt and pepper to taste. Toss for about 3 minutes, until the radicchio is wilted and tender. Stir in the pine nuts and serve at once. *Serves 4*

Broiled Radicchio

Despite the fact that cooked radicchio is not nearly as appealing to look at, it tastes just as delicious.

1	radicchio, cut in half or quarters	1
	olive oil or melted butter	
1	garlic clove, minced	1
	freshly ground black pepper	

Brush the radicchio with lots of olive oil or melted butter and broil, turning only once, until softened but not limp. How long this takes depends on the thickness of the leaves, and the size of the cut pieces. Check it frequently.

Meanwhile, heat a little minced garlic in some olive oil or butter, and drizzle the mixture over the cooked radicchio. Sprinkle with some freshly ground black pepper and serve immediately.

Rapini

Rapini, also known as broccoli raab, is a type of broccoli, as its alias implies. You have probably seen it without knowing what it was. It is easy enough to recognize once you know what it is, or once you know that it is related to broccoli, but it is also easy to overlook rapini. It resembles tiny bunches of broccoli on long stems amidst lots of large, spiky leaves. There may be a yellow flower or two among the broccoli buds, brightening up this beautiful deep green vegetable.

Rapini is available off and on all year but is most easily found from November to mid-May. Look for rapini which has good bright color, fresh-looking leaves, firm, smallish stems and relatively few opened buds. Refrigerate the vegetable, wrapped, for up to 3 days.

Rapini is a good source of potassium and vitamins A and C. It is very low in calories with only about 45 per cup.

How you cook rapini is very much a matter of personal taste. Its aggressiveness can be moderated if you blanch it in boiling salted water for a minute or two, drying it before preparing it for a recipe. But even blanched, some people still find it too strong. It is particularly good with spicy Italian sausages or with dishes with lots of garlic or spices. The flavor can also be mellowed somewhat by blending the vegetable with cream.

Rapini can be cooked the same way as broccoli, but more quickly because it is essentially a green. It seems that most North Americans prefer it cooked quickly, for about 5 minutes or so; however, many people cook it longer. Pete enjoys it steamed for about 5 minutes. He then adds some coarsely grated carrot, some sliced tomatoes and a vinaigrette made with olive oil. It is delicious hot or cool.

Rapini is rather like coffee. Ten years ago we drank it with cream and sugar; now we drink it black. If you have never tasted rapini, try it in the following recipe. It is an unusual addition to any diet.

Rapini Fried Rice

Some people prefer this recipe with half white rice and half long-grain brown, or some long-grain and short-grain brown rice or . . . well, there are various combinations which offer themselves as possibilities. Try the recipe first with the short-grain brown rice. If it is too crunchy or nutty, change to a blend that you are more comfortable with.

3 Tbsp	soy sauce	50 mL
1½ tsp	honey	7 mL
6 ounces	tofu, drained and cubed	175 g
5 Tbsp	peanut oil	75 mL
½ cup	pine nuts, almonds or cashews, toasted	125 mL
1 pound	rapini, washed and cut into bite-size pieces	500 g
2	carrots, coarsely grated	2
3	large cloves garlic, minced	3
1	Serrano or Jalapeño pepper, seeded and finely chopped	1
1½ cups	short-grain brown rice, cooked and cooled for a day or two	375 mL
½ cup	green onions, thinly sliced	125 mL

In a small bottle, mix 2 tablespoons/25 mL of the soy sauce with the honey and 3 tablespoons/50 mL of water. Shake well and set aside.

Sauté the tofu with the remaining 1 tablespoon/15 mL soya sauce and 1 Tbsp/15 mL of the peanut oil in a wok for about 2 minutes; remove from the wok and set aside.

Sauté the nuts in 1 tablespoon/15 mL of the peanut oil until lightly browned. Set aside.

Sauté the rapini and carrots with the garlic and pep-

If you are an enthusiastic fan of aggressive vegetables, you should be familiar with rapini. It has a strong bitter flavor that is wonderful in combination with the right things, but it can be overwhelming with ingredients that are unable to hold their own next to its particular brand of enthusiasm. It is a favorite with Italians and the Chinese whose cuisine delights in aggressive ingredients.

per in 2 tablespoons/25 mL of oil for 3 minutes until slightly softened. Set aside.

Heat the remaining oil in the wok. Add the rice and toss in the hot oil until heated through. Add the rapini, carrots, nuts and tofu. Toss for one minute.

Pour the soy sauce and honey mixture over the vegetables and stir over high heat until well blended. Sprinkle with sliced green onions and serve. *Serves 4*

Spinach

This beautiful, dark green vegetable could be every cook's dream. It is delicious steamed, creamed, puréed, in a salad and as soup; and it is wonderful in combination with other foods—especially cheese, fish, eggs and pasta.

Spinach is available all year, though its peak months are April and May. Most of the time you can buy spinach pre-washed and nicely packaged in cellophane wrap.

If, however, you are buying spinach that needs to be washed, fill the sink with lukewarm water and swish the spinach around. Then lift the spinach out, clean the sink, fill it with cold water and wash the spinach once again. Repeatedly wash with cold water until there is no sand left. Drain the spinach. By not washing the spinach until you use it, you will save yourself the trouble of drying it, letting it cook in the water that clings to the leaves.

Look for spinach with a nice dark green color and crisp leaves. Avoid spinach with yellow or soggy leaves. Spinach is extremely perishable so do not buy it and expect to store it for a while before using it. In fact, you should not expect spinach to keep in the refrigerator for more than 2 or 3 days, whether you buy it pre-packaged or loose.

Dieters should delight in spinach because it has very few calories, about 30 in 4 ounces/120 grams of the raw vegetable. And as all of us know very well, spinach is very good for us; it is an excellent source of vitamin A, a good source of vitamin C, and a fair source of minerals—especially iron—when cooked. So the next time you go shopping, pick up some extra spinach and try some of following treats.

Italian Spinach

3 pounds	spinach, trimmed and washed	1.5 kg
2 Tbsp	olive oil	25 mL
½ cup	almonds, slivered	125 mL
2	cloves garlic, crushed	2
2 tsp	vinegar	10 mL
1 tsp	fresh basil, chopped	5 mL
1 Tbsp	fresh parsley, chopped	15 mL
	Salt and pepper	

Tear the large spinach leaves into smaller pieces. Heat the olive oil in a deep pan. Toast the nuts in the oil, stirring constantly until golden. Add the spinach, garlic, vinegar, herbs and seasonings to taste. Simmer, covered, for 4 minutes, or until tender, shaking the pan to prevent the spinach mixture from sticking. Serve hot. *Serves 4*

This beautiful, dark green vegetable could be every cook's dream. It is delicious steamed, creamed, puréed, in a salad and as soup; and it is wonderful in combination with other foods—especially cheese, fish, eggs and pasta.

Spinach Soup

1	medium onion, finely chopped	1
2	cloves garlic, finely chopped	2
2 Tbsp	butter	25 mL
1 pound	spinach, chopped	500 g
1 cup	peas	250 mL
2 cups	chicken broth	500 mL
1 tsp	fresh dill, chopped	5 mL
1 cup	mashed potatoes	250 mL
1 cup	sour cream	250 mL
	Fresh basil or fresh chives, chopped	

Sauté the onion and garlic in the butter until soft. Add the spinach and peas, and sauté them gently for 3 minutes. Add the chicken stock and dill, and simmer for an additional 4 minutes. Add the potatoes and blend well. You might wish to give this mixture a quick zip in the food processor to ensure that the ingredients are well blended. Mix in the sour cream just before serving. Sprinkle with fresh basil or chives.

This soup can be served hot or cold, depending on your preference. *Serves 3-4*

Spinach Frittata

You may have noticed a lot of frittata, or Italian omelets, in this guide. They are the perfect solution for hungry, disorganized cooks.

3 Tbsp	butter	50 mL
2	cloves garlic, minced	2
1	small onion, diced	1
10 ounces	spinach (1 cello pack), chopped	380 g
¼ cup	wheat germ	50 mL
1 tsp	fresh basil, chopped	5 mL
1 cup	Cheddar cheese, grated	250 mL
1 tsp	Dijon mustard	5 mL
6	eggs, beaten	6
	Salt, pepper and nutmeg	

Heat 1 Tbsp/15 mL of the butter in a large saucepan. Sauté the garlic and onions for 5 minutes, until the onions are transparent. Add the spinach and stir until wilted. Remove from the heat and keep warm.

Mix the wheat germ, basil, cheese, mustard and eggs. Blend with the spinach mixture, and season with salt, pepper and nutmeg.

Put the rest of the butter in a frying pan. Pour in the spinach-egg batter. Cook over low heat until the bottom is set. Then either turn the frittata over (using a plate) or broil the top until it is set.

This fritatta is exquisite with cheese sauce. *Serves 4 to 6*

Spinach and Ricotta Pie

10 ounces	spinach (1 cello pack)	380 g
1	small onion, diced	1
2 Tbsp	butter	25 mL
	Salt and pepper	
1 tsp	fresh basil, chopped	5 mL
1 pound	ricotta cheese	500 g
3	eggs, beaten	3
3 Tbsp	flour	50 mL
½ cup	old Cheddar cheese, grated	125 mL
½ cup	sour cream	125 mL
½ cup	yogurt	125 mL

Pastry for a 9-inch/23-cm pie
Paprika

Sauté the spinach and onion in the butter with the salt, pepper and basil. Mix the spinach mixture with the ricotta, eggs, flour and cheddar in a small bowl. Spread the mixture into the pie shell. Blend the sour cream and yogurt, and spoon it over the top of the spinach, spreading it to the edges. Dust with paprika. Bake at 375° F/190° C for 40 to 45 minutes. *Serves 4*

Spinach Salad

1 pound	spinach, washed and dried	500 g
½	Spanish onion, sliced	½
1 cup	mushrooms, thinly sliced	250 mL
6 Tbsp	olive oil	90 mL
1 Tbsp	soy sauce	15 mL
2 tsp	Dijon mustard	10 mL
1 tsp	lemon juice	5 mL
	Salt and pepper	
4	hard-cooked eggs, sliced	4
6	slices bacon, cooked crisp and crumbled	6
	Parmesan cheese	
	Croutons or a generous handful of toasted pine nuts	

Removing the stems, tear the spinach into bite size pieces. Put them in a salad bowl with the onion and mushrooms.

Combine the oil, soy sauce, mustard, lemon juice, salt and pepper in a small bowl and mix well.

Just before serving, pour the vinaigrette over the spinach, mushrooms and onion. Toss lightly and arrange the egg slices on the top. Sprinkle the salad with bacon, a generous amount of Parmesan cheese and some croutons or toasted pine nuts. *Serves 4*

Super Spinach

Deciding which of the many ways to enjoy spinach can be a problem. The inventive French even have a dessert they make with spinach—a custard into which they blend dried apricots.

2 pounds	spinach, washed, trimmed and coarsely chopped	1 kg
2	medium onions, minced	2
2 Tbsp	olive oil	25 mL
1 tsp	nutmeg	5 mL
4 Tbsp	pine nuts	60 mL
	Salt and pepper	
½ cup	raisins	125 mL
1 cup	yogurt, more or less	250 mL
1 Tbsp	fresh parsley, chopped	15 mL

Sprinkle the spinach leaves with water and place them in a medium-sized saucepan with the onions. Simmer, covered, over medium heat, for 5 minutes, shaking the pan frequently to prevent the spinach from sticking.

Add the olive oil and continue cooking for a few minutes. Add the nutmeg, pine nuts and seasoning. Remove from the heat and add the raisins and yogurt. Sprinkle with parsley before serving. *Serves 4*

Sprouts

During the past ten years, these crunchy little delights have sprung from relative obscurity onto almost every market shelf and restaurant menu in North America. They add a little crispness to sandwiches or salads, and the sprouts from larger grains, such as mung beans, chick peas and lentils, are good in soups and casseroles. Because of their versatility, it never hurts to have sprouts on hand.

One day I bought a bag of mung bean sprouts at Pete's, and as I was walking home with a friend, I opened the bag and offered him some. I live very close to the City Market, but by the time we got home, we'd eaten them all. I had to turn around and go back for more so I could make dinner. Ever since, sprouts have become a regular snack for me. The next time you are tempted to buy junk food, reach instead for a bag of sprouts. You won't regret it. Besides being healthy, they are tasty and versatile.

The length of time you can store sprouts depends on how fresh they are when you buy them, and determining their freshness is quite easy. Take a good look at the sprouts: they should be crisp and appear fresh, small with bright color. Mung beans should be white and crisp, with the bean still attached. When the sprouts begin to get old they get slimy and will leave a film on the plastic in which they are packaged.

Sprouts are an excellent source of protein and a good source of vitamin C. One cup/250 mL of raw mung bean sprouts has 37 calories. Four ounces/120 grams of alfalfa sprouts contain 35 calories.

There is a wide variety of sprouts available. The following are among the most common.

Alfalfa sprouts are tiny alfalfa seeds, about twice the size of a pin head, with tails on them, 2½ to 3½ inches/6 to 8 cm long. They are wonderfully tender, having a delicate crunch and a taste rather like immature lettuce. They are especially nice in sandwiches because they add moisture without making your bread damp and a taste of something different. Never use alfalfa sprouts for cooking.

Clover sprouts are probably the most beautiful of all the delicate sprouts. They have tiny bright green clover leaves with shiny white tails which are anywhere from 3 to 5 inches/7 to 10 cm long. The leaves themselves taste like clover and are thick and fleshy. Though they are not as moist as alfalfa sprouts, clover sprouts have more flavor; they are vaguely bitter, reminiscent of sweet grass and clover. Clover sprouts are especially good with tuna, chicken or in Pete's favorite, roast beef sandwiches. And Pete's comment for these little treats is that you don't have to be a cow to eat them. These sprouts are also not recommended for cooking.

Spicy sprouts are a combination of alfalfa and radish sprouts, mixed together at a ratio of about ⅓ radish to ⅔ alfalfa sprouts. I imagine you could find radish sprouts solo if you really wanted: find out where your neighborhood dragon shops! Radish sprouts alone are very, very peppery. They are far hotter than any radish could ever be, but mix them with alfalfa sprouts and you have spicy sprouts—a well-named combination. Radish sprouts are more robust looking than either the alfalfa or clover sprouts. Their leaves resemble an unopened four-leaf clover, and their color is a slightly dull green. They

The best way to tell whether or not your sprouts are fresh is to take a good sniff; sprouts are young and delicate and their life is not particularly long. When they begin to "go," they smell like it.

have short thick, white tails, and are especially good with eggs, in sandwiches or sprinkled on an omelette. And no, I wouldn't bother cooking with these sprouts.

Crispy sprouts are for hard-core sprout fans—lots of big, crunchy, nutty-flavored sprouts. These sprouts consist of a mixture of sprouted green beans, yellow peas, adzukis and lentils, sometimes in combination with garbanzo beans or chick peas. Since this combination of beans does not sprout with the enthusiasm of the smaller seeds, you get a delicious mix of the beans themselves and the delicately flavored sprouts. Because these sprouts are not as fine in taste or texture as the ones mentioned above, they are well-suited to cooking. You can steam them for a few seconds and serve them with lemon juice or butter and pepper. Toss a handful into a soup, a casserole or the next stir-fry you concoct, where they'll make a tasty addition. They are also delicious piled onto sandwiches. If you are going to use crispy sprouts in a salad, chill them in ice water for half an hour to enhance their crispness.

Mung bean sprouts are the grand-daddy of all sprouts, having been used in Chinese cooking for thousands of years. In fact, it is the reintroduction of mung bean sprouts which is largely responsible for the wide variety of sprouts which we can now find. There are few corner grocery stores in North America where you will not find them. These sprouts have a crisp, moist texture and a bland, vaguely nutlike flavor which makes them a natural addition to salads and main dishes. Since they are slightly more robust than a lot of the other sprouts, they can easily withstand cooking.

Bean Sprouts au Gratin

2 Tbsp	butter	25 mL
2 Tbsp	flour	25 mL
1 cup	milk or cereal cream, heated	250 mL
1 cup	Swiss cheese, grated	250 mL
1 tsp	dry mustard	5 mL
	Salt, pepper and nutmeg	
6 cups	mung bean sprouts	1.5 L
1 cup	fine bread crumbs	250 mL

Heat the butter in a skillet and stir in the flour. Cook for 1 minute, stirring constantly. Add the hot milk or cream and continue to stir the mixture. Simmer until the sauce is thick and smooth. Add ¾ cup/200 mL of the cheese and the mustard. Stir until the cheese is melted and season with salt, pepper and nutmeg.

Add the sprouts to the sauce. Put the entire mixture into a buttered 1-quart/1-L casserole dish and sprinkle with bread crumbs and the remaining ¼ cup/50 mL grated cheese. Bake at 400° F/200° C for 10 to 15 minutes or until golden. *Serves 4*

Sprout Salad

1	English cucumber, sliced	1
1	small zucchini, sliced	1
3	medium-sized tomatoes, sliced	3
½	red pepper, sliced	½
½	green pepper, sliced	½
¼ cup	sunflower seeds	50 mL
2 tsp	fresh basil, chopped	10 mL
2 tsp	fresh dill, chopped	10 mL
¼ cup	yogurt	50 mL
1 Tbsp	mayonnaise	15 mL
1 cup	cottage cheese	250 mL
	Paprika	

Mix all the ingredients together in a large bowl and toss gently. Serve with a huge bowl of your favorite sprouts. *Serves 8*

Since alfalfa, clover and radish sprouts are so delicate, they do not stand up particularly well in a salad, but tend to get rather squashed.

Egg Foo Yung

2 cups	mung bean sprouts	500 mL
6	eggs, beaten	6
2 Tbsp	onion, grated	25 mL
2	green onions, thinly sliced	2
½ cup	snow peas, trimmed and cut in half	125 mL
¼	small red pepper, diced	50 mL
1 cup	small shrimp, peeled	250 mL
	Salad oil	
	Soy sauce	
	Salt and pepper	

Cook the sprouts in boiling water for 1½ to 2 minutes, until they are just tender but still firm. Drain well.

Put the eggs, onion, green onions, snow peas, red pepper and shrimp in a wok or a large frying pan, and sauté the mixture, adding oil, soy sauce, salt and pepper to season. Stir constantly until the egg is cooked and everything is heated through. *Serves 4*

Sweet Potatoes, Yams and Boniato

Sweet potatoes and yams are completely different vegetables, although not everyone knows this. If you have the opportunity to see the two side by side, this confusion would surprise you because they look entirely different. Sweet potatoes are a familiar sight to all of us, but yams, or ñame, as they are called by everyone but North Americans, tend to be large, vaguely round in shape and covered with a thick, dark-brown skin, almost like a bark. The flesh inside may be white, yellow, red or purple or something in between. Although you would never mistake one for the other when you are buying them, sweet potatoes and yams are generally interchangeable in recipes.

Both yams and sweet potatoes are available all year, with sweet potatoes having a peak season from September to March.

Look for well-shaped, clean roots with evenly-colored skins. Choose thick, chunky potatoes of medium size which taper toward the end. Do not buy sweet potatoes with signs of decay or bruises, since they spoil quickly.

As for yams, buy them with unwrinkled skins weighing 1 pound/500 grams or less. Avoid soft yams and those with blemishes or sunken areas. Sweet potatoes may be stored in a cool, well-ventilated place, but not in the refrigerator, for up to 2 weeks. Yams will tolerate the same conditions, but for no more than 1 week.

Sweet potatoes and yams are an excellent source of vitamins A and C and a fair source of potassium. Both have about 150 calories in four ounces/120 grams of boiled flesh.

The simplest way to cook sweet potatoes and yams is to boil or bake them like an ordinary potato, the only difference being that they cook faster and reheat better. Incidently, Pete recommends a sprinkle of nutmeg on sweet potatoes and yams, along with the usual salt and pepper.

At the risk of totally and completely confusing you, I will tell you that the name boniato is Cuban for sweet potato, and that the boniato is the real sweet potato. Irregularly-shaped, as in the illustration below, its skin is sometimes creamy, purple or vaguely red in color. You may cook it as you would any sweet potato. It is superbly delicate in flavor, fluffy and less sugary than our orange-fleshed sweet potatoes. If you are going to cook boniatos peeled, in a stew or boiled, keep them in a salt solution (1 tsp/5 mL of salt in 1 cup/250 mL of water), for they discolor quickly. When you cook boniatos, you'll want about half a pound/250 grams for each person. My own personal advice is to first try them baked. Wash them off and cook them like a sweet potato in a 400°F/200° C oven for 1 hour. The skin gets wonderfully crunchy and the flesh becomes superbly creamy.

Boniato is available all year round, becoming somewhat scarce in late winter. When you buy boniatos, ensure that they are rock hard without any soft spots. Store them as you would sweet potatoes, in a cool well-ventilated spot and for as brief a time as possible, no more than 2 days.

Half a cup/125 mL of baked boniato has 115 calories and lots of vitamin A.

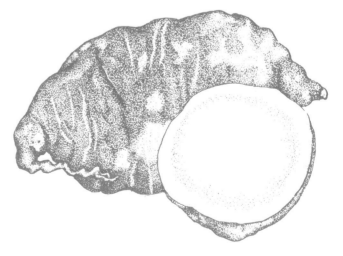

Sweet Potatoes with Orange

3 pounds	sweet potatoes, washed	1.5 kg
¼ cup	toasted cashews	50 mL
¼ cup	light brown sugar	50 mL
2 Tbsp	lime juice	25 mL
½ cup	freshly squeezed orange juice	125 mL
	Rind of 1 orange, grated	
	Salt	
¼ tsp	cinnamon	1 mL
4 Tbsp	butter, cut up	60 mL

Cook the sweet potatoes in boiling salted water for 15 minutes or until tender but still firm. Drain the water cool the potatoes, peel and cut them into ¼-inch/6-mm slices.

Arrange the potatoes in layers in a shallow, buttered baking dish. Distribute the cashews though the layers and sprinkle with the sugar. Mix the fruit juices and rind, adding a pinch of salt and the cinnamon. Sprinkle the liquid over the potatoes and dot with the butter. Bake at 325° F/160° C for 25 minutes or until golden. *Serves 4 to 6*

Curried Sweet Potatoes

2 pounds	sweet potatoes	1 kg
2 Tbsp	butter	25 mL
1	medium onion, minced	1
¼ tsp	cumin	1 mL
¼ tsp	tumeric	1 mL
¼ tsp	ginger	1 mL
¼ tsp	cinnamon	1 mL
1 cup	chicken stock	250 mL
	Salt and pepper	
	Juice of lemon	
¼ cup	freshly grated coconut	50 mL

Boil the sweet potatoes in their skins until almost done. Drain and rinse the potatoes in cold water, then peel and slice them.

Melt the butter in a saucepan and sauté the onions, stirring constantly, for 2 or 3 minutes. Stir in the spices and sauté the onions for another 2 minutes. Add the chicken stock, bring to a boil and reduce the heat. Cook, stirring occasionally, for 3 minutes. Season with salt and pepper as necessary.

Add the sliced sweet potatoes to the liquid and simmer, covered, for 10 minutes or until the sweet potatoes are tender. Sprinkle the potato mixture with the lemon juice and coconut just before serving. (This spicy dish is great with yogurt!) *Serves 4*

Sweet Potato Pancakes

If you are a fan of potato pancakes, you'll become addicted to this version in no time. And if you are not a fan, just try them . . . I bet you'll change your mind.

2	sweet potatoes, grated	2
2	ordinary potatoes, grated	2
2	carrots, grated	2
1 Tbsp	onion, chopped	15 mL
1	clove garlic, minced	1
¼ cup	parsley, chopped	50 mL
4	eggs, beaten	4
⅓ cup	flour	75 mL
	Juice of 1 lemon	
	Salt, pepper, nutmeg and cinnamon	
	Melted butter	
	Sour cream or yogurt	
	chives, chopped	

Put the potatoes, sweet and ordinary, in a colander over a bowl. Sprinkle with salt and let stand for 15 minutes. Rinse and squeeze the potatoes to remove all the liquid.

Mix the potatoes with the carrots, onion, garlic, parsley, eggs, flour, lemon juice and seasonings. Thin the mixture with milk, if necessary. Drop large tablespoonfuls of the batter into a frying pan, and fry the pancakes in melted butter until brown and crisp. Serve with a dollop of sour cream or yogurt and a sprinkle of chopped fresh chives. *Serves 4*

There is an island in the Pacific called Ponape where yams are described as being 2, 4, or 6-man yams, indicating how many men it takes to lift the vegetables. It may be hard to believe, but there are records which indicate that yams have grown up to 6 feet long and up to 600 pounds!

Sweet Potato Quiche

This is heavier than the average quiche. With a green salad, it makes a perfect winter meal.

2 pounds	sweet potatoes	1 kg
3	eggs, beaten	3
¼ cup	cereal cream	50 mL
1 Tbsp	flour	15 mL
1 cup	Mozzarella cheese, grated	250 mL
1 Tbsp	soy sauce	15 mL
½ tsp	cinnamon	2 mL
¼ tsp	mace	1 mL
	Salt and pepper	
	Pastry for a 9-inch/23-cm pie	

Boil the sweet potatoes until soft. Cool, peel and mash them.

In a medium-sized bowl, mix the eggs and cream and blend with the sweet potatoes.

Mix the flour with the cheese and combine these ingredients with the sweet potato mixture. Add the soy sauce, spices and seasonings. Spread the entire mixture into the pie shell and bake at 375° F/190° C for 45 minutes to 1 hour, or until a knife inserted in the center comes out clean. Serve hot. *Serves 6 to 8*

Tomatillos

Tomatillos, or Mexican husk tomatoes, may be purple or yellow when ripe, but nine times out of ten they are used when green. Tomatillos are usually cooked because this process enhances their lemony flavor and softens their usually tough hides. Raw, they have a sweet plum taste or a harsh, acidic flavor.

Tomatillos are available off and on all year. Look for fruit which is hard and firm with clean tight husks and no bruises or signs of shrivelling. Store them unwashed in a paper-lined basket for up to a month.

Tomatillos make a superb and unique garnish if you simply pull back the husk, without removing it. Before cooking, the husk, however, must be peeled off and the fruit inside washed. Cooked, they make a lovely full-flavored, mellow sauce. Tomatillos are traditionally used in Salsa and if you are a Salsa-lover, chances are you'll not be able to get enough of this little fruit.

Salsa

Salsa can be made with tomatoes, or for a little treat, with tomatillos. Try this garden-fresh combination with crunchy corn chips or as a sauce on your favorite white fish.

3	red peppers, finely chopped	3
1	green pepper, finely chopped	1
1	small spanish onion, diced	1
10	tomatillos, finely chopped	10
3 Tbsp	fresh lime juice	50 mL
1 Tbsp	olive oil	15 mL
	Salt to taste	

Combine all the ingredients in a medium-sized bowl and let stand for 30 minutes. *Makes about 2 cups/500 mL*

Tomatillo Salad

This is the easiest recipe for tomatillos that I have ever come across. It is a good introduction to the fruit.

1 pound	tomatillos, peeled, washed and thinly sliced	500 g
¼ cup	olive oil	50 mL
2 Tbsp	lime juice	25 mL
1 cup	Parmesan cheese, grated	250 mL
2 tsp	basil, chopped	10 mL
	Pepper	
	Coriander	

Arrange the sliced fruit on a platter. Blend the oil and lime juice and drizzle over the fruit. Sprinkle with grated cheese and basil. Grind on some pepper. Garnish with coriander. *Serves 4*

Tomatoes

Pete says never, never, never store tomatoes in the refrigerator unless they are absolutely ripe, and even then only for a short time. To help bring out their flavor, they should be kept at room temperature.

There is nothing in the world like a vine-ripened tomato. Although there is little that is not available almost "farm fresh" at Pete's all winter long, not even the most expensive, most luxurious-looking hothouse tomatoes can match the taste of a tomato picked fresh from the garden. My grandfather has some very happy memories of summer afternoons spent in the tomato field with nothing but a salt shaker.

It is important to choose tomatoes which are smooth, firm, nicely shaped and heavy for their size, preferably with good color. Tomatoes with stems attached lose moisture more slowly and will keep fresh longer. Usually the tomatoes found in the markets during the winter months are not yet ripe. The best way to ripen them is to place them stem down in a paper bag in a cool place (although not in a refrigerator), away from direct sunlight, until they become slightly soft. Once they are ripe, tomatoes may be stored in a cool place.

Tomatoes are high in vitamin C and one medium tomato has about 25 calories.

To peel tomatoes, immerse them in boiling water for 15 to 20 seconds; then plunge them into ice water immediately. Let them cool and peel them with a sharp knife.

To seed tomatoes, cut them in half horizontally and squeeze them until the seeds fall out.

Little cherry tomatoes are a nice idea for a salad because all you need to do is give them a rinse and toss them in whole. They tend to look much neater, are less work and taste as good as the larger tomatoes. And as Pete notes, larger tomatoes, once sliced, will add a lot of moisture to a salad.

Cherry Tomatoes Vinaigrette

2 pints	cherry tomatoes	1 L

	Vinaigrette	
¼ tsp	sugar	1 mL
¼ cup	fresh lemon juice	50 mL
¾ cup	peanut oil	175 mL

2	cloves garlic, minced	2
1 tsp	fresh thyme, finely chopped	5 mL
1 tsp	fresh basil, finely chopped	5 mL
1 Tbsp	parsley, chopped	15 mL
2 or 3	green onions, thinly sliced	2 or 3

Mix the vinaigrette and add the washed and stemmed tomatoes. Chill several hours or overnight. *Serves 6*

Stuffed Tomatoes

1½ cups	cottage cheese	375 mL
½ cup	yogurt	125 mL
½ to 1 cup	Parmesan cheese	125 to 250 mL
1	green onion, finely chopped	1
¼ cup	celery, chopped	50 mL
4	large tomatoes	4
¼ cup	coriander or parsley, chopped	50 mL

Mix the cottage cheese, yogurt, parmesan, onion and celery. Cover and refrigerate.

Cut each tomato in 4 or 6 pieces down to within 1 inch/2.5 cm of the base. Separate the sections and place the cheese mixture in the middle. Garnish with chopped parsley or coriander. *Serves 4*

Broiled Herbed Tomatoes

⅓ cup	old Cheddar cheese, grated	75 mL
4 Tbsp	parsley, chopped	60 mL
4 Tbsp	fresh dill or basil, chopped	60 mL
2	cloves garlic, finely chopped	2
3	large tomatoes cut in half	3
2 Tbsp	butter or olive oil	25 mL

Mix the cheese, parsley, basil or dill and garlic together, and sprinkle the mixture on the tops of the halved tomatoes. Dot with butter or drizzle with the olive oil. Broil the tomatoes for 10 minutes, until they are heated through. Garnish with a little extra parsley. *Serves 6*

Pete's Stuffed Baked Tomatoes

8	large ripe, firm tomatoes	8
½ cup	olive oil	125 mL
⅓ cup	minced parsley	75 mL
2	cloves garlic, minced	2
1 cup	uncooked long grain rice	250 mL
1 tsp	saffron	5 mL
2 cups	hot chicken stock	500 mL
½ tsp	cinnamon	2 mL
	Salt and pepper	
	Dill or basil	

Slice off the top of each tomato and carefully scoop out the pulp, leaving the shell whole. Strain the pulp and put aside. Arrange the tomatoes in a shallow baking dish, sprinkling each one with a few drops of the oil.

Heat the remaining oil in a skillet. Sauté the parsley and garlic for 2 minutes. Add the rice and, stirring constantly, simmer for another 3 minutes. Stir the saffron into the stock and pour the hot stock onto the rice and parsley.

Simmer the rice mixture, covered, over low heat for 10 minutes, stirring frequently until rice is almost done. Remove from the heat and season with salt, pepper and cinnamon.

Fill the tomato shells with the rice mixture. Pour the reserved tomato pulp over the tomatoes, ensuring that there is 1 inch/2.5 cm of pulp around the base of each tomato; if there is not enough, add some water.

Bake the tomatoes at 350° F/180° C for 30 minutes or until the rice is tender and the liquid has been absorbed. Watch to make sure the tomatoes don't get scorched. Add water if necessary. Baste occasionally with the pan juices. Serve hot or at room temperature. Garnish with basil or dill just before serving. *Serves 6*

Turnip and Rutabaga

Another vegetable neglected by North Americans! Turnips and turnip greens are widely used in Oriental countries, Northern Europe, France, Austria, Switzerland, Germany and Great Britain. On this side of the ocean, however, that are regarded as a lowly root and too often relegated to stews. Although Pete sells quite a few turnips, I have a sneaking suspicion that this vegetable is not being used to its best advantage.

I displayed my ignorance by looking confused when Pete started explaining the difference between turnip and rutabaga. I had always assumed that rutabaga was an American name for turnip. Not so. Rutabagas look different from turnip; they are longer and rounder, and while turnips tend to have purple-tinged skin surrounding clean, white flesh, rutabagas have a red-brown and beige skin with cream-colored flesh. Rutabagas also taste different; they are sweeter, more flavorful and possess a drier flesh than turnips. To top it all off, most of the rutabagas which are sold in the United States are grown in Canada. But if you are one of those who are relieved by my own ignorance and worried that you may have been committing a grave error by mistaking rutabaga for turnip, fear not. The two are interchangeable in any recipe and the taste and texture is so close that none but the most discerning could tell them apart.

Turnip and rutabaga are available all year round, with their peak season between early November and late March. Choose medium to small turnips (2 to 3 inches/5 to 7.5 cm in diameter) and small rutabagas (3 to 4 inches/7.5 to 10 cm in diameter) which are firm, heavy for their size and have smooth unblemished skins. Large turnips and light rutabagas tend to be fibrous.

Turnips and rutabagas should be stored in cool, well-ventilated, dry surroundings, or in a plastic bag in the refrigerator. A rutabaga can be stored for a couple of months in the former, a week in the latter. If you bought turnips with the greens attached, then cut the greens off, wash them, shake them dry, wrap them in plastic and put them in the refrigerator. A turnip stored in plastic in the refrigerator will keep for 3 weeks, the greens for 2 to 4 days.

Turnip and rutabaga are not the same thing. Rutabagas are longer and rounder than turnips which have a purple-tinged skin and white flesh. Rutabagas are sweeter tasting and have cream-colored flesh.

Turnips are an excellent source of vitamins A and C, especially the greens; they also provide potassium and calcium. Rutabagas have even more vitamin C and are a good source of potassium. Four ounces/120 grams of raw turnip have 33 calories, the same amount of raw rutabaga has 55 calories.

Turnip greens are particularly sharp in flavor so the most popular cooking technique is to boil them, thereby dulling their kick a little. When preparing the greens for cooking, simply put the damp leaves in a pot with a tightly fitting lid with an inch or two of water and boil them, covered, for 5 to 10 minutes, until tender but not mushy. Serve the greens with butter, salt, pepper and a sprinkle of Parmesan cheese.

Pete of course likes turnip and rutabaga as he likes almost every vegetable—boiled, steamed or baked with lots of butter and pepper. For variety, he adds basil, dill or crumbled bacon. He is particularly fond of mashed turnip and apples. When the turnip has boiled for about 15 minutes, he just adds half as much peeled, cored and quartered apple as turnip. He then boils the two together until tender and mashes them as usual, adding a little nutmeg with the seasonings. According to Pete, the apple adds a delicious sweetness to the turnip.

To **bake** turnip or rutabaga, peel and slice the root into ¼-inch/6-mm slices, arranging them in a shallow baking dish. Dot with butter, sprinkle with salt, water and a little freshly ground pepper. Cover and bake for 30-40 minutes until tender.

To **boil** turnip or rutabaga, simply place the whole, peeled vegetable into enough water to cover it and boil for 30 minutes until tender. If you want to speed things up, cut the turnip into chunks.

Turnips or rutabagas are also good in a stir-fry. Simply peel the roots, slice them into ¼-inch/6-mm slices or julienne strips and give the strips about 5 minutes in the wok.

Both vegetables are also delicious raw on a vegetable tray or in salads.

The following recipes refer to turnips but feel free to use rutabagas instead. The cooking time for a rutabaga may be a little longer.

Turnip au Gratin

6 small or 4 medium	turnips (2 to 3 lbs/1 to 1.5 kg), peeled and sliced	6 small or 4 medium
	Salt and pepper	
4	slices bacon	4
1	medium-sized onion, sliced	1
2 cups	cooked rice	500 mL
1 tsp	fresh thyme, chopped	5 mL
1 tsp	fresh basil, chopped	5 mL
4 Tbsp	butter	60 mL
1 cup	Mozzarella cheese, grated	250 mL
2 Tbsp	parsley, chopped	25 mL

Cook the turnips in boiling salted water until tender. Drain. Add salt and pepper to taste. Cook the bacon until crisp, crumble and put it to the side. Cook the onion in the bacon fat until transparent. Mix the rice, onion and crumbled bacon together.

In a baking dish, arrange the turnip in alternating layers with the rice mixture, add a tiny sprinkling of the herbs as you go and dot with butter. Bake at 350° F/180° C for 15 minutes.

Remove the mixture from oven and sprinkle with cheese and parsley, returning it to the oven until the cheese has melted. *Serves 4 to 6*

Curried Turnips

1	medium onion, minced	1
3 Tbsp	butter	50 mL
1 Tbsp	curry powder	15 mL
1 cup	hot chicken stock, more or less	250 mL
2 pounds	turnips, peeled and cut into 1-inch/2.5-cm cubes	1 kg
2	medium apples, peeled and sliced	2
	Salt and pepper	
½ cup	yogurt	125 mL
2 Tbsp	fresh basil, coarsely chopped	25 mL

Sauté the onion in the butter until transparent. Add the curry powder and cook for 2 or 3 minutes, stirring constantly. Add ½ cup/125 mL of the stock.

Add the turnips. Simmer, covered, over very low

heat. After 10 minutes, add the apples. Simmer for another 10 minutes or until the turnip is tender. Add more stock, a little bit at a time, if necessary to prevent scorching. Season with salt and pepper. Remove the turnip mixture from heat and stir in the yogurt. Sprinkle with basil and serve immediately. *Serves 4 to 6*

Winter Squash

There was some discussion between Pete and I about what types of winter squash to present here. It was a bit of a difficult decision because there are so many types of squash which are similar but different. He decided on Butternut, Buttercup and Acorn, since these are the three most popular winter squash and Pete's particular favorites.

Squash was a staple food for North Americans before the advent of Europeans on this continent. The Indians relied on it along with beans and corn. To this day, it is still far more popular with North Americans than Europeans.

Squash keeps for such a long time that you can buy it and store it until you decide how you want to serve it. I always have squash around because I am the ultimate disorganised cook, and I can buy it without deciding ahead how it will be served. A versatile vegetable, squash can be used in soup, in a main course or in a dessert.

Acorn squash, also known as pepper squash, is acorn-shaped with wide ribs. It is usually 5 to 8 inches/12 to 20 cm long and about 5 inches/12.5 cm in diameter. The shell is smooth, hard and thin, and it varies in color from a solid, deep green to a green with bright orange areas. The flesh is pale orange, tender, moist and fibrous with a large seed cavity.

Buttercup squash is sometimes called a turban squash because of the funny turban-like cap at the blossom end. Its shape resembles that of a pumpkin, being 4 to 5 inches/10 to 12.5 cm long and 6 to 8 inches/15 to 20 cm across. The shell is quite hard and thin and its color is between dark ivy and dull blackish green with grayish spots and faint dull gray stripes. The flesh is orange, fine textured, dry and sweet.

Butternut squash is cylindrical, usually about 12 inches/30 cm long, with a bulb at the bottom and only 3 to 5 inches/7.5 to 12.5 cm wide. The shell is hard and smooth, and anywhere from light beige to dark yellow in color. The flesh is yellow and fine-grained. Butternut squash is a particularly good value, since this variety tends to have a lot of flesh.

In all instances, look for squash that is hard, blemish free and heavy for its size. Avoid squash with soft or decaying spots or cracks. Store it in a dry, well-ventilated place for up to a month.

On average, winter squash is an excellent source of vitamin A and a good source of vitamin C, although acorn squash contains less vitamin A. Four ounces/120 grams of baked squash contain 50 calories.

Simplicity Squash Recipe

1	winter squash, split in half	1
	Butter	
	Salt and pepper	

Poke holes in the squash with a fork and either wrap it in saran wrap for the microwave or wrap it in tin foil and bake it in the oven at 350° F/180° C for 15 to 20 minutes, depending on the size of the squash. The foil will keep the squash from drying out and will speed up the cooking time.

Unwrap, dot with butter and sprinkle with salt and pepper. Serve piping hot. *Serves 2 to 4*

When Pete does his taste tests for Mid-day, this is how he cooks his squash, and with a little butter and black pepper, he and the CBC crew are all set. When the filming is done they all enjoy the leftovers.

Pete's Sautéed Buttercup Squash

1	medium-sized buttercup squash, peeled, seeded and cut lengthwise in slivers	1
4 Tbsp	butter	60 mL
	Salt and pepper	
	Nutmeg, or if possible, fresh tarragon, finely chopped	

Simply sauté the squash slivers in the butter until golden-brown and slightly soft. Drizzle the squash with some extra melted butter, and season with salt, pepper and either nutmeg or fresh tarragon. Pete's personal favorite is tarragon, but he insists that it must be fresh! *Serves 2 to 4.*

Baked Butternut Squash

1	large butternut squash, peeled, seeded and cut into 1-inch/ 2.5-cm cubes	1
	Salt and pepper	
2 tsp	anise seed, crushed	10 mL
1/8 tsp	ground cardamom	.5 mL
2 or 3 Tbsp	brown sugar	25 or 50 mL
2 Tbsp	lemon juice	25 mL
1/2 cup	melted butter	125 mL

Place the squash into a buttered 2-quart/2-L casserole. Sprinkle with the salt, pepper, anise seed, cardamom and sugar. Drizzle with the lemon juice and butter. Bake, uncovered, at 350° F/180° C for 30 minutes or until tender. *Serves 4*

Golden Soufflé

1½ cups	puréed, steamed, winter squash	375 mL
	Salt, pepper and nutmeg	
6 Tbsp	butter	90 mL
5	egg yolks	5
7	egg whites	7

Blend the squash with the seasonings and butter and beat lightly. Mix in the egg yolks one at a time, beating each in well.

Beat the egg whites until stiff but not dry. Fold one-quarter of the whites into the purée, mixing carefully. Gently fold the remaining whites into the purée. Pour the mixture into a well oiled 1½-quart/1.5-L soufflé dish. Bake at 375° F/190° C for 25 to 30 minutes. *Serves 6*

Harvest Soup

⅓ cup	diced onions	75 mL
4 Tbsp	butter	60 mL
1	large potato, chopped	1
1 cup	beef stock	250 mL
2 cups	cooked winter squash	500 mL
	Salt and pepper	
¾ tsp	curry powder	3 mL
¾ cup	milk	175 mL
	Paprika	

Sauté the onions in butter until soft. Add the potato, stock, squash, salt, pepper and curry powder. Simmer for 10 minutes, or until potato is tender. Blend in the milk. Sprinkle with paprika.

For a little luxury, add a spoonful of yogurt to each serving. *Serves 4*

This is the pumpkin soup recipe which got me through university. You can use any winter squash you like, including pumpkin.

Baked Acorn Squash

2	large acorn squash, washed and cut in half lengthwise, with the seeds removed	2
	Salt and pepper	
1	small onion, grated	1
4 Tbsp	brown sugar	60 mL
4 Tbsp	butter	60 mL

Place the squash, cut side down, on a shallow baking dish and add ¼ inch/6 mm of hot water. Bake at 350° F/180° C for 20 to 30 minutes or until the squash is tender to touch.

Drain any water left in the tray and turn the squash

over. Sprinkle each half with the salt, pepper and onion, sugar and butter.

Return the squash to the oven and bake for another 10 to 15 minutes.

Honey-glazed Acorn Squash: for a variant of this dish, substitute honey or maple syrup and nutmeg for the onion and brown sugar. *Serves 4*

Yuca Root

If you are searching for something unusual for your next tray of crudités, don't bother with yuca root. In its raw form, yuca root contains so much purric acid that it's poisonous. Cooked, it is an extraordinarily versatile vegetable and can be added to a stew, a stir-fry or any number of side dishes.

If you like tapioca, you'll like yuca root . . . since the flesh of the yuca plant, know as cassava in South America, is used as a base for the pudding which most of us have eaten as children and secretly crave as adults.

In South America, a flour is made from dried, grated yuca root and sprinkled on starchy dishes or used to make a hard flat cake called cassava bread. Pieces of the root are also used in stews where it absorbs flavors and thickens the stock.

Yuca root looks more like a branch than a root. Shaped like a sweet potato and covered with a rough pinky-brown bark, yuca root usually weighs between half a pound and three pounds/250 g and 1.5 kg. The flesh is pure white, dense and heavy. A good source of iron, yucca root contains about 40 calories in ½ cup/125 mL of the cooked vegetable.

When buying yuca, look for roots with firm skin, avoiding those with hairline cracks (a sign of dryness) or any sign of mold. A good sniff will often lead you to a good root, since yuca roots tend to smell acrid or sour when they begin to age. You might even want to ask your grocer to cut a root for you to ensure that the flesh is clean and free from rot.

Yuca root should be used soon after it is purchased, since it does not store well. If necessary, you may keep the root in a cool, dark, well-ventilated place, but for no more than 2 days. Or you can freeze it raw. Just peel and rinse the chunks, wrap them tightly and place them in the freezer.

To use yuca root, simply peel it and remove the fibrous central core. Since the root is very hard, it may be necessary to cut the root into chunks before making an incision in the bark. A knife may then be used to peel away the bark and its underpading.

A versatile vegetable, yuca may be fryed, boiled, sautéed or added to a stew. When cooked, it absorbs the flavor of other vegetables and becomes almost translucent with a sticky, densely buttery chewiness of which Pete is particularly fond. Yuca root is also a natural thickening agent, so be sure to include it in your stews and soups.

The very first time I had yuca root, I just put it in boiling water, added some garlic and simmered the root for 20 minutes. Although this is still my favorite way of eating yuca root, it is also delicious served with a spicy tomato sauce, chopped green onions and coriander.

Pete's Yucca Yummies

These little hors d'oeuvres are one of Pete's chewy, cheesey specialties.

1 pound	yucca root, rinsed, peeled and cut into chunks	500 g
⅓ cup	old Cheddar cheese, grated	75 mL
1 tsp	Dijon mustard	5 mL
1 Tbsp	melted butter	15 mL
3	eggs	3
1 tsp	salt	5 mL
1	Serrano or Jalapeño pepper, minced	1
½ tsp	sugar	2 mL

Grate the yuca root and blend it with the cheese, Dijon mustard, melted butter, eggs, salt, pepper and

and sugar. When well blended, form the mixture into small balls, 1 inch/2 cm in diameter. Deep fry the balls until golden, about 5 minutes. Drain the yuca balls on a paper towel and serve hot. *Serves 5*

Zucchini and Summer Squash

Zucchini is a summer squash, but being the most popular and most common, Pete and I decided to include summer squash with zucchini rather than vice versa. Probably most of us don't even think of zucchini as a summer squash anymore. It is wonderfully versatile, and delicious both raw and cooked. Zucchini are a great favorite at summer fairs because, if encouraged, they will grow to be absolutely enormous. Until about 20 years ago, zucchini was all but unknown, except to people of Mediterranean descent and to the French, but today it is very popular and easy to find.

This section refers most often to zucchini but, unless otherwise indicated, the same descriptions apply to the other varieties of summer squash as well. Every recipe for zucchini can be used with summer squash and vice versa. The most common varieties of summer squash, after the zucchini of course, are the yellow crookneck, the yellow straightneck and the golden zucchini.

Zucchini is available all year round, its peak season being from June to August, while summer squash is, as the name implies, only available during the summer. Look for firm, smooth, glossy, well-shaped zucchini, about 6 to 10 inches/15 to 25 cm long and 1 to 2 inches/2.5 to 5 cm in diameter. Avoid zucchini with soft spots or torn rinds.

To store zucchini, simply put it in a plastic bag in the refrigerator. Although it will keep for 5 days, it is a good idea to use as soon as possible.

Zucchini is a good source of vitamin C and raw, it has only 20 calories in 4 ounces/120 grams.

Sautéed Zucchini and Variations

1½ pounds	zucchini, thinly sliced	750 g
6 Tbsp	olive oil or butter	90 mL
	Salt and pepper	

Heat the olive oil, butter, or some of each in a skillet. Add the zucchini and sauté for 4 or 5 minutes over medium to high heat, tossing well. Season with salt and pepper. Serve hot.

With garlic and herbs: add 3 large cloves of finely chopped garlic to the oil and sauté with the zucchini. Sprinkle with 3 tablespoons/50 mL of chopped parsley and 1 tablespoon/15 mL of chopped fresh basil just before serving.

With shallots: before adding the zucchini, sauté ½ cup/125 mL of finely chopped shallots, in the oil or butter until until they are transparent.

With walnuts: simply add ½ cup/125 mL of coarsely chopped walnuts to the zucchini. Cook with the vegetable. Sprinkle with 2 tablespoons/25 mL of chopped parsley and a few more nuts just before serving.

With cheese: once the zucchini is cooked, sprinkle generously with freshly grated Parmesan cheese and broil for 2 minutes or until the cheese is melted and golden brown.

With tomatoes and peppers: before cooking the zucchini, add a generous handful of halved cherry tomatoes and 1 small green pepper cut into strips to the oil. Sauté the three vegetables together. When the zucchini is tender, sprinkle the mélange with 2 tablespoons/25 mL of fresh chopped basil and a generous amount of grated Parmesan cheese. *Serves 4 to 6*

Chilled Zucchini Soup

2 pounds	zucchini, washed and grated	1 kg
1 cup	green onions, chopped	250 mL
4 Tbsp	butter	60 mL
2½ cups	chicken stock	625 mL
2½ cups	buttermilk	625 mL
	Salt and pepper	
6 Tbsp	dill, chopped	90 mL

Cook the zucchini and onions gently in butter over low heat until soft, about 8 minutes. Stir in the stock and purée the mixture. Add the buttermilk, salt, pepper and 4 tablespoons/50 mL of the dill. Chill for at least 4 hours. Garnish with the remaining dill just before serving.

For a curried soup, add 1 tablespoon/15 mL each of curry and cumin to the zucchini and onions, a few minutes before adding the stock. Omit the dill. *Serves 6*

Pete's Zucchini Muffins

This recipe does not belong to Pete Luckett but to my brother Pete. He makes the most amazing muffins and my mum grows the vast quantities of zucchini, so when the two of them get together, we all feast on these delicacies.

2 cups	zucchini, grated	500 mL
2	eggs, well beaten	2
1 cup	buttermilk	250 mL
½ cup	brown sugar	125 mL
3 Tbsp	honey	50 mL
½ cup	raisins	125 mL
1 tsp	vanilla	5 mL
1 cup	oil	250 mL
1½ cups	whole wheat flour	375 mL
1½ cups	bran	375 mL
2 tsp	baking powder	10 mL
1 tsp	baking soda	5 mL
1 tsp	cinnamon	5 mL
1 tsp	salt	5 mL
¼ tsp	nutmeg	1 mL

Mix together the zucchini, eggs, buttermilk, brown sugar, honey, raisins, vanilla and oil.

In a separate bowl, mix the flour, bran, baking powder and soda, cinnamon, salt and nutmeg. Blend the dry ingredients with the zucchini mixture, just until moist. Spoon the batter into greased muffin tins and bake for 25 minutes at 375° F/190° C. *Makes 12 large muffins*

Zucchini Ginger Jam

My mum makes this jam every summer and it is really wonderful stuff. If you grow your own zucchini this is a great way to use up the squash which sometimes grow too big.

4 pounds	zucchini, peeled and cut into small cubes	2 kg
3	lemons, juiced and rinds grated	3
1½-inch piece	ginger root	4 cm piece
¼ pound	candied or preserved ginger, slivered	125 g
6 cups	sugar	1.5 L

Place the zucchini in a large bowl, cover with sugar and let stand overnight. Drain off the liquid and bring it to a boil with the lemon juice and grated rind. Add the ginger root tied in a cheesecloth bag. (My mum just grates the ginger and leaves it in, making the jam extra gingery.) Simmer for 1 hour. Add the candied or preserved ginger and the zucchini. Simmer one hour longer or until zucchini becomes transparent. Remove the cheesecloth bag, and spoon the jam into hot sterilized jars. Seal. *Makes 4 pints/2 L*

Zucchini is a wonderfully versatile squash. Like carrots, zucchini is delicious both raw and cooked and lends itself to sweet and savory dishes.

Zucchini and Tomato Casserole

1	small onion, minced	1
½ pound	mushrooms, sliced	250 g
1	small red pepper, sliced	1
2	cloves garlic, minced	2
4 Tbsp	olive oil	60 mL
2 to 3 pounds	zucchini, trimmed and cut into ¼-inch/6-mm slices	1 to 1.5 kg
2 Tbsp	fresh basil or dill, minced	25 mL
½ cup	Cheddar cheese, grated	125 mL
4	large tomatoes, peeled and sliced	4
	Salt and pepper	
2 Tbsp	melted butter	25 mL
½ cup	big bread crumbs	125 mL

Sauté the onion, mushrooms, pepper and garlic in the olive oil, stirring frequently, for 4 minutes or until the onion is soft. Add the zucchini. Sauté over medium heat, stirring constantly, for 5 minutes or until the zucchini turns golden, but still firm.

In a buttered 1½-quart/1.5-L casserole, spread a layer of the zucchini mixture. Sprinkle with basil and some Cheddar cheese, cover with a layer of tomatoes and sprinkle with salt and pepper. Repeat the layers.

Combine the melted butter and the bread crumbs and sprinkle them over top of the zucchini mixture. Bake, uncovered, at 350° F/180° C for 20 minutes or until golden-brown. *Serves 6*

Zucchini Frittata

2 Tbsp	olive oil	25 mL
1	small red onion, sliced paper thin	1
2 pounds	zucchini, trimmed and thinly sliced	1 kg
1	large tomato, sliced	1
6	eggs	6
¼ cup	parsley, minced	50 mL
2 Tbsp	fresh basil or dill, minced	25 mL
	Salt and pepper	

Heat the olive oil in a frying pan and sauté the onion for 2 minutes at high heat; add the zucchini and continue cooking for about 2 or 3 minutes. Lower the temperature and lay the tomatoes on top of the zucchini and onion.

Beat the eggs and herbs together. Season with salt and pepper and pour the mixture over the zucchini. Fry over low heat for about 5 minutes or until the bottom is set and browned. Turn the omelette over and cook for another 2 or 3 minutes. Cut into wedges and serve. *Serves 3*

Bitter Melon

I am squeezing things a little by pushing Balsam pear, or bitter melon, in this section, but it is a squash, so look for it in the squash section of your produce supplier. It looks like a wrinkled cucumber, 5 to 8 inches/12 to 20 cm long, green in color when immature and orange when completely ripe. For eating, you'll want one that is greenish-yellow. Inside the melon is a pink or white spongy pulp and seeds. The skin is edible, but do remove the seeds and the core.

The vegetable is well-named because it is in fact bitter. To remove the bitterness, simply soak the vegetable in salty water, give it a good rinse and pat it dry. Bitter melon is at its best when sliced and added to a pork and shrimp stir-fry. It is also good stuffed or curried. If you want to get into bitter melon with any sincerity, consult an Asian cookbook, for bitter melon is an Asian speciality.

Bitter melon is available without much regularity, all year round. Look for melons which are well-shaped and firm, with good skin color and without any dark spots or soft areas. Although the skin of the bitter melon is wrinkled, avoid any vegetables which have withered skin. Store bitter melon in a plastic bag in a cool place for 3 days at the most.

Joe's Bitter Melon Stir-fry

	Pork, cut in strips	
2 Tbsp	peanut oil	25 mL
1	clove garlic, minced	1
1	medium onion, sliced	1
1	tomato, diced	1
	Shrimp, shelled	
	Salt or soy sauce	
3	bitter melons, cut lengthwise, seeded, with core pulp removed, and cut in ¼-inch/ 6-mm slices, soaked in salt water as described above, if desired	3

Joe ran the Nipa Hut, a little lunch counter in the corner of the Saint John City Market. This is his favorite way of preparing bitter melon and a nice introduction to the vegetable.

I have not suggested the amount of pork or shrimp which should be used in this recipe because it varies from person to person, and for this recipe, it doesn't seem to matter much as long as you have some of each. Joe uses about 1 pound of each. I use about 1 pound of shrimp and ¼ pound of pork for four people.

Boil the strips of pork for 5 minutes or until they are cooked. Then give them a quick browning in a frying pan or wok and set them aside until you need them.

Heat the oil in a wok or frying pan. Brown the garlic, add the onion and tomato and sauté the mixture until the onion is transparent. Add the pork and shrimp with some salt or soy sauce and, if you can get it, some pale brown fish gravy. Simmer for 3 minutes. Add the bitter melon and simmer until the bitter melon is soft and the flavors well-blended. Serve hot with rice. *Serves 4*

Fruit

Apples

North Americans consume vast amounts of apples. And no wonder: apples can be eaten raw or they can be prepared a hundred ways. They are a good with meat and cheese and with other fruit and vegetables. In a pie, a salad or as a snack, apples are a staple in the North American diet.

Most of the apples we find in our markets are those which ship and store well; but in the autumn, less popular varieties are readily available for apple lovers. Unfortunately, many types of apples are no longer grown in quantity, simply because they do not travel well, but their scarcity only makes them more of a treat. Pete particularly recommends anything which ends in "pippin"; his favorite is a Cox's Orange Pippin. If you can find one of these, buy it, eat it and think of Pete and England where they are bestsellers.

There are four common types of apples available virtually all year round: Red and Golden Delicious, Granny Smith and MacIntosh. The Red and Golden Delicious apples outsell all the other varieties of apples in North America. The Red Delicious is an eating apple (it loses its shape and some of its taste when cooked); the Golden Delicious, on the other hand, is excellent eaten out of hand or cooked. Granny Smiths, originally from Australia, are enjoying increasing popularity. Although they demand a particularly warm climate for growing, they travel well. "Grannies" are equally delicious eaten raw or cooked. The Delicious varieties and Granny Smith apples are available all year round and in good supply. McIntosh apples are also very popular, but they have one peculiarity—they dissolve when baked. Nevertheless, they are a favorite for out of hand eating or for pies. They are especially abundant in the autumn, and the stored apples are usually in good supply until late summer.

In recent years a new arrival, picked and shipped fresh, has been imported from New Zealand. These apples have a crunchy freshness that is unique to apples which have not been in storage. So if you are fond of fresh apples, keep an eye out for New Zealand's exports in late spring and early summer, in particular, the Gala, Royal Gala and Braeburn varieties.

The popularity of the apple is such that there are recipe books exclusively about apples, how to, what to, when to . . . there is little that has not been done with apples. I *could* tell you how to make a swan out of a Granny Smith apple. But that wouldn't be of much use would it? Instead I will pass on this all-purpose apple recipe which can be added to your collection of apple pie, apple pudding, apple cookies, applesauce, apple bread, apple muffins, apple everything recipes. This culinary gem is something different—something you will be amazed that you ever did without.

Crêperie Apples

When I worked at a crêperie in France, one of our most popular dessert crêpes was "Pommes, crème fraîche, Calvados." This consisted of a crêpe with an apple mixture and a dollop of crème fraîche inside, all rolled up and flambéed with Calvados, an apple liqueur. What a fabulous dessert. I still dream about it! Every couple of days I would make the apple filling, and although it was intended for the crêpes, when the crêperie doors were closed, we found a thousand other uses for it. We spooned it over ice cream, over cake, mixed it with yogurt, poured cream over it, put it on toast, ate it with chicken, duck and pork. Its uses are infinite!

You may wish to adapt this recipe to your particular taste. I use Granny Smith apples because of their tartness.

¼ cup	flour	50 mL
3 pounds	apples, peeled and cut in thick slices	1.5 kg
3 Tbsp	butter	50 mL
½ cup	brown sugar	125 mL
2 tsp	cinnamon	10 mL
1 tsp	nutmeg	5 mL
	Pinch salt	
½ cup	cider or apple juice	125 mL

Put the flour in a paper bag and toss the apple pieces in the flour until they are well-coated.

Melt the butter in a frying pan. Add the apple and

sauté for about 5 minutes. In the meantime, blend the sugar and spices. When the apples begin to turn golden, add the sugar-spice mixture and the salt, and cook for a few more minutes. Then add the cider, turn the heat to low and simmer, covered, for 15 minutes, until the apples are tender. Depending on your taste, you can add more or less juice to this mixture. You can also include some brandy or Calvados, an excellent addition if you intend to serve crêperie apples with ice cream. *Serves 8, depending on how you use it of course.*

Apricots

If you want to eat apricots immediately, choose softer ones; if you won't be using them for a day or two, choose apricots which are less ripe. They will ripen nicely if you just leave them on the counter, out of direct sunlight. To hurry up the ripening process, wrap them loosely in a paper bag.

Apricots have been cultivated in the United States for about 300 years, making them one of the first cultivated fruits in North America. These sweet little beauties are among the earliest fruits to reach the markets each summer, and they dry so well that we can enjoy them all winter too. But ripe apricots do not stand up to shipping, and although new, tougher varieties have been developed, we often exchange firmness for sweetness. My grandmother, who lives 1,000 miles away, has several apricot trees, which some years give the most magnificent crop; other years they produce nothing! Unfortunately, these wonderful little fruit do not travel well, and every time I eat an apricot which is not from one of her trees, I long to taste one of those hopelessly-soft, richly-flavored little jewels. I am a fan of the old-fashioned apricot which, I guess, mean that I am not a proponent of the "bright" flavors of the new hybrids!

Apricots are available from New Zealand and Chile from January to March. Domestic apricots are available from late May to early August. Look for firm, golden-colored apricots. Once they are ripe, you may keep them, in the refrigerator in a plastic bag, for up to 2 days.

Apricots are a good source of vitamin A and C. One medium-sized apricot has about 17 calories.

Apricots are delicious rinsed and eaten out of hand. You can cut them in half, remove the stone and fill the hollow with Brie or any soft cheese, making a nice appetizer. For breakfast, add slices of apricot to your cereal or pancakes. Toss them into a fruit salad or add them to ice cream and top with toasted almonds.

Apricots and Sour Cream

12	apricots	12
½ cup	brown sugar	125 mL
1 cup	sour cream	250 mL
	A pinch of nutmeg	

Halve the apricots and place them in a baking dish. Sprinkle with brown sugar and spread the sour cream over them. Grate on a little nutmeg. Bake at 325° F/160° C for 15 minutes or until apricots are soft. *Serves 6*

Asian Pears

This is the fruit for me! If you are a lover of crisp texture with the richness of a soft fruit taste, then Asian pears are also the fruit for you. The Asian pear tastes like a soft ripe pear, but is crisp and juicy like a firm apple. Their granular texture is offset by mild flavor and aroma. The most common of all Asian pears is sold at Pete's under the name "Japanese pear." Its Japanese name is Nijisseiki, or translated into English, "Twentieth Century." It has the shape, size and color of a large golden delicious apple and although its flesh is not as juicy as that of some varieties, it is slightly sweeter.

There are more than 25 varieties of Asian pears available in North America—of every color and size. They are always extremely crisp, almost unbelievably juicy and well-suited to being sliced transparently thin.

Asian pears are available almost all year, their peak month being September. They are sold ripe, and their storage life is incredible. You may leave them on the counter for up to two weeks. Left unwashed in a plastic or paper bag in the refrigerator, they will keep for up to three months!

Asian pears are a good source of vitamin C and a great source of fiber as are most fruit.

The very best way to eat Asian pears is raw. Because of their juiciness and the texture of their flesh, the pears also cook well, remaining dense and meaty. Try them sautéed with toasted sliced almonds or some slivers of preserved ginger, or make them into a pie, adding some thickener to make up for their juiciness.

An Asian pear is a perfect end to a meal. Serve it slightly chilled with a wedge of lime on the side or sliced horizontally to expose its flower-shaped seed center. An Asian pear is a great dessert for the kids' lunch box or for a snack; it is a refreshing, juicy change of pace and nothing beats its crisp minty freshness.

Bananas

Bananas are one of those rare fruit which ripen better off the tree. They are picked and shipped green, then stored and ripened in special rooms. Owing to the increased demand for exotic fruit, we can look for a few delicious surprises on the banana shelf of our local markets. The apple, or finger banana, sold at Pete's as a baby banana, is a small, fat banana which is rich, super sweet and firm when ripe. Its seeds are slightly crunchy, giving the fruit a unique texture. Red bananas are also available in limited quantities. These bananas really are red until they ripen, when they become almost black or a very dark purple. They have very creamy flesh and are surprisingly sweet.

Bananas are available all year round from Central and South America. The red and baby bananas are available sporadically. Choose fruit which is slightly green at the ends if you like bananas firmer and slightly less sweet, clear yellow with the occasional black spot if you like them softer and sweeter. You can store fully ripe bananas in the refrigerator. The cold will retard the ripening process but will keep the texture of the flesh, despite blackening the skins. Bananas will ripen nicely at room temperature, out of direct sunlight.

Bananas are an excellent source of potassium. One medium-sized banana has about 100 calories.

Baked Bananas

Baked bananas are an easy, delectable dessert. Slit the bananas down one side and bake them in a 325° F/160° C oven for about 15 minutes or until they are soft but not mushy. Drizzle the bananas with some

Cut bananas should be coated with citrus juice to prevent them from blackening. They are delicious eaten out of hand or sliced on cereal, pancakes or waffles. Add them to a fruit salad or a fruit tray. The next time you make a cheesecake that doesn't need baking, try lining the inside of the cake with sliced bananas; simply cover the bottom crust with sliced bananas before you pour in the filling.

melted butter and sprinkle with brown sugar. Bake them for another 5 or 10 minutes until the sugar has dissolved. Serve them with yogurt or sour cream.

Sautéed Bananas

Peel and slice the bananas on a diagonal. Heat some butter in a frying pan and gently add the fruit. Turn once to coat each slice with butter and cook slowly until soft. Sprinkle with some brown sugar and continue cooking until the fruit is glazed. Serve the bananas very hot.

For a special treat, flambé the fruit in Grand Marnier or brandy, and serve with ice cream or yogurt. Delicious!

Blackberries

One of my happiest memories from childhood is picking blackberries, or brambleberries as they are sometimes called, at my grandmother's farm. I would wander down the lane behind the fields and fill a bowl with the wild berries and as much cream as I could find, indulging in these little treasures until I couldn't eat any more. Now I can't eat blackberries without remembering those days.

Blackberries are available off and on all summer, from May until mid-September. It is a good idea to plan on using blackberries within 2 days of purchasing them. As with all berries, Pete's advice is; "Don't keep 'em, eat 'em." To keep them in perfect condition, refrigerate them, unwashed, on a cookie sheet lined with paper towel; cover them with another layer of paper towel and wrap them in plastic. Rinse the berries quickly before serving them.

Blackberries are delicious in a fruit salad or on breakfast cereal. Try tossing a handful into pancake or waffle batter. Serve them *au naturel* with cream or ice cream and a little sugar. For visual appeal, sprinkle a few onto a slice of cantaloupe, or serve a mixture of sliced strawberries and blackberries with a little sour cream or yogurt. Try them on meringue, with ice cream or on fresh pound cake.

Blackberries are a good source of vitamin C and 1 cup/250 mL has only 75 calories.

There are several types of blackberries, including the red Loganberries, all of which grow on upright or on trailing bushes.

Blackberry Concentrate

The idea of mixing fruit and vinegar surprises some people but this concoction produces the most delicious syrup. You can mix it with water, about 4 Tbsp/60 mL with 10 ounces/300 mL of water, and make a delicious thirst quencher, or you can pour this syrup over ice cream or yogurt for a summer dessert.

1 cup	white vinegar mixed with 1 cup/250 mL water	250 mL
1 quart	blackberries	1 L
2 to 3 cups	sugar	500 to 750 mL

Pour the vinegar and water over the berries and let them stand for at least 24 hours.

Press the whole mixture through a strainer, squeezing as many of the berries through as possible. Add the sugar and boil for 30 minutes, stirring occasionally. Cool the syrup and keep it in the refrigerator until you are ready to use it. This syrup also freezes well. *Makes 1 quart/1 L*

Blueberries

Three hundred and fifty years ago the blueberry was already an established North American native. Indians were gathering, drying, and using blueberries as an integral part of their daily diet.

Canadians now produce and consume more blueberries than any other nation in the world. Blueberries grow in other countries but nowhere are they so enthusiastically greeted as in Canada and the United States. They grow with wild abandon over much of North America, and although there are several types of blueberries, high-bush and low-bush are the most common varieties. The larger berries tend to come from the cultivated high-bushes while the smaller, wild blueberries come from the low-bushes.

Blueberries ship well and are transported around the country, so no matter what your local season, the fresh fruit is available from early summer to early fall. Look for plump, firm little berries with a slight grayish hue. To store the berries, either refrigerate them in the box or, if you want to keep them in perfect condition, place them between layers of paper towel and wrap them in plastic. Blueberries can be stored in this manner for 4 days, but like all berries, they are perishable and you are wise to use them as soon as you purchase them. To freeze blueberries, simply lay them, unwashed, on a cookie sheet in a single layer, place them in the freezer and, when they are firm, put them in bags. It isn't necessary to thaw them before cooking.

Blueberries are an excellent source of vitamin C; one serving, about four ounces/120 grams, contains only 23 calories!

Blueberries can be found in a wealth of recipes, from muffins and pies to cakes and bang-bellies. They are delicious simply rinsed and served with ice cream, sour cream or yogurt and some sugar and cinnamon. They are super with crème de cassis or Cointreau.

In some ways blueberries are the ultimate fruit, with nothing to hull, nothing to peel, nothing you can't use, nothing to throw away. Whether you are a lover of wild or cultivated berries, all of them are juicy, slightly crunchy little morsels of tart-sweet flavor.

Blueberry Cake

4	eggs	4
1 cup	sugar	250 mL
1 cup	oil	250 mL
2½ cups	all purpose flour	625 mL
3 tsp	baking powder	15 mL
½ cup	orange juice	125 mL
¼ tsp	salt	1 mL
	Rind of one orange, grated	
3 cups	blueberries	750 mL

In a large bowl, beat the eggs. Add the sugar, beating until almost white and beat in the oil. Sift the dry ingredients, reserving ½ cup/125 mL flour for flouring the berries. Alternately add the dry ingredients and the orange juice, mixed with the salt and orange rind, to the mixture. Fold in the floured berries, and pour the batter into an oiled bundt pan.

Bake at 325° F/160° C for 45 to 60 minutes.

Breadfruit

In the South Sea islands breadfruit is called "the staff of life." It is usually stored in water and sold whole.

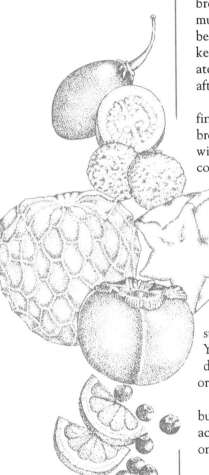

Breadfruit is eaten as a vegetable. The green fruit, which is about the size of a large cantaloupe, is covered with bumps, almost like scales. Inside, it is rather like a potato, both in texture and taste. When slightly ripe, breadfuit resembles partially baked bread. When completely ripe, the fruit develops a muskiness present in many tropical fruits; its texture becomes soft and slightly runny. Breadfruit does not keep once it becomes ripe and must be used immediately, although in some tropical countries, it is eaten after it has fermented.

Breadfruit is available all year round and is easier to find in an area with a Caribbean population. A good breadfruit will weigh close to 5 pounds. Look for fruit with large, well-developed "scales." It should be completely green if you want to keep it for some time. Avoid fruit with hard spots, dents and dark areas.

Breadfruit is jammed with calories, with around 120 in 4 ounces/125 grams. It is also loaded with vitamin C and potassium.

Most popularly used like potatoes, breadfruit makes a gorgeous side-dish, baked for 1 hour at 425° F/220° C. It is also good boiled, steamed, mashed, creamed, puréed, fried or roasted. You might like to try roasting it, eating it sliced or deep-frying the slices and reheating them in a spicy or cheese-flavored sauce.

If you live in an area where breadfruit is common, buy some and try it. Some will warn you that it is an acquired taste. They are right. It is. But I'm told that once you've acquired it, you will never let it go.

Cactus Pears

Tuna is the fruit of a cactus native to Mexico. Surprised? Thought it was a kind of fish, right? Tuna, Indian fig or prickly pear are all names for the cactus pear: a spiky egg-shaped fruit, usually disarmed by the time it has reached the shelves of our markets. Mexico produces more cactus pears than the world produces apricots—a statistic which gives you some idea of just how popular the fruit is.

Most of the cactus pears sold in Canadian markets are grown in the desert areas of the United States, with occasional imports from Central and South America. There are two main varieties. One type has a dull, gray-maroon exterior and scarlet flesh. The other has a greyish green-yellow skin and yellow flesh. Both varieties of fruit taste the same, contain the same edible seeds, are the same shape and the same size. A combination of the sliced flesh from both varieties is an exquisite contrast of color.

Although the fruit is usually harmless by the time you buy it, some authorities recommend wearing rubber gloves or using tongs to handle the fruit, to avoid being pierced! Pete considers this procedure totally unnecessary. To remove the skin, simply hold the fruit and slice off both ends; make a lengthwise slit in the skin and peel it away from the flesh. Cactus pear skin comes off surprisingly easily, revealing a barrel-shaped fruit.

Cactus pears are available from August to December. Look for ripe fruit which is a deep color all over and which gives a little to gentle pressure. Choose fresh-looking fruit; avoid those with mould. You may store the ripe fruit in a plastic bag in the refrigerator for 5 days. Cactus pears will ripen at home, on the counter, out of the sun; when tender, retire them to the refrigerator.

Cactus pears are a good source of vitamin C and rich in potassium and fiber. One cactus pear has 45 calories.

Pete prefers that cactus pears be served chilled. If you serve them raw, have a little fun with their color: try mixing them with kiwi, oranges or bananas in a salad or on a fruit plate.

Cactus pears are among the most attractive garnishes in the markets. Drop a slice of cactus pear into a cocktail or serve it with roasted or grilled meat. Lime juice will accent the flavor.

Cactus Pear Smoothie

2	cactus pears, peeled and sliced	2
1	very large banana, peeled and sliced	1
4	ice cubes	4
2 Tbsp	honey	25 mL
	Squirt of lime juice	

½ cup	milk	125 mL
½ cup	yogurt	125 mL

In a blender, purée the pears and the banana for one minute. Add the remaining ingredients and whirl until smooth. *Serves 2*

Cactus Pear Sauce

This sauce is delicious served hot with ice cream, sour cream or yogurt. It also makes a lovely complement to fresh fruit. It can be served hot, warm or cold.

3	cactus pears, peeled, slice and puréed	3
1 Tbsp	cornstarch	15 mL
¼ cup	sugar	50 mL
2 Tbsp	lime juice	25 mL
1 Tbsp	butter	15 mL
1 tsp	vanilla extract	5 mL

Blend the purée, cornstarch and sugar. Cook over medium heat until the mixture boils and thickens. Remove from the heat and add the lime juice, butter and the vanilla. *Makes 1 cup/250 mL*

Carambola

The carambola, or star fruit, is a beautiful garnishing fruit. It is ellipsoidal, with four to six ridges running its entire length. When sliced, it makes exquisite star shapes. I make a fruit plate composed of peeled, sliced kiwi fruit, sliced strawberries and sliced carambolas; the combination of colors and shapes couldn't be more beautiful.

Carambola come in yellow or white, although the white variety is rare. You can buy green carambola, but these are simply the yellow fruit before it is ripe. Carambola is a versatile fruit, and can be added to vegetable or fruit salads as easily and as decoratively as to a seafood or poultry dish; it is also particularly attractive in drinks. The carambola, originally a native of India and Sri Lanka, is now produced in

Thailand, Tropical Africa, Brazil, India and, happily for North Americans, in Florida.

The taste of the star fruit is rather difficult to describe. The one problem is knowing whether you are getting a wonderfully sweet plum-and-roses tasting fruit or a lemon-lime tart fruit. Although there is virtually no certain way to be sure which is which, Pete can usually tell. But that is due to years of experience. As a general rule, the sweeter carambolas tend to have thick ribs, while the more sour ones have narrow ribs. A white carambola, a different variety from the yellow, will definitely be sweet.

Carambola are available from January to May and from July to October. If you can buy the fruit unripe, do so; it will ripen at room temperature. What's more, since the fruit is delicate and doesn't stand up very well to the poking and pinching which customers will occasionally inflict on it, it will probably be safer on your kitchen counter than on a grocer's shelves.

When fully developed, a ripe carambola will give off the most wonderful aroma, a fruity, flowery perfume, and according to Pete, the ridges of the fruit will probably be brown. If you are using the fruit chiefly for its appearance, try to avoid ones with brown marks on them—these marks don't affect the taste but they mar the appearance a little.

Store the fruit at room temperature; even ripe, it will keep for 3 days. If you won't be using them for a week, keep carambolas where they will not be damaged, in the warmest part of the refrigerator.

Carambola are a good source of vitamin C. A medium-sized fruit has only 40 calories.

Sliced carambola can be sautéed in butter for a few moments and served as a garnish with beef or pork. If you are broiling fish, place slices of carambola—preferably a slightly sour one—on the fish before grilling it. A lovely treat is carambola sautéed with shrimp. It only takes 2 minutes to cook, and may be served with a squeeze of lemon juice. Slice up star fruit and add it to your next fruit salad or as a garnish on your next vegetable salad, but don't use too much—half of one fruit is plenty in a salad for four.

Carambola and Avocado

These fruit were made to go together.

2	ripe avocados, halved lengthwise and thinly sliced	2
	Orange juice	
4	small carambolas, thinly sliced	4
	Salt and pepper	

Dip the avocado slices in the orange juice. Arrange slices of carambola and avocado on a serving plate. Squeeze on a little orange juice and sprinkle with salt and pepper. *Serves 4*

Cherimoya

Cherimoya, soursop or sherbet fruit, as Pete will enthusiastically tell you, is his favorite tropical fruit. It is not hard to see why. He describes it as being every tropical fruit blended together and poured into a skin. But what a skin! In all honesty, cherimoyas are not attractive from the outside. They look interesting, but not appealing. They have greenish-grey skin and what appears to be an attempt at scales on the outside. Despite their rather rough and ready appearance, cherimoyas are extremely delicate; even a leaf brushing on the skin during the growing period will leave a mark on this leathery covering. But the exterior belies the beauty of the fruit inside, which is both appealing to the taste buds and attractive to the eye.

The skin is filled with a creamy white flesh which is studded with beautiful, inedible, large black seeds. Apparently, steps have been taken to develop a seedless cherimoya but, like watermelon, half the fun of eating this fruit is spitting the seeds out, unless you are at a posh dinner party— but when was the last time you were served cherimoya at a dinner party?

Cherimoyas are expensive. They require complicated and time-consuming pollinating techniques and because they are so tender, they must be harvested by hand and shipped with extreme care; considerable effort is put into their packing so that they arrive, after having been shipped by air, in North American markets looking as unblemished as possible.

The taste of a cherimoya is a taste of heaven and it is greatly enhanced by the smooth, creamy texture of the fruit. You hardly need to use your teeth on a cherimoya; just mush it around in your mouth until it dissolves. Sweet, almost fermented and slightly musky, cherimoya tastes like paradise or what I imagine paradise to taste like. One mouthful and you can sense the warmth of a tropical breeze on your cheeks, feel the sun filtering through the leaves of a palm tree and hear the waves lapping at the white sand.

Cherimoyas are in season when we most need to dream of tropical climes—from November until the end of April. They are picked hard and left to ripen en route to your table, or mouth. You can buy them green and hard, and let them ripen at home, out of direct sunlight, turning them frequently so that they ripen evenly. A ripe cherimoya can be anywhere from pale green to a darkish green with brown speckles; it may even turn slightly gray when ripe. Watch out for darkened fruit, which may not ripen properly, the dark spot indicating that they may have been subjected to cold. Markings on the skin, called surface scars, will not affect the quality of the fruit. You can buy either large or small cherimoyas since their size has no effect on the taste; if they are sold individually rather than by the pound, buy a big one and get more for your money. A large one will probably last you all day.

Cherimoyas are high in calories: a 4-ounce/120 gram serving has about 100 calories. They are a good source of vitamin C and contain niacin and thiamin, two of the B vitamins.

The best way to eat cherimoya is all by yourself. That way you get more. They are exquisite slightly chilled, cut up and eaten like watermelon. A quick 30 minutes in the freezer and you will have sherbet fruit, just like an exotic sherbet. Since the fruit will darken once exposed to the air, squeeze some lemon or lime juice on the cut surface to protect the creamy white

The flavor of cherimoya has been described as being a combination of various tropical fruit: mangos, pineapple, banana and papaya. But the best description of the fruit's flavor is Pete's: every tropical fruit you ever tasted blended together into a thick cream.

color. You can serve cherimoyas cut in half or quarters so that they can be eaten with a spoon. Remember to cut out the small central core. Cherimoyas may also be puréed by pushing pieces of the fruit through a sieve and mixed with a little lime or lemon juice to give the fruit an edge. Try the purée mixed with a little cream and a sprinkle of nutmeg, or blended with other delicate fruits like raspberries, grapes or melon.

Cherimoya Soufflé

This isn't really a soufflé but it is similar in texture. It was concocted by Pete for a friend who complained that he found the cherimoya a little overwhelming.

1	ripe cherimoya	1
3 Tbsp	orange juice	40 mL
	or	
1½ Tbsp	lime juice	25 mL
¾ cup	whipping cream, whipped	175 mL
	A sprinkling of nutmeg	

Purée the flesh of the cherimoya with the fruit juice. Gently fold in the whipped cream. Sprinkle with nutmeg and chill well. *Serves 4*

Cherimoya Soufflé Sauce

1	ripe cherimoya	1
1 tsp	lemon or lime juice	5 mL
½ cup	coffee cream	125 mL

Purée the flesh of the cherimoya with the fruit juice. Stir in the coffee cream. Chill. This is a delicious sauce for delicate fruit or ice cream. *Makes 1 cup*

Atemoya

Atemoya is a cousin of the cherimoya. It looks like a wax artichoke which was stored on the mantlepiece and melted a bit. It also looks like a cherimoya with rounded scales. In color, it is a grayish green. In taste, it is uncannily like cherimoya, but milkier, as opposed to creamier. Its texture is similar to that of the cherimoya, although it has fewer pips. Serve it chilled as you would cherimoya. And why not be totally decadent? Pour a little cream over the fruit.

Atemoyas are available from late August to November. Take them home unripe and ripen them on the counter. If they split, as they often do en route to perfect ripeness, don't worry, just cover them with a clean tea towel. Do not refrigerate the fruit until it is ripe or you will ruin it. Once ripe, it will yield to gentle pressure, and you can keep it for a day or two in the refrigerator. The cold will darken the skin of the fruit but that will not affect the taste.

Atemoya is high in calories, with 93 in ⅓ cup/75 mL, and is a good source of protein and potassium.

I'm going to let you in on a secret. At a dinner party once, Pete served atemoyas. He covered the halves with 1 inch/2.5 cm of sour cream and a generous sprinkling of brown sugar. Then he chilled them for about 15 minutes. There is no more magnificent dessert in the world. I promise!

Cherries

One day at Pete's we received a case of cherries, and it was immediately obvious that every single cherry had been packed by hand! Each tiny berry was neatly placed in line with those below, above and beside it. All the stems pointed in the same direction; not one of the cherries was squashed, damaged or even out of line. I gazed at this in astonishment when Pete's right hand man, Geoff, came up to me. "Amazin' in't it? You gotta treat 'em li'l beau'ies wif' such care." Wow, he wasn't kidding! I wasn't surprised when I saw the price per pound. They were expensive, but they were magnificent too! Those particular cherries were unusually early, which also accounted for their price.

In the summer months cherries can be found relatively easily and at a reasonable price. Cherry lovers in North America are particulary lucky because more cherries grow here than any other country in the world; they are also the sweetest and best.

There are, of course, two different types of cherries: tart and sweet. Certain types of tart cherries can be eaten out of hand, but generally they are used in cooking. Ninety percent of the crop is processed and

"Don't keep 'em, eat 'em!" Pete's words are as true for cherries as for any berries. Since they are very perishable, cherries should be eaten as soon as possible after purchase.

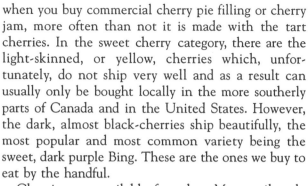

when you buy commercial cherry pie filling or cherry jam, more often than not it is made with the tart cherries. In the sweet cherry category, there are the light-skinned, or yellow, cherries which, unfortunately, do not ship very well and as a result can usually only be bought locally in the more southerly parts of Canada and in the United States. However, the dark, almost black-cherries ship beautifully, the most popular and most common variety being the sweet, dark purple Bing. These are the ones we buy to eat by the handful.

Cherries are available from late May until early August. You may be lucky enough to find some New Zealand imports around Christmas; however, only a small quantity is imported, so if you are frantic for them, be prepared to search a little. The ripest cherries are also the biggest, the sweetest and the most richly colored. In sweet and tart cherries, look for fruit which is plump, firm and brightly colored.

Cherries are very perishable. They should be eaten as soon after purchase as possible. However, if you must, cherries may be stored in the refrigerator for up to 3 days, if you arrange them between paper towels on a cookie sheet and wrap them in plastic.

Sweet cherries are a good source of vitamin C; tart cherries are a good source of vitamin A. Four ounces/ 120 grams of raw sweet cherries have 80 calories; 4 ounces/120 grams of sour cherries have 65 calories.

In my opinion, the best way to eat sweet cherries, is to give them a quick rinse and eat them raw. If you want something a little more adventurous, you can cut them in half, remove the stones and add them to a fruit salad. Stewed cherries are good with ice cream or yogurt. Tart cherries, or a mix of tart and sweet cherries, make a wonderful deep-dish fresh fruit pie. Garnish a plain cake or a lonely meringue with a mixture of fresh and stewed cherries. For real, true-blue adventure, combine stoned, halved cherries with a little brandy, let them marinate for about 15 minutes and blend in some sour cream, or sour cream and yogurt. Garnish with some minced tarragon and toasted slivered almonds. You can also use Grand Marnier and add a little grated orange rind to the sour cream. Go ahead, create something!

Coconut

This hairy, hard-shelled fruit is a delight for kids. It is amazing how many children will try to convince their mums to buy a coconut when they see them at Pete's. I still remember the excitement among my brothers and sister and I when we managed to squeeze a coconut onto the shopping list. Not many North Americans realize that in many tropical and sub-tropical regions, coconuts are the an important source of food, as common as apples for us.

Coconuts are available all year, being most plentiful in October, November and December. A good coconut will be clean on the outside, without any damp spots or mould. It should be heavy for its size, and when you shake it, you should be able to hear the liquid inside.

If you want to keep a coconut for a while, store it in the refrigerator; but the fruit will also be fine on the counter for a week or two if you can guard it from the kids. The grated flesh will keep in the refrigerator for 2 weeks.

Getting into a coconut can be difficult if you don't know the formula. Here is the easiest way to get the most out of this fruit. One end of a coconut is usually more pointed than the other, and on the rounder end, there are three little depressions called the eyes. Drill two holes in the eyes and drain out the liquid. One way of extracting the liquid is to stick a straw in and drink it; the other is to let the fruit sit upside down on a bowl or mug and let the liquid drip out. This juice is superb added to fruit salad or mixed with rum. Incidentally, this is not coconut milk.

For the next stage you have two choices. The first is to pound away at the coconut until you manage to break it. The second is to put it in the oven at 350° F/180° C for 15 minutes, until the shell begins to crack; let the nut cool briefly and then whack it with a hammer along the crack. The shell should split open. You can then pry out the flesh out with a knife or a clean screwdriver.

Three-quarters of a cup/175 mL of coconut meat contains about 150 calories. It is a good source of potassium and fiber; it also contains saturated fat—a rarity for a fruit or vegetable.

Use fresh coconut in place of dried, packaged coconut without having to adjust the recipe. Try grating it coarsely and adding it to a fruit salad, or serving it with curry.

Coconut Milk

Use coconut milk and some grated coconut to make an interesting sauce for fish or chicken. Try a little coconut milk in a cocktail, or with your favorite dessert.

1 cup	fresh coconut cut into ½-inch/ 1.25-cm chunks	250 mL
1 cup	hot water	250 mL

Whirl the coconut and the hot water in a blender or food processor for 20 to 30 seconds until the chunks have all but disappeared, or until the mixture is thick and pulpy.

Let the liquid steep for 30 minutes. Strain through a double thickness of cheesecloth, wringing it well to remove the liquid. Discard the coconut.

The milk, covered and refrigerated, will keep for up to 3 days. *Makes 1 cup/250 mL*

Cranberries

Although the lowly cranberry was relegated to jelly and sauce for a long time, it is finally coming into its own and recipes abound for cranberry cookies, cranberry bread, cranberry coffee cake, cranberry muffins and cranberry pudding. It is about time, for this tart little berry has been overlooked for too long.

North America is the only producer of cranberries. I know, because cranberry juice is one of my favorites and I have searched a large part of continental Europe for the ruby liquid, but to no avail.

There are three types of cranberries: bog, bush and rock. The ones most of us buy in plastic bags for Thanksgiving and Christmas are bog cranberries. This wild fruit is cultivated all along the eastern seaboard as well as in Wisconsin and British Columbia. Occasionally, you'll find bush and rock cranberries for sale locally from late summer to mid-autumn.

Cranberries are abundant from September to the end of November, and they freeze like a dream: Simply drop the bag in the freezer; you don't even need to thaw the berries before cooking. Look for plump, firm berries and avoid withered or shriveled ones. Cranberries keep for up to 8 weeks—much longer than most berries.

Cranberries are a great source of vitamins A. One cup/250 mL has only 55 calories, that's without sugar, of course!

Cranberry Wine Sorbet

2 cups	fresh or frozen cranberries	500 mL
½ cup	sugar	125 mL
½ cup	red wine	125 mL
1½ cups	orange juice	375 mL
2 tsp	grated orange rind	10 mL

Combine all the ingredients in a saucepan and simmer over medium heat until the cranberries are cooked and split open. Cool. Purée the mixture in a blender or food processor.

Pour the purée into an ice cream canister and freeze according to the manufacturer's instructions, or pour the cranberry liquid into a loaf pan and cover with foil or plastic wrap. Freeze for 4 hours or until firm. Scrape the mixture with a knife or fork until it looks like crushed ice. You can also break the frozen sorbet and whirl it in a food processor just before serving, chilling the bowl first. *Makes 3 cups/750 mL*

Cranberry-Blueberry Pie

Pete told me about this pie. It is deliciously different and hopelessly easy.

2 cups	cranberries	500 mL
2 cups	blueberries	500 mL
¾ cup	sugar	175 mL
2 Tbsp	cornstarch	25 mL
¼ tsp	nutmeg	1 mL
2 Tbsp	grated orange rind	25 mL
	Pastry for a 9-inch/23-cm pie shell	

Mix the ingredients in a medium-sized bowl and pour the mixture into the pie shell. Bake at 425° F/220° C for 15 minutes; reduce the oven temperature to 375° F/190° C and bake for another 35 minutes.

Just before serving, add a dollop of sour cream flavored with a small amount of Cointreau.

Dates

For a sweet, energy booster, dates are hard to beat. Contrary to popular opinion, dates are not dried fruit. They are fresh, but because they are so dry and sugar-packed, they are often mistaken for dried fruit.

I am not sure why Pete keeps selling dates at his stall. He maintains, with great vehemence, that the staff eat more than they sell. On behalf of the staff, I would like to say that probably, all put together, we eat far fewer dates than he does. Who can blame him, or us, for that matter?

There are three types of dates; soft, semi-dry and dry. The soft dates are invert or liquid-sugar dates and the dry, cane-sugar dates. Although there are more than a hundred different varieties of dates, North Americans are most familiar with less than ten.

The most common date is the Deglet Noor, which translated means "Date of the Light." It is a semi-dry date, probably what most of us expect a date to be: superb, plump, smooth-skinned with a beautiful golden-brown color. Chances are good that when you buy packaged dates, you are getting Deglet Noor.

Pete's favorite date is the Medjool which is often sold loose, as fresh fruit. Big, soft and immensely sweet, the Medjool is wrapped in a dark, rather wrinkled skin.

The Barhi is the softest and tenderest date. It has a thin, slightly crunchy skin and flesh which dissolves in your mouth. The Zahidi, Halawy and Khadrawy dates are all invert-sugar dates. The Halawy, usually imported from Iraq, is semi-dry and often steamed to fatten it up. The Thoory, a light, golden-colored date is the driest variety, sometimes called a bread date, and a favorite snack for athletes.

If stored properly, dates will keep indefinitely. You can put them in plastic bags in the freezer and forget them for as long as five years! Although you can keep them in the refrigerator for up to a year, it is important to keep dates away from foods with a strong odour, such as fish or onions, because dates have a tendency to absorb smells, doing little to enhance their taste.

Dates contain some of the B vitamins and, despite their sugary sweetness, only 25 calories in a single fruit.

Great eaten out of hand for a quick energy renewer, dates are also a delicious addition to a wide variety of dishes. Try sprinkling a handful on your breakfast cereal, pancakes, waffles or French toast. Include a few coarsely chopped dates the next time you make bran muffins. For something really different, add some cut up dates to a fruit salad, or to a chicken or tuna salad. An exquisite treat for an appetizer or a light dessert can be made quickly and easily by filling a few date halves with cream cheese, topping each half with a walnut, or by sliding pieces of Brie into date halves and warming them a little. You can use chopped dates in place of raisins in any recipe. If you like playing with your food, toss a few into a bowl of ice-cream, yogurt or sour cream. Now that you have a few ideas . . . experiment a little and see what you can come up with!

Feijoas

A *feijoa is not a pineapple guava.* If you ever hear anyone refer to a feijoa as a pineapple guava, you have Pete's permission to correct them. No, even better, you have a request from Pete to correct them. A feijoa tastes vaguely like pineapple, among other things, and like guava, it is a member of the Myrtle family; but it is not a guava.

A delicious, if rather innocuous-looking fruit, a feijoa is about 2½ to 3 inches/6 to 8 cm in length and shaped like a football with flattened ends. The thin skin can be anywhere from mild lime green to a dark olive in color. Inside is a dense, somewhat gritty, tan-colored flesh similar in texture to that of a very ripe guava with tiny, edible seeds.

Feijoas are on the market in the winter and autumn from California and in the summer and spring from New Zealand. If the fruit is not completely ripe when you buy it, it will ripen uncovered, out of direct sunlight. To speed things up, put a feijoa in a paper bag with a ripe apple until the feijoa feels like a soft ripe pear and smells wonderfully fragrant. But don't wait for much of a change in color; the skin may become only a little darker. Once ripe, feijoas may be refrigerated, uncovered, on a tray lined with paper towel, for up to

A delicious treat for breakfast is half a feijoa with a little lime or lemon juice, or if the fruit is a little tart, with a sprinkle of sugar. If you feel like really indulging, scoop a little of the flesh out of the center of a halved fruit, drop in a dollop of vanilla ice cream or a citrus-flavored sherbet and pour a little Cointreau over top.

2 days. Feijoas are a good source of vitamin C; four ounces/120 grams of the fruit have 40 calories.

Feijoa will darken quickly once cut, so if you want to serve them sliced, in a fruit salad or on pancakes or waffles, a squeeze of lemon will help.

For a delicious dessert, serve halved, poached feijoas with unwhipped 32 percent cream. If you have a large budget, are simply extravagant or lucky enough to be able to buy feijoas inexpensively, scoop the flesh out of several feijoas, purée it in a food processor or blender, and serve it over sliced bananas, strawberries and oranges. Sprinkle with minced crystallized ginger and you have the dessert of a lifetime!

Feijoas in Orange Syrup

½ cup	water	125 mL
¼ cup	sugar	50 mL
¼ cup	frozen orange juice concentrate	50 mL
	Half an orange rind, grated	
3	large ripe feijoas, peeled, halved and sliced	3

In a saucepan, bring the water, sugar, orange juice and rind to a boil. Add the sliced feijoas. Lower the heat, cover and gently poach the feijoas for 5 minutes or until the fruit has become slightly soft. Chill for at least 4 hours.

This concoction is great with vanilla ice cream, or with lemon or lime sherbet. But beware of using too much. It is highly concentrated! *Makes 1½ cups/375 mL*

Figs

Most of us are probably more familiar with dried figs than we are with the fresh fruit. Dried figs are fifty percent sugar while the fresh contain only twelve percent. Fresh figs are delicate and must be handled with extreme care. They can be white, green, purple or black, depending on their variety. The flesh can be anywhere from a deep pinkish-red to a yellowish-white, and can be either a mass of tiny edible seeds or seedless. The very best figs are tree-ripened, but since they are so perishable, they are usually picked and shipped before they are ripe. All these considerations mean that we rarely get good figs in Canada, but at Pete's we often get beautiful figs. And in some ethnic markets in larger cities, you may occasionally stumble across an excellent fig or two.

Fig season lasts for most of June and from August to late September. Perfectly ripe figs, which should be used immediately, are soft to the touch. When buying figs, avoid those with brown or greyish spots on the skin which indicate that the fruit has turned sour and should not be eaten; they can sour and ferment easily. If you must store them, lay them on paper towel, cover them with plastic wrap and keep them in the refrigerator, but for no more than 3 days.

Fresh figs are a good source of calcium, phosphorus and iron. Two large fruit have about 100 calories.

A ripe fresh fig is delicious simply eaten out of hand; you can eat the skin if you wish, or you can eat the flesh out of the skin. You can wrap fig halves in prosciutto or salami as an appetizer. Try some fresh fruit with crusty French bread and cheese or sprinkle fresh figs with kirsch or lime juice and a dollop of fresh cream. A delicious and easy dessert can be made by cutting an "X" in the bottom of a fresh fig, stuffing it with some cream cheese and a little mixed spice, wrapping it in foil and baking it in a hot oven for 15 minutes. For an extra special treat, serve this dessert with fresh gingersnaps.

Figs and Cream

16	fresh Black Mission figs, peeled, or unpeeled and cut into quarters	16
	Raspberry liqueur	
1/4 cup	fresh raspberries	50 mL
1 cup	whipping cream	250 mL

Divide the figs among four separate bowls. Sprinkle with liqueur. Mash the raspberries and blend them into the cream, which can be whipped or not, depending on your preference. Divide the raspberry mash among the four bowls and chill for 2 hours. *Serves 4*

Figs, Cognac and Cream

A decadent version of Figs and Cream.

8 to 10	fresh figs	8 to 10
3 Tbsp	sugar	50 mL
2 Tbsp	Cognac	25 mL
¾ cup	whipping or sour cream	175 mL
¼ cup	Curaçao	50 mL

Cut the figs in half from top to bottom. Lay them cut side down on a large plate or tray. Sprinkle with sugar and drizzle the Cognac over them. Cover and refrigerate for an hour or more.

Mix the cream and Curaçao and refrigerate.

To serve, put the figs in bowl and pour the cream over top. *Serves 2 to 4*

Grapefruit

We all know what a great beginning to the day grapefruit is: its tang is what we need to get us going. For a change, try eating one peeled, like an orange, in segments. It's delicious.

Have you ever wondered where the grapefruit got its name? It certainly wasn't because it tastes like grapes, because it doesn't. Don't get your hopes up, because I'm not going to tell you. I would tell you if I knew, but no one seems to know for sure where the name came from—not even Pete. But it is probably because the fruit grows in clusters like grapes.

Grapefruit are certainly a popular fruit and Pete sells them by the truck-load. The best quality citrus fruit is the Indian River fruit, grown in Indian River, Florida, which has the perfect soil and climate conditions for growing good citrus fruit. The pink and white grapefruit are different in color, but not in flavor or juiciness.

Grapefruit are available all year round, and although they are most abundant from January to June, they are most flavorful and juicy from March and April. Look for fruit with smooth, thin skins that are either well-rounded or slightly flat at both ends. Fruit which is heavy for its size promises juiciness and since the grapefruit is almost three quarters liquid, juiciness means flavor. Avoid coarse, rough or puffy fruit, or those with a pointed end—an indication that the flesh will be dry and nearly flavorless.

Grapefruit like temperatures around 50°F, so unless

you are keeping them for over a week, leave them on the counter. If they are going to be around for more than a week, store them in the refrigerator.

We all know what a great beginning to the day grapefruit is: its tang is what we need to get us going. If they could come up with a grapefruit that was good with coffee, or a coffee that was good with grapefruit, we'd be all set.

One 8-ounce glass of fresh grapefruit juice has more than enough vitamin C to give you your daily requirement, and half a grapefruit has only 50 calories. You might try eating one, peeled, in segments; they are delicious and nutritious like this.

Grapefruit Mousse

3	large eggs, separated	3
½ cup	sugar	125 mL
2	large grapefruit, puréed	2
	Rind of 2 oranges, finely grated	
1 Tbsp	unflavored gelatin, softened in ¼ cup/50 mL cold water	15 mL
1 cup	cream, whipped	250 mL
	Salt	

Mix the egg yolks and all but 2 tablespoons/25 mL of the sugar. Beat well. Stir in the puréed grapefruit. Simmer the mixture in the top of a double boiler for 5 minutes or until thick, stirring frequently. Remove from the heat and stir in the orange rind and gelatin. Transfer the mixture to a large bowl and place it in the freezer, stirring occasionally, until the mixture is thick enough to mound slightly.

Beat the egg whites with the sugar and salt until they are stiff but not dry. Whip the cream.

Remove the grapefruit mixture from the freezer and fold it into the whipped cream a little at a time. Then fold one quarter of the grapefruit-whipped cream mixture into the egg whites. Fold the egg whites into the rest of the grapefruit-whipped cream mix. This must be done with great care so that you do not lose the lightness you have beaten into the egg whites.

Put the mousse into individual dessert dishes or a large glass bowl. Chill for at least 5 hours. Serve garnished with a few sliced strawberries. *Serves 6*

Broiled Grapefruit

2	grapefruit, halved	2
1 Tbsp	melted butter	15 mL
4 Tbsp	honey	50 mL
	Nutmeg	
4 Tbsp	Crème de cassis	50 mL

Place the grapefruit in a pan close enough together so that they stand upright. Drizzle the melted butter and honey on each half and dust with a little nutmeg.

Pour some water into the bottom of the pan and broil the fruit for 8 minutes, or until they are very hot. For a little excitement, drizzle some crème de cassis on each half grapefruit.

Grapes

Grapes don't ripen once they leave the vine so they are ready to eat the moment you buy them.

There is a bewildering array of grapes of various sizes, colors and tastes: Thompson seedless, Flame seedless, Ruby seedless, Tokay, Emperor, Almeria, Calmeria, Cardinal, Ribier and Muscatels. There are grapes with seeds and those without. Some grapes are small, others are large. They may be red, green or black.

Grapes sell quickly at Pete's and if an employee can't find anything else to do, he can always work on the grape display. One of Pete's most oft-uttered phrases is, "Jump on that grape display!" Grapes are a favorite food, all you have to do is rinse them.

Grapes are available all year. The first six months of the year see our shelves filled with imported grapes, mainly from Chile; the last six months load us down with the fruit from California. When buying grapes, look for plump, firm fruit. White, or green grapes as they are more commonly called, have a tinge of amber at their sweetest. Darker grapes, red and purple ones, should have no signs of green. Although seedless grapes are more popular, grapes with seeds usually have a richer, fuller flavor. Grapes don't ripen once they leave the vine, so they are ready to eat the moment you buy them. Refrigerate them in a plastic or paper bag up to 4 days, depending on the variety, but since they are extremely perishable, they should be eaten as soon as possible after purchase.

Grapes contain small amounts of several nutrients and the number of calories they contain, ranging from 70 to 140 calories per cup/250 mL, depends on the type of grape.

Grapes are most commonly eaten out of hand, after a quick wash. They are the perfect complement to ripe soft cheeses, before or after a meal. Try adding a handful to your next vegetable salad for the occasional sweet bite. For an attractive centerpiece, dip grapes, still on the stem, first into beaten egg whites and then granulated sugar, refrigerating them until firm. For an attractive fruit plate, arrange a small bunch of Ribier, or another black grape, with strawberries and sliced kiwi fruit. The color combination is beautiful. For a delicious, nutritious snack for the kids, pop some Flame grapes into the freezer. They'll love them!

Grapes, Honey and Cognac

¼ cup	mild, fragrant honey	50 mL
3 Tbsp	Cognac	40 mL
1 tsp	lime juice	5 mL
1 pound	green seedless grapes, rinsed, drained and dried	450 g
	Yogurt or sour cream	

Mix the honey, Cognac and lime juice together. Add the grapes and toss carefully. Chill overnight. Serve with a dollop of yogurt or sour cream. *Serves 4*

Guava

This luscious tropical fruit may be a little difficult to put your finger on since it occurs in 140 species! But don't rush to your nearest market to see how many types of guavas they sell because most varieties are not easy to find outside their habitat—Australia, India, South Africa, South America and the Caribbean. Guavas can be rounded or pear-shaped; the flesh may range from a hot pink to a gentle salmon color, or it may be white or yellow. The fruit may be infested with seeds or virtually seedless, and sweet or sour, they may taste like pineapples, lemons, strawberries or bananas. The skin is usually a yellowish-green or a dull yellow.

The one constant is the fragrance or odor of guavas. Pete has described the smell as varying from that of a pair of sweaty old sneakers to the Garden of Eden. A ripe guava has a rich, heady floral aroma; the less ripe fruit smells much less appealing.

The peak season for guavas is summer, starting a little early and ending a little late, when they can be purchased either at the peak of their ripeness, or taken home unripe and left on the counter to ripen, filling your kitchen with their sweet aroma. When ripe, guavas will be yellow in color and yield to gentle pressure. Use guavas promptly once ripened, or store them in the refrigerator in a plastic or paper bag for up to 5 days. But remember, handle the ripe fruit with care, guavas bruise easily.

Guavas are full of vitamin C and a good source of potassium. Four ounces/120 grams of the raw fruit have about 70 calories.

The pink-fleshed guava is especially exciting because its color is so wonderfully adventurous. It is a must in a fruit salad, especially in combination with the emerald kiwi, the clear yellow carambola or the velvet orange mango. Pink guava purée is glorious added to whipped cream, snow pudding or rice pudding or spooned over sponge cake. A brief tour with a spoon leaves slashes of pink and streaks of flavor through an otherwise ordinary dessert. But if you are not lucky enough to find a pink guava, you only lose out on visual appeal; no matter what colour, the taste is just as miraculously delicious!

A guava can also be delicious eaten out of hand. You can either peel it or eat it from the inside out. If you are a curry lover and have not been savoring the delectable fruit after a curry, do so without delay. A slightly chilled guava is perfect after a spicy meal, cleansing and refreshing. A few slices of peeled guava added to an apple pie before baking will make an exquisite dessert you'll not soon forget, and guava purée with pheasant or duck is an unusually welcome treat. Guava can be a delicious addition in the most unlikely situations. Come on: be daring; explore!

Guava and Avocado Dessert

A delicious and interesting dessert demonstrating the versatility of the avocado while displaying the wonderful taste of the guava.

1	large avocado, peeled and diced	1
4	fresh guavas, peeled and diced	4
	Juice of 1 orange	
	Juice of 1 lime	
1 Tbsp	sugar	15 mL
½ cup	yogurt	125 mL
	Sugar to taste	
	Cream	
1 tsp	vanilla	5 mL
	Orange slices or sliced strawberries	

Mix the diced avocado and guava with orange juice. Add the lime juice and sugar to taste. Chill the mixture.

Sweeten the yogurt with the sugar and add enough cream to thin it out just a bit.

Place alternating layers of yogurt and the guava mixture in a glass bowl or individual parfait glasses. Decorate with orange slices or sliced strawberries. *Serves 4*

Kiwano

This truly exotic looking fruit is a cherished favorite of the African hippopotamus. At least, that's what Pete says. But if we believe that, then we have to believe that mangosteens are Bruce Springsteen's favorite fruit. I leave the choice of belief or disbelief to you. If they are a favorite of the hippos, that is because they do not have to pay for them. It is just about as expensive as any exotic fruit on the market and you certainly aren't paying for taste.

A kiwano looks like a very large punk Easter Egg and is indeed beautiful in appearance. Its color can range from deep yellow to golden-orange. In shape, it is spherical and covered with little round-ended spikes. Inside is a soft, textured flesh looking rather like kiwi fruit, but packed with white edible seeds.

Kiwanos were discovered by a New Zealander on holiday, a clever New Zealander on holiday. He took the fruit home with him and grew acres and acres of it and started shipping it around the world, marketing it as a brand new fruit.

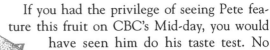

If you had the privilege of seeing Pete feature this fruit on CBC's Mid-day, you would have seen him do his taste test. No doubt three-quarters of the viewers were watching the spoonful of gorgeous, emerald-colored, seed-laden fruit as it moved towards Pete's mouth. We all waited for his ecstatic "Delicious!" Instead we got "Yuck!" Kiwanos are cucumber jelly in one of the most beautiful coverings Mother Nature ever designed. Although they may be superbly refreshing, if you live in one of the hottest climates on earth, and especially if you're a hippo, in North America, these exotic-looking fruit should probably be purchased exclusively for their appearance or not at all.

Kiwi Fruit

Although this fruit is native to China, it did so well when introduced to New Zealand that it was renamed after that country's national symbol—the kiwi bird. Although kiwi fruit is grown in Israel, California, Italy, Spain, France and Chile, to name a but few of the countries, most of the fruit found in North American markets comes from New Zealand or California. This exotic fruit exploded onto the North American marketplace and has become so popular that it is now almost as easy to find as apples. There is no doubt but that this little brown fruit is here to stay. (It is rather interesting to note that several years ago the kiwi fruit, then known as the Chinese Gooseberry, made an attempt to "explode" onto the fruit market. Its lack of success is now largely attributed to its unappealing former name.)

Thanks to the New Zealand-California balance,

kiwis are in good supply all year round, with Californian fruit in our markets from October to May and New Zealand fruit from May to October.

When purchasing kiwi, choose fruit which is firm. You can allow them to ripen as much or as little as you like. Just keep them uncovered and out of direct sunlight for a few days. If you want them to ripen more quickly, put them in a paper bag with a ripe apple, banana or pear. If you are buying kiwis to eat immediately, choose ones which are uniformly soft or firm without squishy areas. They should yield to gentle pressure. Fruit which is too soft will be mealy and lacking flavor. Once ripe, kiwis will retain their texture and flavor, if stored in a paper or plastic bag and refrigerated, for up to a week. One small kiwi contains enough vitamin C for your daily requirement; 4 ounces/120 grams of the flesh—one fairly large kiwi—contain 40 calories.

A real treat when working on the kiwi display at Pete's is to find a split kiwi fruit. All we do is break the fruit in half and eat it right out of the skin. The skin is edible but not too many people enjoy it. My brother, who is a kiwi fruit fanatic, worked hard at eating kiwi fruit with the skin, but he gave up after about a month, claiming that it was not worth the effort.

The fruit is not easy to peel, but can be done with a sharp knife or a vegetable peeler. Inside is beautiful emerald flesh surrounding an edible, white center, around which are swirls of tiny black seeds. Peeled and sliced, kiwis are beautiful in fruit salads or served with fresh or poached fruit. In combination with strawberries, they make a splendid garnish on sponge or angel-food cake. They are also delicious with shrimp and scallops, especially if you add a little freshly grated ginger root.

Both the flesh of the kiwi and the skin have some surprising uses; they can be used to tenderize meat by simply laying slices of the fruit or strips of the skin on the meat. In 30 minutes, the meat will be tender enough to grill and infinitely more flavorful.

The same enzyme which tenderizes meat prevents gelatin from setting, so kiwi should only be used as a garnish for gelatin molds. Some glazes, if used on kiwi fruit, will become watery if they are allowed to stand, so don't glaze kiwi fruit unless you plan to serve it right

Kiwis are one of the hardiest fruits for shipping and handling. They are picked green and they have their own built-in protection in the form of a fuzzy skin, which, although thin, is tough. If they are refrigerated the moment they are picked, they will not ripen until moved to warmer temperatures.

away. Another enzyme in kiwi will separate milk, but don't worry about mixing kiwis with ice cream or other milk products; if the two are mixed, just serve them immediately.

Cooking with kiwi fruit is generally not recommended; the fruit loses some of its tang and turns a rather unpleasant shade of olive green. And since the fruit is so beautiful and so wonderfully refreshing, there is no reason to eat it anything but raw.

Kiwi Fruit Sorbet

This is a wonderful end to a meal. The last time I made it, I served it in individual cups, surrounded by sliced strawberries and topped with whipped cream. It looked magnificent and tasted even better.

⅔ cup	sugar	150 mL
¼ cup	fresh lime juice	50 mL
¼ cup	fresh lemon juice	50 mL
2 cups	kiwi fruit, puréed	500 mL
¾ cup	orange juice	175 mL

Stir the sugar into 1½ cups/375 mL of water and bring it to a boil. Simmer for 5 minutes and then cool the mixture, refrigerating it for 1 hour.

Add the lime and lemon juices to the kiwi purée and chill. Blend the syrup, the purée and the orange juice. Pour the mixture into an ice cream canister and proceed according to the manufacturer's instructions.

Like most sherbets, kiwi fruit sorbet profits from a rest in the freezer for a day or two. *Makes 1¼ quarts/1.25 L*

Kumquats

Occasionally when I am making fruit baskets at Pete's, I happen to be lucky enough to find a box of kumquats to decorate the baskets. This is bliss, for not only do the tiny oblong, orange-colored kumquats make a fruit basket look heavenly, they are the best things to pop in your mouth and munch on every once in a while. The combination of the silky-sweet peel and the lip-curling, sour pulp makes them wonderfully out-of-the-ordinary, strangely delicious and refreshing. And, from an aesthetic point of view, these cheerful, bright-orange creations are hard to beat.

Kumquats are a winter fruit, appearing in November and if we're lucky, lasting until late April or early May. Look for firm fruit, which are not squishy-soft. Don't be afraid to give a kumquat a gentle squeeze. If you buy kumquats planning to use them within a few days, leave them out; otherwise you can store them in the refrigerator for up to 2 weeks. They tend to spoil more rapidly than oranges because they are so thin-skinned.

Kumquats are an excellent source of vitamin C. Four of these tiny fruit contain 75 calories.

There is no need to waste anything with kumquats. All you do is wash them and use them. No peeling, nothing to cut off, nothing to throw away. Since they make beautiful garnishes, they may be blanched in boiling water for 15 seconds, chilled in ice water, dried, sliced thinly and tossed by the handful into a fruit or vegetable salad. They may also be used with fish, meat or duck. If you want to add a little color and pizzazz to your fruit bowl, toss them where they will look splendid nestling among black grapes. If you can manage to get your hands on some strawberries too, you will be astonished at how beautiful a combination the three can be. But of course the easiest way of all to eat these little wonders is to give them a quick roll between your finger and thumb, blending the flavor of skin and flesh, and pop them in your mouth. What a treat!

Kumquat and Broccoli Salad

Pete never lets kumquat season pass without making this salad at least once. He doesn't remember where he got the recipe but he says that he has never forgotten it. It is not only great tasting, but great looking too.

1	bunch broccoli	1
10	kumquats	10
4 Tbsp	extra virgin olive oil	60 mL

Kumquats are the ideal garnish. All you do is wash them and use them—no peeling, no trimming. Put kumquat slices on your next carrot cake after it has been iced.

1	clove garlic, minced	1
2 Tbsp	lime juice	25 mL
½ tsp	sugar	2 mL
	Salt and pepper	
	Pinch of savory	
10	black olives	10

Peel broccoli stems and cut them into smallish pieces; cut the head into florets. Steam for 3 minutes, or until the broccoli is bright green but still firm.

Boil the kumquats in the broccoli water for 15 seconds. Chill the fruit in ice water. Cut half the kumquats into quarters; slice the rest thinly.

Heat the oil and garlic very slowly, until the garlic becomes a very light beige, about 5 minutes. Add the lime juice, sugar, salt, pepper, savory and quartered kumquats, and purée the mixture in a blender or food processor.

Add the purée to the broccoli and sliced kumquats and toss well. Chill. Add the olives just before serving; sprinkle with salt and grind on some pepper. *Serves 2*

Lemons

Where would we be without lemons? On fish, on salads, in mayonnaise, in sauces, in butter for vegetables, in desserts, cakes, soufflés, pies and sherbet—so much is enhanced by a little lemon juice. Sliced lemons provide a colorful and tasty garnish, lemon rind is a zesty addition to just about anything. It may seem an odd parallel, but the lemon is perhaps the onion of the fruit world. Just as there are few vegetable recipes that aren't enhanced by the addition of onion, so there are few fruit as indispensible as the lemon.

It was the Gold Rush of 1849 which first drew attention to the lemon. High in vitamin C, this yellow citrus fruit was used as a cure and as a preventative for scurvy; miners were willing to pay exorbitant sums for a single lemon. This instant demand caused lemon trees to be planted in such numbers that we are still reaping the benefits more than 100 years later.

Lemons are available all year. The lemons you'll see in Canadian markets come from California, Florida,

South America and Spain. When buying lemons, look for fine-textured skins and for fruit which is heavy for its size. Coarse-skinned lemons, or those which are light in weight, don't have as much juice. Pale yellow lemons, or fruit with green overtones, are likely to be acidic. Deep yellow lemons are more mature and generally not as sour. Lemons may be kept for several weeks in the refrigerator or on the counter.

If you or any of your acquaintances should happen to contract a dose of scurvy, lemons are the answer. Lemons are an excellent source of vitamin C, a good source of calcium, phosphorus and potassium. Four ounces/120 grams of the peeled fruit contain about 25 calories.

Lemons are indispensable— as a garnish, a flavor and a source of vitamins, with fish, in desserts, cakes, sauces and a hundred other ways.

Lemon Poppy Seed Bread

If you are a lemon lover, you will become devoted to this bread after one mouthful!

4	eggs	4
1½ cups	oil	375 mL
1½ cups	cereal cream	375 mL
2 Tbsp	lemon juice	25 mL
½ cup	poppy seeds	125 mL
	Rind and juice of 2 lemons	
1½ cups	sugar	375 mL
3 cups	flour	750 mL
1½ tsp	baking soda	7 mL
2 tsp	baking powder	10 mL
1 tsp	salt	5 mL

Beat together the eggs, oil, cream, lemon juice and poppy seeds.

In a separate bowl, combine the lemon rind, sugar, flour, baking soda, baking powder and salt. Stir the dry ingredients into the egg mixture and blend until smooth and uniform.

Pour the batter into 2 greased loaf pans. Bake at 325° F/160° C for 1 hour.

Blend ¼ cup sugar with the juice from the 2 lemons and pour the liquid over the loaves while they are hot and still in the pans.

Limes

Lemons and limes are more than vaguely alike. They have the same distinctive shape and the taste is similar, but limes are less acidic and much more fragrant.

Do you know why Englishmen are called limeys? When we were discussing limes, Pete told me; being a limey, it is not surprising that he should be informed about this sort of thing. He says that during the California gold rush, lemons were almost as dear as the gold itself. Why? Because they could provide enough vitamin C to prevent scurvy. In an effort to combat this complaint without paying the ludicrous prices demanded for lemons, the English soldiers were rationed one lime a day. Brits have therefore been known as limeys ever since.

Limes are a funny little fruit, largely overlooked by most cooks. This is an unfortunate occurence, because limes add a little zap which brightens up many foods. There are many different types of limes, the Persian being the most common.

Nothing is more refreshing on a really hot day than lime sherbet. Add some slices of lime in your iced tea or, like Pete, insist on lime in your gin and tonic. Try squeezing a lime over your salad, or garnish your fish or even your meat with a few slices of lime.

Limes are available all year round, since they are now grown in a number of tropical countries, as well as in California and Arizona. Look for limes which are firm and bright; heavy fruit will be juicy. Since the skin on a lime is thinner than that of a lemon, be careful when handling them. Limes will keep well in the refrigerator for 3 weeks.

Limes are an excellent source of vitamin C. A 4-ounce/120-gram lime has less than 30 calories.

Spiced Limeade

On the hottest, driest day of the year, this thirst quencher is what you need.

½ cup	sugar, or to taste	125 mL
2	sticks of cinnamon	2
5	whole cloves	5
	Juice of 6 large limes	
	Ginger ale	
1	lime, sliced	1
	Sprigs of mint	

Simmer the sugar, cinnamon and cloves in 1 cup of water for 10 minutes. Cool and add the lime juice.

Fill some glasses with crushed ice or ice cubes, and fill each one half-full with the lime juice mixture. Top up the glasses with ginger ale, and garnish with a slice of lime and a generous sprig of mint.

Lime Butter

This easy butter is delicious on broiled or fried fish, and on hot vegetables.

1 cup	soft butter	250 mL
2 tsp	finely-grated lime peel	105 mL
8 tsp	lime juice	40 mL

Beat the butter until light and fluffy. Blend in the lime juice and peel. Mix well.

Loquats

One morning when we were setting up the stall, Pete handed me a rather odd-looking little fruit and said, "Try this, I think they're absolu'ely beau'iful!" I looked dubiously at the little thing in my hand, steeled my nerves and ate it. (Pete has been known to invite new employees to eat a hot pepper. An unpleasant surprise!) To my delight, it *was* delicious!

Loquats have one big problem. In a market which places so much importance on appearance, ripe loquats look rather insignificant; they are small and they bruise easily. Throughout the Mediterranean and in countries where loquats are popular, such as Portugal, China and India, for example, loquats are eaten and enjoyed without regard to their less-than-perfect appearance.

A loquat looks something like an apricot, one to two inches/5 cm in length and usually ovoid-shaped. It has a downy skin which is a dark golden-yellow and firm flesh ranging from cream to orange with one or more large seeds. In taste, it walks the tightrope between tart and sweet and can vary from mild to densely rich.

Loquats are delicious with kiwi and strawberries or raspberries. The fruit in syrup is great at any time of day, as a snack or with a meal. Try them in meringue shells or with a plain white cake.

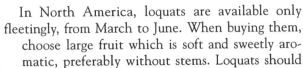

In North America, loquats are available only fleetingly, from March to June. When buying them, choose large fruit which is soft and sweetly aromatic, preferably without stems. Loquats should be refrigerated only if they are moments away from spoiling. Otherwise, you'd be smarter to cook them in a syrup to preserve all of their wonderful taste and aroma.

Loquats are a first-rate source of vitamin A and a good source of potassium. They are also low in calories, with only 50 in four ounces/120 grams of the flesh.

Most loquats don't need peeling. They can be quartered and seeded or, if you like, you can cut the fruit in half, like Pete, without worrying too much about the seeds. Just be sure to remove the stems.

Loquat Heaven

1 cup	loquat chunks	250 mL
3	bananas, sliced	3
1	orange, unpeeled or peeled and sliced	1
1 cup	pineapple chunks	250 mL
½ cup	grated coconut	125 mL

Toss together the loquat, bananas, orange and pineapple. Sprinkle with the coconut just before serving. *Serves 4*

Loquats in Syrup

1 cup	water	250 mL
½ cup	sugar	125 mL
	Peel and juice from 1 small lemon	
1 pound	ripe loquats, rinsed and stemmed, with the blossom ends cut off	500 g

Simmer the water, sugar, lemon juice and peel, covered, for 3 minutes. Let the syrup stand for about 10 minutes to let the flavor develop. Add the fruit to the syrup and simmer gently, covered, for five minutes or until the fruit is tender. Cool, uncovered, in the syrup and chill.

Loquats in syrup keep for months in a plastic container in the freezer. *Serves 4*

Lychees

These perfectly wonderful little fruits are almost indescribable. Known as lychees, litchis and lichees, they are usually expensive, about twice the price of mushrooms; but they are without any doubt worth the price, no matter what it is.

One day a customer approached my cash with a rather large bag of lychees. I told her the price, which was almost twenty dollars, and asked if she wanted to put some back. She smiled serenely and said "No, it's all right. They are worth every penny." I have to agree.

When we have them at Pete's, it is rare that Pete will pass the lychee display without picking up a few to savor. And they are a fruit to be savored. They are small, about 1 to 2 inches/2 to 5 cm in diameter, and have a warty, thin, tough skin which ranges in color from a warm rose to a dull brown. Inside this rather inconspicuous outside lies a true tropical delight. The flesh of this fruit is tight, translucent and a shiny white in color. The consistency is similar to that of a peeled grape and the taste is rather musky and grapey, with a hint of violets—a juicy paradise for your tastebuds. In the midst of this delectable flesh is a smooth mahogany-colored pit, beautiful but inedible.

If you know where you can get some lychees, rush out—right this minute—and buy them. If the shop is closed, be there when it opens tomorrow. Even if you only have enough money to buy one, buy it. You won't regret it.

Lychees are available from December to May and in July and August. Grown in Israel, China, Taiwan, South Africa and Thailand, they are also grown in Florida, but in extremely limited numbers since they are very susceptible to the cold.

Look for full, heavy lychees, which still have some of the stem attached. Fruit with a hint of red color tends to be fresher. Don't worry if the shell is mottled with brown; this occurs very soon after the fruit have been picked. But avoid shriveled or cracked fruit or those which seem too soft. Although they will lose

No one in his right mind would recommend that you cook lychees. Pete says that the only way to eat these little fruit is fresh. They are delicious with chicken, duck or veal in a light wine-based sauce. Just add them in the final seconds of cooking, so that they become warm but aren't actually cooked.

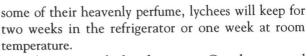

some of their heavenly perfume, lychees will keep for two weeks in the refrigerator or one week at room temperature.

Lychees are packed with vitamin C and are a good source of potassium. Surprisingly, for all that sweetness, they contain only about 80 calories in 4 ounces/120 grams.

No one in his right mind would recommend that you cook lychees. Pete maintains, rightly, that the only way to eat these little fruit is fresh. They are excellent stuffed with cream cheese, thinned with a bit of milk or mayonnaise and top-ped with a walnut or two. They are also superb in a fruit salad: simply peel them and remove the stones by cutting the fruit in half, gently loosening the pit and lifting it out. But best of all, simply put a bowl of lychees in the middle of the table, give everyone a plate for skins and pits and watch them enjoy!

Mangoes

Mangoes are relatively easy to find, in season, which is fortunate for those of us who love them.

The fruit is common in the tropics and no longer the rarity it once was in North America. A ripe, fresh mango is almost unbeatable in terms of its flavor and, if properly cut, the texture is blissful. Mangoes tend to be very fibrous and, without a knife, they are difficult to eat out of hand, taking about about half an hour to consume and at least an hour to get the fibrous bits of the flesh out from between your teeth—but let me assure you that it is more than worth it. In flavor, a mango is a cross between apricots and peaches, although even sweeter and with a hint of something tropical. The texture is smooth and dense. If you have been unlucky enough to taste a mango that was less than deliciously delightful, try again. Let them win you over.

The best way to deal with a mango is to cut it down each side, from top to bottom. *Do not* try to twist the fruit away from the stone; the two are firmly connected! Insert your knife into the middle of the fruit and cut the flesh away from the stone. Then lay the fruit halves skin side down on a cutting board, and slice the flesh, but not the skin, lengthwise and then crosswise. (This technique deals with the stringiness of the fruit and makes it much easier to eat.) Then all you have to do is push the skin so that the flesh pops up and voilà, mango cubes beautifully displayed on their own serving dish! If you are adding the fruit to a salad or a dessert, simply slice the cubes of flesh from the skin.

Mangoes are available from January to August, with their peak season in early summer. Coming in 101 different shapes and colors, they can be round, heart-shaped, kidney-shaped or oval; they might be green, yellow, orange or red or any combination of these colors. Look for mangoes with nice tight skins, and avoid those with loose, wrinkled-looking skin or soft spots.

A ripe mango should yield to gentle pressure like a ripe peach. The stem end will smell sweetly fragrant; the aroma faint but still there. Avoid fruit which smell acidic.

An unripe mango will ripen on your counter, uncovered, out of direct sunlight. Mangoes do not like the cold, although the fruit is especially good if chilled briefly before serving. Gentle thumb pressure is the best way to tell if a mango is ripe because, despite the variety of colors mangoes come in, few of them go through any noticeable color change as they ripen. If you must store the fruit, keep it in a plastic or paper bag in the refrigerator for no more than a day or two.

Mangoes are an excellent source of vitamins A and C and a good source of potassium. Four ounces/120 grams of the flesh have 75 calories.

For a truly exotic sauce, purée mango flesh in a food processor or blender and spoon it over fresh fruit, or sauté sliced mangoes in butter, sugar and your favorite liqueur and serve it over ice cream, yogurt, or a simple light cake. Mangoes are, of course, delicious simply eaten out of hand, without any embellishment.

Mangoes are delicious raw or cooked. Try mango cubes on your waffles or pancakes, as a delicious addition to fruit salad or, surprisingly enough, as an accompaniment to roast meats or poultry. Sautéed mango with grilled chicken is a delightful combination.

Pete's Mango Heaven

This is the next best thing to paradise. Try it with yogurt, ice cream or sour cream.

2 Tbsp	butter	25 mL
1 Tbsp	lime juice	15 mL
1 Tbsp	brown sugar	15 mL
1	ripe mango, about 1 pound/ 500 g, peeled and cut into about 10 slices	1
1	large firm, ripe banana	1
3 Tbsp	Grand Marnier	40 mL
3 Tbsp	brandy	40 mL
	Freshly grated coconut	

Melt the butter in a frying pan and add the lime juice and sugar, stirring until the sugar is dissolved. Add the sliced fruit and cook for 2 minutes on each side until heated through and slightly soft.

Add the alcohol and flambé. Garnish with the grated coconut. Serve immediately. *Serves 4*

Mangosteens

Yet another delight from southern climes! Mangosteens are miraculous little things, one of the most fragrant tropical fruits you will find anywhere. They are not particularly remarkable on the outside; a short, thick, dark-green stem is attached to the fruit where four symmetrical sepals meet the reddish-purple shell. Inside the tough, hard skin are two comparatively large, inedible seeds and a spherical collection of pure white syrupy sections, one of the most tender-fleshed fruit you will ever experience.

Mangosteens are bought ripe because they are sold ripe, because they are picked ripe, because they do not ripen once harvested. So you can savor one of these delights without having to exercise your patience! This fruit, which is often sold by weight, is expensive, especially so because it is heavy and most of the weight is in the inedible skin. The actual fruit is usually no more than 2 inches/5 cm in diameter. The shells, which are full of tannin and are used in the Far East for tanning leather or making ink, make getting at the fruit a bit of an adventure. The best way to release the fruit is to cut through the shell with a knife, being careful not to slice the flesh, and gently pry out the sections of the fruit.

Mangosteens are available off and on all year. They are grown in Indonesia, Thailand and Central Brazil. Because of their thick shell, they keep well in the refrigerator for up to a week or on the counter for 3 days.

Mangosteens are a good source of vitamin C. Four ounces/120 grams of the flesh have 75 calories.

The best way to eat mangosteens is raw. You can serve them with half their shells off or without the shell, all by themselves, in a fruit salad or folded into whipped cream.

Mangosteen-Champagne Sorbet

6	mangosteens, peeled and pushed through a sieve	6
⅔ cup	champagne or sparkling white wine	150 mL
1	egg white	1
1 Tbsp	sugar	15 mL
½ cup	raspberries, puréed or pushed through a sieve	125 mL
1	kiwi, thinly sliced	1

Mix the mangosteen pulp with the champagne. In a seperate bowl, beat the egg white until stiff, gradually adding the sugar. Fold the fruit into the egg white and freeze, stirring occasionally, so that the sorbet remains light.

Serve with the raspberry purée and decorate with slices of kiwi. *Serves 3 to 4*

Pete's Tropical Paradise

One evening Pete asked me to get some thing together for him for dessert: a coconut, some bananas, and about 6 mangosteens.

I asked him the next day "How was the dessert?" He got a dreamy look in his eye and said "Beau'iful, absolu'ly beau'iful." I asked him what he had done and he explained that he had poached the bananas in the coconut liquid for about 5 to 7 minutes. He then added some coarsely grated coconut flesh and the mangosteens which he poached for 2 minutes, just until warmed through. Pete then flambéed the whole thing in Cointreau and served it over ice cream. And if that doesn't sound heavenly, I don't know what does! If you are feeling particularly adventurous and in the mood for a truly exquisite dessert . . . you now know what to try!

Melons

A good melon is one of the chief delights of the fruit world. A slice of ripe, juicy melon is a wonderful way to start or end a day. Look for Ogen or Galia melons from Israel which are wonderfully sweet and heavily scented.

When we have cantaloupes cut in half and ready to eat on the reduced shelf at Pete's, I take one home and eat half for supper and the other half for breakfast. True indulgence, but one hundred percent enjoyable!

One of the saddest stories I know involves my mother, my grandmother and a field of Crenshaw melons. (At least we think they were Crenshaws. They were grown from special seeds, imported by a friend from Arizona!) About twenty-five years ago my grandmother, who has a farm in the fruit belt in Ontario, had a field of melons which were painfully close to being ripe. She and my mother went out to have a look at the fruit and decided that it would be ready to be picked and eaten the next day. The whole family went to bed with dreams of the luscious treats. They got up the next morning, raced out to harvest the fruit and found that every last melon was gone! The horses had beaten them to it; they had gone into the field and eaten every Crenshaw. I don't think my grandmother has ever grown melons again. Even now, when she tells that story, a tear comes to her eye. Mine too!

Summer and melons go together, and even in midwinter a slice of melon is a slice of sunshine.

Cantaloupe, honeydew and watermelon, the more common melons, are available all year round; other melons have definite seasons. At Pete's, we have them from New Zealand, Chile, Mexico, California and Israel, to name just a few places. Most melons are sold slightly under-ripe and can do with a day or two at room temperature. Look for melons which are evenly ripe, without soft or damp spots. Ripe melons should be stored in the refrigerator and tightly wrapped in plastic, since a ripe melon will give off ethylene gas and cause other produce to spoil.

Melons are a good source of vitamin C; cantaloupe and honeydew are rich in potassium and most melons with red or deep-orange flesh provide some vitamin A. Four ounces/120 grams of melon flesh have between 30 and 40 calories.

Cantaloupes are available year round; they are especially abundant in the summer months during the California harvest. To make sure that they're perfectly ripe, give cantaloupe a day or two at room temperature before serving them; the flesh will be softer and juicier. Look for melons that are slightly oval, at least 5 inches/12 cm in diameter and have a golden background color. Both pronounced netting and a very small crack or two at the stem end are signs of sweetness. The fruit should also give a little when pressed.

Honeydews are usually available from May to November. The ripe fruit should have an aroma and be a little soft at the stem end. An unripe melon will ripen at room temperature, if kept out of direct sunlight. *Green Honeydews* are yellowish-white, tinged with green with a satiny blush. Choose melons which weigh at least five pounds and are smooth and firm. *Orange Flesh Honeydews* are a cross between a cantaloupe and a honeydew. The outside looks like a honeydew but inside, the flesh looks and tastes like a cantaloupe. When ripe, the skin should be a light pink.

Casabas are golden-yellow in color with a hint of green at the stem end. They will keep, uncut, in a cool place for a month.

The **Santa Claus** looks like a small watermelon with the flesh of not-quite-so-sweet honeydew. As with green honeydews, look for melons which weigh at least 5 pounds and have bright-yellow stripes.

The **Canary** melon is Pete's favorite. A ripe canary will be sweet, juicy and fragrant and will have a firm, crisp texture. Look for a melon weighing from 4 to 5 pounds, and canary yellow in color.

The **Myan** melon was developed by horticulturalists in Texas to be grown specifically in the Guatemalan highlands where, in fact, most of them are now grown. The Myan is a cross between a honey-dew and a casaba melon. The taste is slightly richer than a honeydew, the color rich and creamy, the flesh a very light green. Myan melons are ready to eat by the time they reach your market.

Watermelon: the only way to be sure that you are getting a good watermelon is to buy it cut. If you are buying a whole watermelon and want a crisp, sweet-fleshed melon, look for one which has dull skin and a velvety bloom of symmetrical shape. The background color of the skin should be turning from white or pale green to a creamy, light yellowish color.

Speciality melons: keep an eye out for the Ogen or Galia melons from Israel. Both are wonderfully sweet and heavily scented. The Galia tastes like an ultra-sweet, juicy cross between a honeydew and a cantaloupe. It has thick, light-colored flesh and a barky, golden skin when ripe. Galia melons are available from October to January.

Melons are a very versatile fruit, mainly because the fruit is sweet and delicately flavored. Try melon wrapped in prosciutto or smoked ham; serve slices of melon topped with ice cream or fruit sorbet; put melon balls in your next fruit salad. Halve a cantaloupe and fill it with cubes or balls of different types of melon, drizzle the whole thing with some fruit-flavored liqueur and serve it with yogurt or vanilla ice cream.

Cantaloupe Ice Cream

A super way to eat cantaloupe. Cold, refreshing, delicious and beautiful.

1	medium cantaloupe, flesh removed from rind	1
2 Tbsp	lemon juice	25 mL
¼ cup	honey	50 mL
¼ cup	sugar	50 mL
3 cups	coffee cream	750 mL
1 tsp	vanilla extract	5 mL

Cut fruit into small pieces and purée it with lemon juice in a blender or food processor.

In a separate bowl, blend the honey, sugar and

cream. Add the melon purée and the vanilla. Stir until the sugar is dissolved.

Pour the mixture into an ice cream maker and freeze according to the manufacturer's instructions, or pour it into a large square pan, cover with foil and put it in the freezer for 4 hours or until firm, stirring 2 or 3 times. *Makes 2 quarts/2 liters*

Honeydew Sorbet

A superbly refreshing ice.

1½ cups	sugar	375 mL
1½ cups	water	375 mL
1	medium honeydew, flesh removed from rind and cut up	1
2 tsp	lime juice	10 mL

Put the sugar and water in a medium-sized saucepan, stirring over medium heat until the sugar is dissolved. Cook until the syrup reaches 220° F/104° C when measured with a candy thermometer, or until the syrup makes a thread when poured from a spoon.

Cool the syrup at room temperature for 10 minutes.

Purée melon and lime juice in a blender or food processor. Pour the purée into the syrup, and blend.

Pour the mixture into an ice cream maker and freeze according to the manufacturer's instructions, or pour the mixture into a large square pan, cover the foil and put it in the freezer for 4 hours or until firm, stirring 2 or 3 times. *Makes 2 quarts/2 liters*

Nectarines

There are many, many varieties of nectarines, but only two types—the freestone and the clingstone. Most of the nectarines which are now available are red, rather than peach-colored, and have firm, sweet flesh. Nectarines are a versatile fruit, standing up well to cooking and combining well with other fruit, meat, poultry or dairy products. They can be substituted for peaches in any recipe, but be prepared to make allowance for the fact that they are not quite as juicy.

Happily for nectarine eaters, the harvesting of the

California fruit (the main source for most of North America) extends from early June until the middle of September, so we can enjoy them throughout the summer. Nectarines are also available from New Zealand and Chile from Christmas until mid-March. Look for fruit which has an orange-yellow background with red areas. The fruit should be plump and bright, and anywhere from firm to moderately hard.

If you are buying a nectarine for lunch or to eat on your way back to the office, choose one which yields to gentle palm pressure. The fruit should almost be as soft as a ripe peach. Avoid fruit which is shriveled, dull or hard, indicating that the it was probably immature when picked. Nectarines, like peaches, don't get more sugary once they have been harvested. You can, however, ripen nearly-ripe fruit at room temperature, out of direct sunlight. You can also store the ripe fruit in a paper or plastic bag in the refrigerator for up to a week.

Nectarines are a good source of vitamins A and C. One medium-sized fruit has 70 calories. As an added bonus, nectarines are a "detergent fruit," excellent for your teeth.

Nectarines are delicious simply washed and eaten out of hand. Try them sliced on cereal or pancakes; add slices of nectarine to fruit, fish or chicken salads. Sautéed, grilled or baked, nectarines are a delicious addition to meat or poultry dishes. Try serving nectarines with ice cream or plain yogurt, or poaching them in a water, sugar and white wine to serve them over pound cake or fresh sponge cake.

Nectarine Sort-of Pie

A delicious and original end to a meal.

3	eggs, well beaten	3
½ cup	milk	125 mL
½ cup	pastry flour	125 mL
	Pinch of salt	

	Filling	
2 cups	nectarines, sliced	500 mL
3 Tbsp	honey	50 mL
1 Tbsp	lemon juice	15 mL

| Sour cream |
| Cinnamon |

Beat the eggs, milk, pastry flour and salt together and pour the mixture into a buttered 9-inch/23-cm pie pan. Bake at 450° F/230° C for 15 minutes, pricking as needed to release some of the air. Bake at 350° F/180° C for another 10 minutes or until golden. Let the crust cool for a few minutes.

In a medium-sized bowl, blend the nectarines with the honey and let them stand for at least 5 minutes.

Sprinkle lemon juice on the cooked batter and cover with the nectarines and honey. Spread with sour cream and sprinkle with cinnamon. *Serves 6*

Oranges

Under this rather broad heading you can expect to find any orange-colored fruit larger than a kumquat. It is not really fair to lump mandarins, Clementines, Satsumas, Minneolas, tangelos and tangerines together under "oranges," because they are not oranges. However, it does seem the simplest way to deal with this diverse group of citrus fruits.

All members of the orange family are excellent sources of vitamin C, with approximately 62 calories in a single fruit.

The best of the orange season extends from November until April because this is when the Florida and California seasons are in full swing. The oranges from these two states are some of the sweetest and juiciest in the world. The season starts with several different types of seeded **Valencia** juice oranges, available from November to March, the two most common types being the Pineapple and the Hamlin. Both tend to be fibrous, although flavorful. Valencias are good for eating but are renowned for their juice. They are more fibrous than the Navels. California Valencias are on the market from late May until early-mid November. From Christmas, until mid-May, California provides the North American market with its most popular eating orange, the seedless **Navel**. It is the only orange which is consistently seedless, but it does not have the juiciness of the Valencias. The Navel orange usually peels easily and

Question: Are Florida or California oranges better? Pete explains: California oranges tend to look better—cleaner and brighter—but they are thicker skinned and less juicy than their Florida counterparts. A California fan can tell you that a California orange is infinitely better than a Florida orange, and vice-versa. But one thing that never varies is that most of California's oranges are grown to be eaten; Florida's are grown for processing.

separates into tender segments without any tough pith. Pete does, however, issue a warning: although Navels have a reputation for being sweet, and indeed, as the season progresses, some of the sweetest oranges are Navels, be careful with the early fruit as it can be a little sharp. California grows more Navels than Florida, and since North Americans are now beginning to see significant imports of Navel oranges from countries in the southern hemisphere, such as Argentina, Pete thinks that in a few years we will have a good supply of fresh Navels year-round.

It is worth noting that there are "specialty" oranges available in small quantities, at higher prices and for short periods of time. For about one month each year, we sell **Seville** oranges at Pete's. They are set well away from the rest of the oranges and adorned with a large sign which advises the unwary of their incredibly tart nature. I was warning one customer about eating them and she looked at me and said "Oh, I buy them to eat them." I asked her if she had ever eaten them before. "Sure have! I like them." My mouth fell open and I looked at her as if she was a lunatic. Then she grinned and added, "I like eating lemons too." Most of the Seville orange crop is processed and used in orange marmalade. The Seville orange rind is coveted for this purpose but the flesh is unpleasantly tart for most palates.

The other specialty orange worth mention is the **Blood** orange. Usually available for longer than the Seville orange and later in the year, their supply is also limited. These oranges are very popular in Mediterranean countries. They are inclined to be tart-sweet with a faint berry-like flavor. From the outside they look like any other orange, although they have a red blush. Inside they have the most incredible flesh, ranging in color from pink to burgundy, sometimes with beautiful slashes of brilliant red. Most Blood oranges are imported from Southern Italy.

Mandarin is a very broad term which encompasses all the different tangerines, satsumas and clementines. The original Japanese mandarin is now called a **Satsuma** and is grown in Japan, North America and Spain. More often than not, it is sold simply as a tangerine. It is a smallish, basically seedless fruit which is sweet and juicy. The **Clementine**, another variety of mandarin sometimes called the Clemie, is Pete's favorite in the mandarin family. It is seedless, with an easy-to-peel skin and a rich flavor. Grown chiefly in Morocco and southern Spain, it is available from December until February. The last member of the mandarin family, the **Tangerine**, is so called because it was developed in the North African country of Tangiers. There are numerous tangerine varieties; they are all generally small and fairly soft, having a deep-orange, pebbly skin and soft, sweet flesh. Most tangerines are available in profusion from December through February and in declining quantities through March and April.

Last but not least, we find the hybrid family of **Tangelos**, of which there are several types. Be careful of the fruit which arrives on the market in November because, as with other early oranges, it is inclined to be bitter. The most popular and very best tangelo, according to Pete, is the **Minneola**, which is available from Florida, in February and March. The Minneola tangelo, as distinct from the Minneola tangerine, is exquisitely juicy and flavorful, so tender "it'll mel' in your mouf, darlin' " and virtually seedless. It is not a particularly sweet fruit. Sometimes called a Honeybelle, it is hard to miss, being rather large and having a knobbly bump at one end. Tangelos are available from December to April.

The last "orange" which should be brought to light is the **Temple** orange, also known as the Royal mandarin by California growers, although it is neither an orange nor a mandarin, but a cross between a tangerine and an orange: a Tangor. Resembling a large tangerine, the Temple is very seedy, but wonderfully juicy and superbly sweet. Look for Temples from January until May.

Pete's Seville Thrill

12	Seville oranges	12
6 quarts	cold water	6 L
¼ cup	lemon juice	50 mL
8 cups	white sugar	4 L
6	red maraschino cherries, chopped	6

Peel the oranges and cook the peel in 6 quarts/6 L of cold water. Simmer until tender. Save 4 cups/1 L of the liquid and set aside.

Scrape the white pith from the peel and shred it to desired thickness and length. Add the retained liquid, lemon juice, the pulp and juice from the oranges. Bring to a boil, add the sugar and simmer for 2 to 3 hours. Add chopped maraschino cherries before pouring the mixture into hot, sterilized jars. *Makes 12 8-ounce/500-mL jars*

Papayas

Papaya, delicious raw, can also be enjoyed cooked. Chunks can be added around a roast and puréed papaya is delicious on meat, fish or poultry, especially with a squeeze of lemon juice.

Although we'll probably never see them, the rarely imported Mexican variety of papayas can grow as large as soccer balls and weigh from 10 to 15 pounds! The flesh of this variety is often a glorious salmon pink, although it varies from region to region. Ninety percent of the papayas which we find in our markets are the Solo variety, shipped from California and Hawaii. This South American fruit can be eaten ripe, as a fruit, or unripe, cooked like a zucchini.

The first time I tasted one was at Pete's. We had cut some of the ripe ones in half, garnished them with a few thin slices of lime and were selling them on the reduced shelf. I bought one and tasted it without the lime, and it immediately became clear to me why we were selling them with a slice of lime: the flesh is subtly sweet and demands the tart freshness of a lime.

Papayas are beautiful when cut in half. The flesh is a deep orange with a central cavity filled with tiny black seeds; when ripe it has a soft, juicy texture and a vaguely musky aroma.

Unfortunately, papayas are picked when still green in order to survive the rigors of shipping, so most of us in North America will never taste the extraordinary flavor of a tree-ripened papaya. Nevertheless, the ones I have tasted at Pete's are pretty wonderful, and if that's as close as I get, then I'm happy.

Papayas are available more or less all year because the plant has no specific fruiting or flowering time. Never buy green fruit as it may not ripen properly at home. Look for partially yellow fruit, and do not be put off by a spotted appearance, since the yellow coloring under all the marking is the important thing.

If the fruit is unripe, put it in a dark place at room temperature or, to speed things up, put it in a paper bag with a ripe banana. The fruit, when ripe, should give under gentle thumb pressure like a ripe avocado. Do not put papayas in the refrigerator unless they are completely ripe, even then do not keep them there for more than 2 days, and do not serve papaya chilled; cool temperatures deaden the taste.

Papaya is an excellent source of vitamins A and C and a good source of potassium and fiber. Raw papayas also contain the enzyme papain which allows the fruit to be used, like kiwi, as a meat tenderizer. Despite its sweetness, it has only 55 calories in 1 cup/250 mL of the flesh.

Papaya, like so many tropical fruit, is not cheap and it seems unfortunate to cook it when it is so delicious raw. But just in case you happen to run into a bumper crop of cheap papayas, I'll mention some things you can do with cooked papaya and some ways to cook it. Unripe papaya does cook well, retaining its shape and remaining firm. It is great cut in cubes and included in a kebab. Chunks of it can be added around a roast and cooked like roasted potatoes. Unpeeled halves are a natural container for salads or they can be filled with savory meat combinations and baked. Cooked, puréed papaya is delicious on meat or fish, or on poultry with a squirt of lime juice. Sautéed papaya is delicious with ice cream, on thin pancakes with a squeeze of lemon or lime, or on thin slices of pound cake. Uncooked papaya is wonderful alone, or in a fruit salad with slightly acidic fruits like pineapple, coconut or oranges. Above all, don't forget the lime. The fruit is lovely arranged with kiwi slices and strawberries or with a scoop of ice cream dropped into the pit cavity.

Papaya Ginger Ice Cream

There is a place in Toronto that makes truly magnificent ice cream, including the most heavenly papaya ginger ice cream. This recipe produces something which is very close to the original.

| 1 | completely ripe papaya, seeded, peeled and sliced | 1 |

2 Tbsp	candied ginger, finely minced	25 mL
3 Tbsp	white rum, or to taste	50 mL
¼ cup	sugar	50 mL
2 tsp	maple syrup, or corn syrup	10 mL
2 cups	milk, chilled	500 mL

Toss the papaya, ginger and rum together in a bowl. Sprinkle with the sugar and let the flavors blend for about an hour, letting the fruit stand at room temperature and occasionally giving it a gentle stir. Purée the papaya and its "marinade" in a food processor and with the processor still running, gradually pour in the milk. Add more rum and sugar if you like. Pour the mixture into an ice cream maker and proceed according to the manufacturer's instructions.

This ice cream improves if stored in the freezer for a day or two.

Passion fruit

For years I thought this fruit was named for the reaction that it elicited from its eaters. Not so. It was named by Christian missionaries who saw the symbols of Christ's Passion in the flowers of the passion fruit tree. Nevertheless, I am sure that I am not alone in my passionate feelings toward this little treat. I was familiar with the flavor of passion fruit before I actually ate one. One summer in France, I worked at a crêperie where we had a great deal of trouble finding passion fruit juice, a vital ingredient in some cocktails! When we finally found it, I decided to taste it to find out what all the fuss was about. It was wonderful. I was delighted when six months and 4,000 miles later, I encountered passion fruit once again, this time at Pete's. I bought one, tasted it and, surprisingly, it tasted exactly like the juice. Even if the fruit did not evoke such powerful and pleasant memories, I think that I would still find some passion for the little wrinkled purple thing.

There are several types of passion fruit, but only two that North Americans really need to know about: the small brownish-purple ones (2 to 3 inches/5 to 7 cm in diameter) which sometimes sport purple labels saying "Wrinkled is ripe" and the larger (2 to 3 inches/5 to 7 cm in diameter) yellow or orange hard-shelled fruit. The small round fruit is sold at Pete's as passion fruit, the larger spherical fruit as granadilla. They taste very similar: tart but sweet, rather like a mixture of jasmine, banana and lime, and are so rich and powerful that it is almost as difficult to forget as it is to describe.

It's helpful to know what the flesh of the fruit looks like. I bought a granadilla at Pete's a few months ago, broke the shell open and did a tour among my co-workers, offering them all a taste. They all, without exception, declined, and I must admit I was not especially surprised. It doesn't look like much just sitting there. A granadilla, for instance, has a hard, smooth shell which protects the flesh from drying out. Inside are a lot of black seeds sitting in what looks rather like cloudy grapefruit flesh. The seeds are edible and provide a little crunch in what looks and feels like semi-set jello.

The purple passion fruit is much the same except that this gelatinous fruit is yellow and surrounded by a thin, tough skin which is wrinkled when the fruit is ripe. As for the taste? The granadilla is slightly more subtle in flavor than the passion fruit and a little more perfumed without the edge. Both are totally heavenly!

Granadillas, Florida's passion fruit, are available from late summer until about Christmas time. Passion fruit from New Zealand are available from early spring until early summer. At Pete's we have also had passion fruit from Colombia and Ecuador. So, with occasional breaks when the supply of passion fruit is a little low, these tropical delights are available all year.

It is hard to get a passion fruit that is past its prime, because its prime lasts for quite a while. If the skin is wrinkled and shriveled, buy it! The fruit is ready to eat. If the skin is smooth and firm and the fruit still rounded, keep it at room temperature until the skin is dimpled and the fruit sounds loose and damp when shaken. Granadillas are a gorgeous orange-yellow when ripe and because of this shell, completely un-wrinkled. Passion fruit should be stored in the refrigerator when completely ripe, preferably in a protected spot so that it won't be knocked or squashed by anything else.

There are several ways to eat passion fruit or gran-adillas. The way Pete prefers is simply to cut away the

Like many tropical fruit, passion fruit blends particularly well with other fruit. Try passion fruit with bananas, kiwi fruit and grapes since these four seem to get along especially well. But be careful not to overwhelm the fruit; mix it with delicately-flavored ingredients or eat it, as Pete prefers it, with absolutely nothing else.

skin or shell and scoop out the flesh—an especially delicious treat if the fruit is slightly chilled. Some people like to add a drop or two of lemon or lime juice, others like passion fruit with a little sugar. The flesh is superb with vanilla or fruit ice creams, or you can mix it in with whipped cream or sour cream and serve it with fruit salad.

Passion fruit has some vitamin C and, unless strained, is a good source of fiber. One passion fruit has about 15 calories.

Passion Fruit and Mango à la Pete

This is true decadence and absolute bliss.

4	passion fruit	4
1	ripe mango	1
1 Tbsp	butter	15 mL
2 tsp	sugar	10 mL
2 Tbsp	Cointreau	25 mL
2 Tbsp	brandy	25 mL

Scoop the flesh and seeds out of the passion fruit and cut the flesh from the skin. Stone the mango. Mix the fruit with the butter and sugar. Add the brandy and Cointreau and flambé the mixture.

If you really want to go overboard on decadence, serve it with ice cream. But be warned . . . you may never recover! *Serves 1 to 4, depending on your generosity*

Peaches

Serve peach slices on your cereal in the morning, or add them to pancakes, waffles or French toast. The fruit is delicious with roast chicken or pork, grilled or raw.

Often referred to as "The Queen of Fruit," the peach is among the four most popular fruit in North America. Little will delight a family more than a shopper returning home with a six-liter basket of ripe peaches.

Look for local peaches at your market and at farmers' markets, since there are many varieties of flavorful peaches which are not widely available simply because they do not travel particularly well. The newer varieties of the fruit are firmer, bigger but not as sweet, yet since they stand up better to the rigors of packing and shipping, they are more commonly available.

Basically there are two types of peaches: freestone and clingstone. In a ripe freestone peach, the stone will almost fall out into your hand when you cut the fruit in half. In a clingstone, the fruit is firmly attached to the stone and needs to be pried out, no matter how ripe the fruit is. Most of the fruit available early in the season is clingstone or semi-freestone; many of the later varieties are freestone. Clingstones tend to have firmer flesh; freestones have a little more flavor.

The peak season for domestic peaches is from mid-May to early October. During the winter months, from late December to March, fruit is imported from Chile and New Zealand. You cannot tell whether or a peach is fresh by looking at the red blush. What is important is the background color. In a good fruit, it will be cream colored, or better yet, yellow. Avoid fruit whose background color is green. It means that the fruit has probably been harvested when immature and will not ripen properly. Unripe peaches will ripen at home on the counter out of direct sunlight or more quickly in a loosely closed paper bag.

For eating out of hand you will want soft, ripe peaches. For cooking and using later on, choose firm, ripe fruit. Ripening peaches at home will not make the fruit sweeter but will soften it and make it juicier. Keep the ripe fruit in the refrigerator in a plastic or paper bag for up to 5 days.

Peaches are a good source of vitamins A and C and potassium. A medium-sized fruit has about 45 calories.

A fresh peach is delicious simply eaten out of hand. Give it a good rinse and if you are not partial to fuzz, peel it. By rubbing your thumb over the fruit, you can remove most of the fuzz and still get the added fiber of the skin.

You can also make a wonderful all-purpose concoction of peaches and honey by slicing some peaches, setting them in a bowl and drizzling a little honey over them. How much depends on how sweet your peaches and how sweet your tooth. Cover this mixture and let it sit. The whole thing blends together

The easiest way to peel a peach is to peel it the same way you peel a tomato. Give the fruit about 15 to 30 seconds in boiling water, lift it out, immerse it in ice water and when cool, peel it with a knife.

wonderfully, with the juice of the peaches and the honey making a delicious light sauce which really enhances the fruit. Serve the fruit alone or with sour cream, yogurt or ice cream. Add a little raspberry sauce for a Peach Melba. With fresh pound cake, some whipped cream and a little Cognac or brandy, you have a gourmet delight.

Peach and Blueberry Bliss

2 pounds	peaches peeled, pitted and sliced	1 kg
1 pint	blueberries, washed	500 mL
½ cup	sugar	125 mL
1 cup	all purpose flour	250 mL
1 tsp	baking powder	5 mL
¼ tsp	salt	1 mL
1	egg	1
5 Tbsp	butter, melted	75 mL
1 tsp	cinnamon	5 mL
1 tsp	vanilla extract	5 mL

Put the peaches in a well-oiled 2-quart/2-L casserole. Cover with the berries and sprinkle with a little of the sugar.

Mix the remaining sugar, baking powder, salt and cinnamon in a medium-sized bowl. Add the egg and mix until coarsely blended and the dry ingredients are dampened. Sprinkle the sugar mixture over the fruit and drizzle with melted butter.

Bake, uncovered, on the highest shelf in the oven for 15 minutes at 375° F/190° C, then bake for another 10 to 15 minutes at 400° F/205° C or until the topping is golden.

Serve the casserole hot, warm, cool, cold, anyway at all. Try it with ice cream or yogurt. *Serves 6*

Peach-Orange Frozen Yogurt

Even more refreshing than ice cream on a hot day is frozen yogurt, and this one is really special.

¼ cup	sugar	50 mL
1 Tbsp	unflavored gelatin	15 mL

½ cup	golden corn syrup	125 mL
1 cup	orange juice	250 mL
5	large ripe peaches, peeled, halved and pitted	5
1 Tbsp	lemon juice	15 mL
3 cups	plain yogurt	750 mL
1 tsp	vanilla extract	5 mL
	Grated rind of ½ an orange	

Mix the sugar and gelatine and blend in the corn syrup and orange juice. Simmer over low heat until the sugar and gelatin dissolve. Cool for 15 minutes.

Purée the peaches and lemon juice in a blender or food processor. Blend the fruit with the gelatin mixture.

Whisk the yogurt in a large bowl and gradually blend in the gelatin and peach mixture. Stir in the vanilla and orange rind.

Pour the mixture into a loaf pan and cover with plastic or foil. Freeze until firm, stirring a few times while freezing. *Makes 1½ quarts/1.5 L*

Pears

I grew up without any particular fondness for pears. They seemed to me a rather dull version of an apple, but working for Pete over the last few years has given me a new appreciation for these heavenly creatures. I think now I would choose a pear over an apple any day.

The key to pears is eating them at their peak—not too early and not too late. I tended to be impatient and eat the fruit too soon, sacrificing flavor for texture. Never again. The flavor of a fresh, ripe pear is only enhanced by its buttery softness. Boscs, d'Anjous, Bartletts or Packhams are all sweet, juicy delights in their own right. They are an excellent source of fiber and each one contains about 99 calories.

Pears are available all year, with different types at different times. For cooking, choose Boscs, d'Anjous and Bartletts at the firm-ripe stage. For eating, pears should be soft-ripe, yielding to gentle pressure. Have you ever wondered why there are so many unripe pears in your market? Maybe it's different where you shop, but at Pete's, most of the pears sell before they are ripe. It is because they have a finer flavor and are smoother textured when they are ripened off the tree, so they are picked, shipped and sold mature, but green.

Occasionally at Pete's we come across a crate of pears which has ripened, but for the most part, we put them out and sell them before they are perfectly ripe. If you buy your pears unripe, remember that they can take up to 7 days to ripen completely. Be patient; they are worth it! Bartletts and Packhams become a beautiful rich yellow when they are ripe; D'Anjous may remain green or turn slightly yellow and Boscs become a warm cinnamon. To ripen pears, keep them in a warm spot in a loosely closed paper bag. If you wish, you can keep the pears in the refrigerator for a week or two to slow the ripening process.

Bartletts, probably the most popular domestic variety of pear, are the first to appear on the North American market, being available from July to November. They are bell-shaped, with a thin, clear, yellow skin when ripe. There is also a red Bartlett which is a surprisingly bright crimson but like the regular Bartlett in taste and shape. They also tend to be a little smaller than their yellow cousins. A fresh, ripe Bartlett is extremely juicy with a rich flavor and smooth white flesh.

D'Anjous are available from October to May. Anjous, as they are commonly called, are largish pears with a short neck. The flesh is a yellowish white, with a juicy, spicy flavor. The texture is buttery and can be a bit granular near the center. The fruit may be yellow, greenish yellow or even green when ripe. The stem end however, should yield to gentle thumb pressure. The importance of letting Anjou pears ripen cannot be overstated. I ate them for years while they were still hard and granular and, unfortunately, almost flavorless. Let them ripen completely and they become a delicious, mellow fruit.

Bosc are often called the "aristocrat of pears," and it is easy to see and taste why. This winter variety has a completely different type of appeal than the others, tending to be smaller with a slender, tapering neck and beautiful dark yellow skin overlaid with a brownish color. The flesh is yellowish white, juicy, crunchy and buttery with a tendency to be slightly granular in the middle. A superb pear for eating fresh or for cooking.

Packhams, a later winter variety, are medium to large, with a bumpy surface. This leading spring import variety looks rather like a Bartlett—although perhaps not quite as symmetrical—and like a Bartlett, it turns from green to yellow as it ripens. The skin is thicker on a Packham than a Bartlett, but the flesh is more buttery and the flavor noticeably richer.

One cannot continue without mentioning the **Passe Crassane** and **Comice** pears. Both of these varieties are hard to find, but if you are lucky enough to trip over some in a market during the autumn or winter months, *do not pass by.* They are the most glorious of all pears, and their taste is exquisite. The Passe Crassane, imported from France, is an apple-shaped pear with skin like that of a ripe Bosc. The richly flavored flesh is juicy, sweet and granular, with a dry after-taste. Pete describes it as having a flavor that will "blow your taste buds away!" The Comice is also roundish with a thick, greenish-yellow skin which is occasionally russeted. Its juicy flesh will literally melt in your mouth.

While discussing pears, Pete could not help but express dismay at the fact that Canadians eat pears like apples. He explained that the way to eat a pear is to pull the stem out and eat down, from the top to the bottom. It was a relief to discover that I eat pears correctly!

Pears are delicious eaten out of hand, if properly ripe. For an easy appetizer, wrap pear wedges with slices of smoked meat or ham. Firm ripe pears are also a tasty addition to a fruit or poultry salad. Serve pears for dessert with blue cheese or Brie. Sliced, drizzled with orange liqueur, dusted with cinnamon and served on sour cream or yogurt, they are bliss! Try sautéed pears with chopped, preserved ginger and a scoop of vanilla ice cream. For a light dessert, poach pears in a thin syrup for 10 minutes.

For eating out of hand, pears should be soft-ripe, yielding to gentle pressure. They have a finer flavor when they are ripened off the tree, which is why you should usually buy them under-ripe.

Pear Tart

	Pastry to line a 9-inch/23-cm pie pan or a 10-inch/25-cm flan pan	
5 or 6	firm ripe pears, cored, thinly sliced and peeled, if you wish	5 or 6
	Sugar	
1 Tbsp	vanilla extract	15 mL
3 Tbsp	butter	40 mL
	Icing sugar	

Line a pie or flan pan with the pastry. Arrange the pears on the pastry, sprinkle them with a little sugar, drizzle them with vanilla and dot them with butter. Bake for 30 minutes at 425° F/218° C or until golden. Remove from oven, sprinkle with icing sugar and broil for a few minutes, just so the sugar melts and glazes the pie. Don't let it burn.

Gingery Poached Pears

This recipe is a specialty of some friends of mine in Toronto and one of Pete's favorite desserts for a spicy meal.

6	medium-sized firm pears, Bartletts or Boscs	6
1 cup	water	250 mL
¼ cup	sugar	50 mL
	Rind of 2 lemons, finely grated	
	Juice of one lemon	
3 Tbsp	preserved ginger, finely diced	50 mL
2 Tbsp	Cognac or rum	25 mL

Using a saucepan big enough to hold all the pears upright, mix the water, sugar, lemon juice and rind over moderate heat until the mixture comes to a boil. Stir in the ginger and remove from heat. Carefully peel the pears. If they won't stand up alone, trim the bottoms a little so they do. Stand the pears in the syrup in the saucepan. Cover and cook the pears, basting frequently, over medium heat for 15 to 20 minutes, or until the pears pierce easily with a toothpick. When the pears are tender, place in a large serving dish or in individual bowls.

Boil the syrup, uncovered, for another 5 to 10 minutes. Add the Cognac or rum and pour the sauce over the pears, basting frequently until cool. Cover and chill. *Serves 6*

Pepinos

Pepino means cucumber in Spanish, a name well-suited to this melon. Its flavor is refreshing like a cucumber and rather bland like a cucumber; even the texture is cucumber-like. The flavor varies from one specimen to another, but it is usually a very subtle blend of honeydew and cantaloupe, a nuance which may be too subtle for North American tastes. The texture is certainly that of a melon, smooth and juicy but not as sweet. When I asked what the fruit tasted like at Pete's, someone described it to me as "a cross between bananas, pineapple and strawberries." I tasted it, and although Geoff, Pete's right-hand man, was enthusiastic, I was a little baffled. Its taste was almost unnoticeable. I had a sneaking suspicion that the first one we tasted was under-ripe. I tried another one and the flavor was more pronounced but still very subtle. Try one for yourself and see. Pete enjoys them, and he is very particular, so they must be good! He adds that the fruit has to be very ripe before it is eaten and most people simply don't wait long enough.

Although pepinos are worth trying, I doubt that there will be a line-up of customers waiting to stock up on them the next time they are in season. They have been around for about 60 years and are still not very popular, except in Japan, where subtlety in food is prized.

The tiny pepino is available from February to mid-May from New Zealand and Peru, and from August to December from California. It is exotic in appearance and does not at all resemble a melon. Usually between 2 and 4 inches long, it is shaped like a teardrop with satiny smooth skin and a pale yellowish base covered with streaks or splotches of purple, which deepens to a gold color when the fruit is ripe. Pepinos will ripen nicely at room temperature, out of direct sun. Once the skin under the purple markings is golden, the fruit is ready to eat. Although it will keep for a few days in a plastic or paper bag in the refrigerator, its delicate nature means that it is not at its best for very long so eat it when its at its best. When ripe, the fruit should feel like a ripe plum, firm but not squishy.

Pepinos are low in calories, like most melons, and high in vitamin C and potassium.

Like all members of the melon family, pepinos are

Pepinos are a very delicate fruit. Hold one to your nose and inhale deeply. The aroma is superb and distinctly sweet, although very faint.

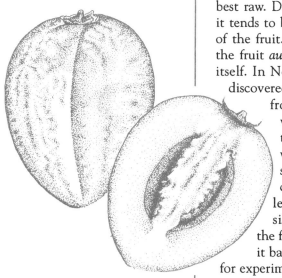

best raw. Distributors say that the skin is edible, but it tends to be tough and does not enhance the flavor of the fruit. The Japanese and South Americans eat the fruit *au naturel,* with nothing, in nothing, all by itself. In New Zealand, where the fruit is just being discovered and where most of our pepinos come from, the melon is served in 101 different ways, from an hors d'oeuvres, to garnishes, to desserts. Try thin slices of pepino wrapped in prosciutto, or lightly sautéed sliced pepinos served with meat. For dessert, try one with a squeeze of lime or lemon. Pete's favorite pepino dessert consists of scooping the flesh out of halves of the fruit, mixing it with ice cream and heaping it back in the empty half skins. It is crying out for experimentation. Buy some and see what you can create!

Persimmons

An unripe persimmon is perhaps one of the most cosmetically beautiful fruit, so perfect that it almost looks unreal. There are two major varieties of this Chinese native available in North America. The heart-shaped **Hachiya** and the **Fuyu** which looks rather like a ripe tomato.

Persimmons are available from September until Christmas, being most abundant from mid-October until the end of November. In November and December, California persimmons are on the market and, to quote our friend Pete, "dirt cheap." Occasionally, you will find persimmons earlier in the year, from Chile, Brazil or Israel, but as yet, these fruits are very expensive because of the shipping costs.

If you buy persimmons before they are ripe, simply store them in a cool, dark place or in a loosely closed paper bag with an apple or banana until they are ripe. A hard Fuyu tastes like a cross between a date and an apple and can be eaten and enjoyed before it is ripe, but the Hachiya must feel like a sack full of water before it is ready to eat. It is very difficult to watch the fruit pass through what looks like perfect ripeness to overripeness, but trust the word of an expert. Pete says that to North American eyes the ripe fruit will appear overripe, but please be patient: once the fruit looks a little ugly and shriveled, it is perfect for eating. If anyone tells you that you can ripen persimmons by freezing them, don't listen—the fruit will soften, but it retains a bitter taste and becomes mushy. If you want to keep the fruit once it is ripe, you can store it briefly in the refrigerator in a plastic bag.

The persimmon is an excellent source of vitamins A and C and has lots of fiber and potassium. A 4-ounce/120-gram serving contains about 90 calories.

This gorgeous little fruit is amazingly versatile and can be used in breads, cookies, puddings, cakes or pies, although it seems rather a waste for a fruit which is virtually perfect solo. Try cutting a Hachiya in half and simply spooning the fruit into your mouth—you really can't eat it without a spoon. You might like to try scooping the flesh into a bowl and eating it with cream or milk. Or try pushing the flesh through a sieve and using it as a sauce for other fruit, a light cake or a pudding. If you want to enhance the sweetness of the flesh, add some freshly squeezed lime juice. Cutting the fruit in half, sprinkle it with brown sugar and, dotting it with a little butter, place it under the broiler for no more than one minute, just 'til the sugar begins to bubble. Serve it with sour cream, whipping cream, yogurt or ice cream— buttered almond ice cream is especially good. The Fuyu can be sliced while still firm and added to vegetable or fruit salads, or it can be enjoyed on its own. The peel is edible but may be removed if you prefer it that way.

Persimmon Pudding

1 cup	sifted flour	250 mL
½ tsp	baking soda	2 mL
½ cup	sugar	125 mL
½ tsp	salt	2 mL
¼ tsp	cinnamon	1 mL
¼ tsp	nutmeg	1 mL
1 cup	persimmon pulp	250 mL

2	eggs, well beaten	2
1 cup	milk	250 mL
1½ Tbsp	butter, melted	25 mL
½ cup	sliced almonds	125 mL

Mix the flour, soda, sugar, salt and spices. In a separate bowl, mix the persimmon pulp, the eggs, milk, butter and nuts. Blend the two mixtures into a soft batter, adding a little more milk if it is too dry. Pour the batter into a buttered casserole and bake at 350° F/180° C for 30 to 45 minutes. Serve hot with whipped cream. *Serves 4*

Persimmons are deceptive little creatures and have surprised a lot of unwary consumers They look perfectly ripe when they are nowhere near it. So now, when you are ready to try a persimmon, make sure, especially if you have a Hachiya in your hand, that it is ripe before you use it. It should look shriveled and a little ugly.

Pineapples

Pineapples, named because of their resemblance to pine cones, should be picked at their peak of ripeness and flavor because they have no starch to convert to sugar; pineapples do not ripen once they have been harvested. Pineapples will soften somewhat and lose some of their acidity, but they do not get any riper.

Pineapples are available all year, with the peak season occurring from April to June. When choosing a pineapple, look for one that is as plump and as large as possible. Deep green, crisp-looking crown leaves are a good sign of freshness. Check out the core on the base of the pineapple for any blackness, which indicates that the pineapple has started to ferment. Don't bother trying to pull out the central leaves of the crown—this won't tell you anything except whether or not the leaves come out easily—which isn't really much good to anyone. A sweet ripe fruit may have a fragrant pleasant aroma—a good indication but not a guarantee, because some lovely fruit will not smell.

There are some renegade pineapple sellers on the market who will harvest the fruit before it is ripe. At Pete's, we have had some exquisite fruit from several of these unknowns. But on the whole, you will be more likely to get a good fruit if you buy one marketed by a name you recognize.

Pineapples do not store particularly well, so use the fruit as soon as possible. If you will not be using it promptly, you can leave it out on the counter, away from direct sunlight, for up to 2 days. A cut pineapple can be kept in plastic in the refrigerator for 4 days, but it too should be used as soon as possible. Four ounces/120 grams of fresh pineapple has 60 calories.

Raw pineapple is an excellent source of vitamin C and contains an enzyme called bromelin which tenderizes meat and prevents gelatin from setting.

Although some markets offer fresh peeled, cored, sliced pineapple this is not true for all of them. So if you are not blessed with a fruit market possessing a pineapple peeler and corer, do not despair. Cutting the fruit for yourself is not particularly difficult. First, slice off the bottom of the pineapple so that it will sit on the counter comfortably, then stand it on its end and cut the skin off with long vertical strokes of a sharp knife. Remove the eyes individually with the tip of a knife, or cut long thin diagonal grooves around the fruit on either side of the eyes. (The latter is slightly more decorative.) Then slice the fruit in quarters lengthwise and cut out the core. You can give the core pieces to the kids for something to chew on. It is tasty but so fibrous that you simply chew it for a while and then spit out the pulp. It is also a favorite snack at Pete's, indulged in by the one chosen to put pineapples through the peeling and coring machine.

The sweet juicy taste of pineapples make them a natural addition to a fruit salad and delicious in combination with chicken, turkey, tuna or cheese, either a mild, solid or cream cheese. A half-pineapple hollowed out can also make an attractive bowl for pineapple dishes. Try filling one with a combination of melon balls or cubes, sliced strawberries, sliced kiwi, grapes or orange sections, and grate some fresh coconut on top. Add some pineapple chunks to your next coleslaw for a juicy delicious surprise. For an interesting tasty appetizer, wrap cubes of pineapple with smoked meat or ham. For a great low-calorie snack or dessert, top a slice of pineapple with a scoop of cottage cheese. Explore a bit—pineapple is a natural in almost any combination.

Pineapple Orange Sorbet

½ cup	light corn syrup	125 mL
2 cups	sour cream	500 mL
1 to 1½ cups	pineapple, finely chopped, with juice	250 to 375 mL
6-ounces	orange juice concentrate (1 can frozen orange juice)	375-mL

Blend the corn syrup and sour cream until smooth. Add the pineapple and orange juice. Pour the mixture into an ice cream canister and freeze according to the manufacturer's instructions, or pour the mixture into a baking pan, cover and freeze for 4 hours, stirring 2 or 3 times. *Makes 1½ quarts/1.5 L*

Pineapple Tropical Cream

Add a little Cointreau or tropical liqueur for a touch of something special.

2 cups	shredded pineapple	500 mL
¼ cup	sugar	50 mL
1 Tbsp	lime juice	15 mL
1 cup	whipping cream, whipped	250 mL
¼ tsp	ground nutmeg	1 mL

Combine the pineapple, sugar and lime juice. Fold in the whipped cream and nutmeg. Chill. *Serves 4*

Plums

The plum is a fruit that comes in almost every color, shape and flavor imaginable. But there are two clear distinctions—Japanese and European plums. During the peak seasons, most North Americans have easy access to both types of plums, although the Japanese varieties, grown in California, are more common. Medium to large and famous for their juiciness, they come in various shapes but are *never* purple or blue. European varieties, on the other hand, are *always* blue or purple and generally smaller and firmer, with a milder flavor. It is the European plums which are dried to make prunes.

Plums are available from early June to early October and during the winter months, from mid-January to mid-March. It can be tricky to tell ripe fruit if you are buying the dark-skinned plums, but look for fruit which is deeply colored. A ripe plum will have a little give when lightly squeezed.

Store ripe plums, unwashed, in a plastic or paper bag for up to 4 days in the refrigerator. Fruit will ripen if left on the counter for a few days, out of direct sunlight; to hurry things up a little, put the fruit in a paper bag and leave it loosely closed, but keep an eye on them as the fruit ripens quickly.

Plums are rich in vitamins A and C. The European variety has a little less than half the calories of the Japanese; an average Japanese plum has 55 calories, a European 20.

Plums are often cooked to bring out the best flavor of the fruit. Stewed plums are a delicious treat, particularly with kids! Particularly suited to poaching, give them about 5 to 10 minutes in sugared water. Prick the skin before cooking, so they don't explode, and serve them with cognac or port.

Plums are delicious eaten out of hand; give them a wash and they are ready. Pete's personal favorite for out of hand eating is the Laroda, a beautiful, juicy, red-skinned plum available early to mid-summer. The Japanese variety of plum is nice in fruit or chicken salads. Try plums sliced in cream, or fill the pit cavities of a European-type plum with a soft cheese like Camembert.

Deep-Dish Plum Pie

It seems logical to make a pie with only a top or a bottom, especially when dealing with fresh fruit. It gives you more fruit to enjoy and fewer calories!

Don't be alarmed by how easy this recipe is. Both Pete and my mum make a plum pie this way, and it is both easy and delicious. The only problem is getting it sweet enough, but not too sweet. I like it a little tart, something which might be worth keeping in mind when you make this pie.

5 cups	plums	1.25 L
¼ cup	sugar	50 mL
2 Tbsp	flour	25 mL
2 tsp	cinnamon	10 mL
	Pastry for the top of one 9-inch/23-cm pie	
	Sugar and cinnamon	

Choose your favorite casserole or deep pie dish and assemble enough plums to fill it. Then cut the fruit in half, remove the stones and place the pulp in a casserole. Layer the fruit with the sugar and flour, mixing the cinnamon in with the sugar. Cover the casserole with pastry and seal it to the sides of the dish. Cut slits in the top to allow the steam to escape and bake at 400° F/200° C until the pastry is golden and the fruit bubbling. Remove from the oven and sprinkle the crust with a little sugar and a touch of cinnamon. I told you it was easy!

Pomegranates

Pomegranates originated in Persia where they reputedly kept numerous travelers alive on treks through the desert and where they gave the brilliant red color to Persian rugs. The broken skin and juice of pomegranates make an excellent dye. The thick skin that made them invaluable in desert treks also made them one of the most common exotic fruits—available a long time before importing exotic fruit was as popular as it is now. (I remember buying a pomegranate for lunch at a corner store about twelve years ago.) The fruit will keep for a long time, well protected by its skin.

A pomegranate is a fruit which must be eaten at a leisurely pace. The name comes from the Latin *pomum granatum* meaning apple of many seeds. From the outside, the fruit does, indeed, resemble a *pomum*. It is the size of a large apple having a leathery skin which is a mottled, deep, reddish-purple. Inside there are hundreds of little seeds, each surrounded by translucent, crimson flesh, held in place and shown to advantage by a coarse, ivory colored, inedible membrane. A mouthful of the little ruby gems is a mouthful of tangy-sweet, juicy flavor.

Pomegranates are available from fall to early winter. Look for large fruit with deep color. A heavier fruit will have more juice. The skin should appear as if it is having trouble holding itself together around its rosy contents. Pomegranates will keep in the refrigerator for 3 months. You can pack the seeds in an airtight container and pop them in the freezer where they'll keep for about 3 months. When you want to use them, just scrape out as much as you think you'll

In many Eastern and Mediterranean cultures, pomegranate seeds are used as a garnish. Their wonderful sweet-sour flavor enhances almost everything. Try adding a handful to your next green salad!

need and sprinkle them, still frozen, into the dish which you are preparing.

Pomegranates are loaded with potassium and vitamin C. You can count on about 110 calories per fruit.

Removing the skin is a fine art, yet surprisingly simple when you know how. When I was growing up, I ate pomegranates by breaking them in half and digging the seeds out with my fingers—a dangerous method if you care about your clothes. Now I simply split the skin carefully with a knife from the calyx—the little crown—to the stem end and peel back the skin. The seeds can then be gently removed, while taking care not to pierce the flesh.

Grenadine

2 cups	pomegranate seeds, cut from 2 large pomegranates	500 mL
2 cups	sugar	500 mL

Mix the seeds and sugar in a saucepan (not an aluminum one) and mash them until all of the little juice sacs have been broken. Let the liquid mixture stand overnight or up to 24 hours.

Bring the liquid to a boil, stirring constantly. Turn the heat to low and simmer for 2 minutes. Strain juice through a cheesecloth, wringing it to extract the liquid. Pour the liquid into a sterilized jar and cover it with a clean towel until cool. Remove the cloth, cap the jar and refrigerate.

This drink was traditionally made with pomegranates but as with many things these days, it is often made with substitutes. Making the real thing isn't difficult and not only is it better for you, but the taste is far superior to today's commercial grenadine.

Quince

I remember the first time I saw quince: it was at Pete's, not too long ago. They are a rather unusual looking fruit but I immediately felt drawn to them, first because they looked rather lonely—we only had about twenty at the stall—and second because my father's favorite jelly is quince jelly. I had been asking what a quince was for years and received vague explanations, but I couldn't help but feel a little excitement when I saw the real thing!

This member of the apple family, which was once

very common, has become less so over the years, probably because it was most often used for jams and jellies. Unfortunately, it has now become a specialty item which, like Seville oranges, is available only in small quantities.

Quince can be the shape of a delicious apple or a pear, and can vary in color from golden to yellow with red flecks; it can also be smooth-skinned or covered with a woolly fuzz. There is little that is constant about the quince except its aroma, which is strongly musky with a hint of pear or pineapple. In fact, you can put a quince in your closet for a few months to scent your clothes.

Quince are available in the fall, imported from California, from September until November. Look for large, smooth fruit because there is a lot of waste and work in preparing smaller or gnarled fruit. If you can't find unmarked fruit, don't forget that the fruit should most often be cooked—a process which covers a multitude of sins. Quince will keep for a couple of months individually wrapped in a double layer of plastic and stored in the refrigerator. But be sure to put them in a corner of the refrigerator where they won't get bumped, since the fruit bruises very easily.

Quince are rich in fiber, are a good source of vitamin C and provide some potassium. There are 65 calories in four ounces/120 grams of the raw fruit.

Baked Quince

The fruit in this dish turns a wonderful pinky gold and the taste of baked quince and honey is gorgeous. Serve it warm with ice cream, sour cream or yogurt, or to accompany chicken or pork.

2 pounds	quince, peeled, cored and sliced	1 kg
5 Tbsp	mild honey	75 mL
2 Tbsp	lime juice	25 mL
6 Tbsp	water	100 mL
¼ cup	sliced almonds	50 mL

Overlap the quince slices in a large rectangular baking dish and drizzle with honey to coat the slices. Sprinkle the fruit with lime juice and water. Cover tightly.

Bake at 300° F/150° C for 45 minutes or until the quince are tender. Remove the cover and turn the heat up to 425° F/218° C; sprinkle with the almonds and bake for 10 minutes until the liquid is thickened and the slices golden. *Serves 4*

Quince and Almond Tart

One of Pete's regular customers brought us each a sample of this tart one day. We *all* asked her for the recipe the next time she was in.

3 cups	water	750 mL
2 cups	sugar	500 mL
	Juice of 1 lime	
3 to 4 pounds	quince, peeled, cored and sliced, with the seeds placed in a cheesecloth bag	1.5 to 2 kg
1	stick cinnamon	1
2	whole cloves	2
	Pastry for bottom and latticework top of a 9-inch/ 23-cm pie	
4 Tbsp	almonds, lightly roasted	60 mL

Boil the water, sugar and lime juice for one minute; add the quince, the cheesecloth bag containing the seeds and the spices. (The pectin in the seeds will help thicken the syrup.) Bring the mixture to the boil, turn down the heat and simmer for 1½ hours or until the juice is thick, stirring occasionally. Remove the seeds, cloves and cinnamon. (If you want to stop here, you will have quince jam!)

Fill a pastry-lined pie or quiche dish with the quince mixture and cover with a lattice work top. Bake at 375° F/190° C for 20 to 30 minutes. Remove the tart from the oven and sprinkle with the almonds. Cool for at least 4 hours or overnight. Serve with whipped cream, sour cream, vanilla ice cream or yogurt.

Rambutans

Rambutans are eaten the same way as lychees and can be used as a substitute for lychees, but you will have to allow for the fact that the fruit is not as sweet or as juicy. The most wonderful way to serve rambutans is peeled and seeded, with coffee ice cream.

Rambutans are funny-looking little fruit, looking more like creatures than fruit. About 2 inches/5 cm in diameter, reddish brown in color and covered with soft, flexible spikes, they look like an odd form of miniature hedgehog. They are also known as hairy lychees, a name which refers not only to their spikes but to their taste as well: the hairy for the spikes, the lychee for the taste. I may be alone in thinking that rambutan suffers in comparison to the lychee, because I am hopelessly partial to lychees. Rambutans are not as sweet, not as juicy and not as richly flavored or scented as lychees.

When eaten on their own, without comparison, rambutans are a nice, delicately flavored, delicately scented tropical fruit, tasting and smelling vaguely like a mix of lychee and coconut. Covered with a thick, slightly flexible skin with a lengthwise seam running around the outside, the rambutan hides a tight, white, slightly opaque flesh, which has a texture similar to a lychee although drier and more granular. The flesh is thin around the brown, oblong, inedible seed, with a hard central section on the area which surrounds the seed.

Rambutans are available off and on from April to October. Look for fruit which feels firm but not hard. Fruit with a rosy hue tends to be fresher; a brown, shriveled skin is a sign of old age. Rambutans may be kept in a plastic bag in the refrigerator for up to a week.

Rambutans may be enjoyed the same way as lychees, eaten raw by simply cutting the skin open along its seam. The flesh is also nice wrapped in thin strips of ham or prosciutto and served as an appetizer.

Rambutans are wonderful in a light syrup flavored with lemon and crystallized ginger, or in any recipe which calls for lychees, although you must compensate for the fact that rambutans are not as sweet or as juicy as lychees.

Raspberries

Although most of us are familiar enough with the red raspberry, it is interesting to know that this fruit is also black, golden, purple, yellow and amber, although it is unlikely that you will run across anything but the red raspberry, which is still the popular favorite and the most common. Most of us have delicious memories of fabulous desserts made with this delicately flavored and textured berry. It is perhaps the most elusive of berries, its delicate, sweetness making it the perfect complement to other fruit and its juicy, richness making it a true delight when eaten alone.

If you have a produce supplier who is a keen importer, raspberries will be available from the end of May into December. The season for locally produced berries is much shorter and varies from region to region.

Raspberries should be stored for as short a time as possible, placing them on a cookie tray between pieces of paper towel, wrapped in plastic. When buying them, look for plump, well-shaped berries with no signs of dampness or mold. Raspberries which have been picked in damp or moist conditions have a particularly short shelf life.

Raspberries are an excellent source of vitamin C and a good source of folate; they have 70 calories per cup/250 mL.

Like most berries, raspberries are delicious alone, with cream, ice cream, sour cream or yogurt. Try them with your favorite breakfast; they are super on cereal, pancakes or waffles. Try mashing a few with a little sugar and spoon over ice cream, in a meringue, on a light cake or over strawberries. If you have never had raspberry shortcake, give it a try. It's a wonderful surprise!

Pete calls raspberries "one-day wonders" because they are the most fragile of all the berries and must be handled with great care. Raspberries should be eaten not stored.

Raspberry Supreme

1 to 2 pints	raspberries, washed	500 mL to 1 L
3 Tbsp	Grand Marnier or orange flavored liqueur	50 mL
½ cup	whipping cream	125 mL

1 Tbsp	sugar	15 mL
½ cup	yogurt	125 mL
¼ cup	toasted slivered almonds	50 mL

Reserving ½ cup/125 mL of the raspberries, divide the fruit between 4 dessert dishes. Pour the liqueur over the berries.

Whip the cream, add the sugar and fold the whipped cream into the yogurt. Mash the reserved berries and fold them into the cream mixture. Spoon the cream mixture onto the berries and liqueur, and sprinkle with toasted slivered almonds. *Serves 4*

Rhubarb

Rhubarb is wonderfully easy to grow and appears early in the spring, about the same time as fiddleheads.

Because we tend to eat rhubarb with sugar and in desserts, rather than with meat and potatoes, we consider it a fruit, although technically it is a vegetable. There are two types of rhubarb: hothouse grown and field grown. The field grown rhubarb has large stalks which are streaked red and green. The younger stems, on which the leaves are not yet full grown, are usually the most tender, having a more delicate flavor than the larger stalks. When buying rhubarb, look for firm, crisp, fresh stalks. If the leaves are attached, they should be stiff and vivid green in color. Avoid rhubarb with wilted leaves or flabby-looking stalks.

Hothouse rhubarb, whose very name sends Pete into raptures, is available in limited supply in early spring. Pete says there is nothing like sweet, tender hothouse rhubarb which is mild pink and nearly stringless, but most people are unwilling to pay the price for it.

Since rhubarb is sold ripe and ready for use, all you have to do is wash it before cooking. If you wish to keep it for a while, you may store it in the refrigerator, unwashed and in a plastic bag, for as long as a week.

Rhubarb is a good source of vitamin C and provides some calcium. Extremely low in calories, it has only 20 in 1 cup/250 mL of the raw diced fruit. However, beware: a 4-ounce/120-gram serving of cooked, sweetened rhubarb has about 160 calories depending, of course, on how sweet you like it.

Stewed Rhubarb

1 pound	rhubarb, cut into 1-inch/2-cm pieces	500 g
½ cup	sugar	50 mL

Add the rhubarb to a saucepan with a small amount of water and simmer for 5 minutes. Add the sugar and simmer for an additional 5 minutes or until the sugar is dissolved.

This is great with yogurt, on ice cream, on pancakes, with custard, all by itself or almost any way you care to serve it.

The easiest thing to do with rhubarb is to cut it up into 1-inch/2.5-cm pieces and cook it without a lid in a small amount of sugar and enough water to cover.

Rhubarb Soup

A friend brought this recipe back from Sweden. I'll admit that I was a little dubious at first, but one mouthful won me over. This is great at either the beginning or the end of a meal. I have not tried it in the middle but it would probably be good there too.

2 pounds	ripe rhubarb cut up into 1-inch/2.5 cm pieces and cooked in	1 kg
8 cups	of water	2 L
2	sticks cinnamon	2
	½ lemon, sliced	
1 cup	sugar	250 mL
2 Tbsp	cornstarch	25 mL
1	egg yolk, beaten	1
½ cup	cereal cream	125 mL

When the rhubarb is tender, remove it from the cooking liquid and purée it in a blender or food processor. Heat the purée and the cooking liquid with the cinnamon and lemon for 5 minutes. Add the sugar. (Taste it, you may like it sweeter.)

Mix the cornstarch with ⅓ cup/75 mL water and stir into the rhubarb juice. Simmer for another 5 minutes, and remove the lemon and cinnamon. Just before serving the soup, mix the egg yolk with the cream and stir the egg mixture into the soup.

I like to garnish the soup with thin slices of preserved ginger if I am serving it as a dessert. *Serves 8*

Strawberries

Strawberries ripen only a little after picking. The size has little to do with taste.

For most Canadians, the strawberry season starts with the influx of berries from California and Florida in early May and lasts until the end of July. Strawberries are of course available just about all year long, but they are shipped half way round the world to get to us, and are usually not as fresh when they arrive.

Strawberries will ripen only a little after they are picked so look for boxes of ripe berries which are not hulled. Don't hull them until you have washed them or they will absorb water. The size of berry has little to do with its taste, so look for boxes of berries which are the size best suited to your needs. Many people find smaller berries are sweeter and have a more concentrated flavor.

Your best bet, because strawberries don't store especially well, is to plan to use them within 3 days of buying them. To keep them in tip-top shape until you use them, lay the berries unwashed on trays lined with paper towel; then cover them with more paper towel and a layer of plastic. Fresh local berries don't need to be treated with such kid gloves—they are usually fine in their quart boxes.

You can freeze strawberries easily enough too. Simply hull them and lay them in a single layer on a baking tray; when they are frozen hard, transfer them to the plastic freezer bags where they will keep for up to 10 months.

Strawberries are a great source of vitamin C and have only 50 calories per cup/250 mL.

Well, well, well—how to use strawberries. It would probably be easier to tell you how not to use these little creatures. They are gorgeous *au naturel*, with whipped, sour or coffee cream, or in yogurt with a sprinkling of sugar. For a real treat, dip a few fresh strawberries in dark or milk chocolate. Try them with a little Grand Marnier and a little whipped cream and you will be in the midst of decadence—a wonderful place to be with strawberries. They are superb in ice cream or with a fresh sponge cake and, of course, in strawberry shortcake. (I don't know how you usually make strawberry shortcake, but try the procedure with tea biscuits and whipped cream if you haven't. The "unsweetness" of the biscuits only makes the berries taste sweeter.)

Strawberry Pie

This is my mum's recipe and even Pete agrees that berries don't come much better than this.

1 quart	fresh strawberries	1 L
1	9-inch/23-cm baked pie shell	1
¼ cup	water	50 mL
¾ cup	sugar	175 mL
2 Tbsp	cornstarch	25 mL
	Whipped cream	

Mash enough berries to make ¾ cup/175 mL pulp and set aside. Fill the pie shell with the remaining berries, leaving them whole unless they are extra large and need to be cut in half, using as many berries as you need to make sure the shell is well-filled.

Add the water, sugar and cornstarch to the mashed berries and boil over medium heat until thick, stirring frequently. Pour the mixture over the berries in the pie shell and chill for at least 30 minutes. Top with whipped cream.

Strawberries Extraordinaire

Ha, this is something I didn't mention when telling you how to eat strawberries. Actually I'd rather not tell you about it now either . . . some things should remain secrets but this is so completely extraordinary Pete has forced me to share it with you.

1 quart	fresh strawberries, use local ones for best flavor	1 L
3 ounces	cream cheese, softened at room temperature	85 g
3 Tbsp	Grand Marnier	40 mL
3 Tbsp	mild honey	40 mL
1 cup	whipping cream, whipped	250 mL
3 Tbsp	grated orange rind	40 mL
	Fresh mint leaves	

Wash the berries quickly in a sieve under running water and drain on paper towel.

Beat the cream cheese, the Grand Marnier and the honey until very smooth. Fold in the whipped cream.

Divide the berries into 6 large wine glasses or crystal dessert dishes and add the cream cheese mixture. Chill for 4 hours, sprinkle with grated orange rind and garnish with mint leaves. Sounds wretched, right? *Serves 6*

Tamarillos

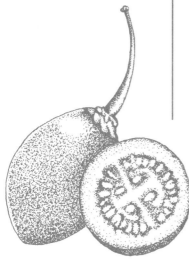

No matter how you use tamarillos, they have to be peeled. Either use a vegetable peeler or immerse the fruit in boiling water for about one minute, then plunge the tamarillo into ice water, pierce the skin and slip it off.

The exquisite little tamarillo, or tree tomato, is memorably beautiful. Scarlet or a warm yellow, it is as smooth skinned and perfectly formed as its cousin, the eggplant. Shaped rather like a pointed egg, the flesh is the texture of a plum, a beautiful orange-yellow color with two deep red swirls of tiny edible seeds.

The unusual astringent flavor of this fruit is especially suited to cooking and benefits from the addition of a little sugar. Of the two varieties, the yellow tends to be sweeter and milder.

Tamarillos are available from March to October, with the fruit being most plentiful during the summer months. Because tamarillos hold up wonderfully well to shipping and storing, nine times out of ten you will find them in perfect condition in markets. A ripe tamarillo will yield to pressure like a firm, ripe plum. It will also develop a fragrance somewhere between that of an apricot and a tomato. Unripe fruit will ripen at home, on the counter, out of direct sunlight. Ripe fruit will keep in the refrigerator in a plastic bag for up to 3 weeks.

Tamarillos are a good source of vitamins A and C and are low in calories. Half a cup/125 mL has only 50 calories.

Tamarillos can be served as a vegetable—sliced, marinated in dressing and then added to a salad. They can also be served as a fruit: let them sit in honey for a couple of seconds and serve them on ice cream or yogurt.

Tamarillos in Syrup

This is the easiest and most versatile way to prepare the fruit. It can be served with ice cream or whipped cream or as a condiment with meat or spicy curries.

4	tamarillos, peeled and sliced into ¼-inch/6-mm thick slices	4
4 tsp	sugar	20 mL
½ tsp	cinnamon	2 mL
¼ tsp	cloves	1 mL
2 tsp	lemon juice	10 mL
	Salt and pepper	

Arrange the sliced fruit in a shallow baking dish and sprinkle with the sugar, cinnamon, cloves, lemon juice, salt and pepper. Bake at 375° F/190° C for about 20 minutes or until tender, basting once or twice with the syrup. *Serves 4*

Ugli fruit

Canadians should be most knowledgable about this Jamaican fruit, since it was first tested in our markets and we responded admirably. Although ugli fruit are indeed ugly, especially in the eyes of North Americans who take so much stock in the appearance of things, they are seed-free, juicy and tartly-sweet. Ugli fruit are about the size of a grapefruit, having rather loose, extremely rough, badly disfigured skin, and can range from light green to yellow-orange in color. Once you get your thumb under it, however, the skin virtually falls away, revealing a gorgeous warm orange-colored flesh. Because the juice sacs are bigger than in ordinary citrus fruit, the flesh of an ugli is particularly luscious.

Ugli fruit is available from January to early June. Look for fruit which is heavy for its size, showing no indication of dryness at the stem end. Although the fruit should have a little give, don't worry about the outer appearance of the fruit. If it didn't look awful, it wouldn't be named ugli fruit, would it? Surface scarring, uneven coloring, dappling, patchiness . . . it's all

Ugli fruit is a superb addition to any salad in which you ordinarily use oranges or to bitter salad greens such as radicchio or Belgian endive. It will turn your fruit salad into a real paradise and is wonderful in gelatin desserts, too.

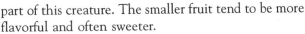

part of this creature. The smaller fruit tend to be more flavorful and often sweeter.

You can store the fruit in the refrigerator for up to 3 weeks. If you plan to use them within a couple days, leave them on the counter; their thick skin offers good protection against drying out.

Ugli fruit is a good source of vitamin C and fiber and has about the same number of calories as grapefruit.

Use ugli fruit as you would a grapefruit or an orange. Eat half for breakfast or take one with you for lunch. And take lots of paper napkins; although this fruit is delicious and easy to eat out of hand, its juiciness makes it a messy fruit to eat, especially since the sections tend to split easily. Ugli fruit is delicious solo— don't feel you have to do anything to it but eat it!

White Sapote

The world of tropical fruit is rather confusing when it comes to the names of various fruit: feijoa is wrongly called pineapple guava, granadilla is actually a kind of passion fruit, the notorious cactus pear is also known as prickly pear, Indian fig and tuna among other things, and the cherimoya is sometimes called sherbet fruit or custard apple. Apparently the white sapote is another fruit whose name is in dispute and calling this particular fruit simply "sapote" is incorrect. Sapote, which comes from the Mexican "zapote," simply means soft fruit—a dangerously vague description. So use its proper name: white sapote. Mind you, unless you live in Mexico or have an unusually stubborn fruit supplier, asking for sapote will probably get you a white sapote.

The white sapote is a superb fruit. It is rather nondescript on the outside, looking rather like a green cooking apple with a slight point at the blossom end. Its pale cream-colored flesh is light textured, almost buttery, smooth, soft and very juicy. It has a delicate, extra sweet, mild flavor with a hint of something tropical—a combination of peach or apricot and banana. The fruit has no core, but it does have a collection of seeds, between 2 and 6, scattered throughout the flesh. In size, the fruit is between an orange and a grapefruit. Its thin, edible, easily bruised skin is green but sometimes turns yellow when ripe, when it will yield to gentle pressure like a ripe plum.

It is tricky to determine exactly when white sapotes will be available in your markets, but look for them between August and November; they tend to peak in September. Buy the fruit while it is still firm and let it ripen at home, on the counter, out of direct sunlight. But don't turn your back on this fruit, since it ripens very quickly, sometimes in only a day or two and in no more than 3 days. Once ripened, the fruit may be refrigerated in a plastic or paper bag for the better part of a week.

White sapotes are a good source of potassium, vitamin C, iron and fiber. One medium sized fruit has about 135 calories.

The skin of a white sapote is edible, though it may be slightly tart. Sapotes are delicious eaten out of hand like an apple; just bear in mind that the seeds are inedible. You can also peel the fruit, slice it and dip it in lemon juice to prevent darkening. The sapote should not be cooked although it is delicious in fruit salads, especially in combination with strawberries and kiwi. The fruit is excellent sliced and served with a squeeze of lime or lemon juice, and topped with cream or whipped cream. Purée the fruit and blend it with orange juice for a different and delicious drink. Or treat the fruit purée as a sauce for other fruit.

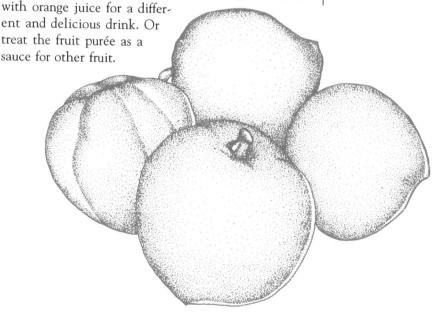

The white sapote has a delicate, extra sweet, mild flavor with a hint of something tropical—a combination of peach, apricot and banana. The fruit has no core but it does have a collection of inedible seeds, between 2 and 6, scattered throughout the flesh.

Sapote Shake

When was the lat time you had a sapote milkshake?

1 cup	white sapote pieces, peeled and seeded	250 mL
1 cup	vanilla yogurt	250 mL
½ cup	orange juice	125 mL
2 Tbsp	honey	25 mL
¼ tsp	ginger	1 mL
1	egg	1

Put all the ingredients into a blender or food processor and blend until smooth. *Serves 2 generously*

Index